BOOK OF FOOTBALL RECORDS!

BOXTREE

First published 2009 by
Boxtree an imprint of Pan
Macmillan Ltd
Pan Macmillan,
20 New Wharf Road,
London N1 9RR
Basingstoke and Oxford
Associated companies
throughout the world

www.panmacmillan.com

Editor: Tim Street
Art Director: Darryl Tooth
Production Editor: Oli Reed
Thanks to: Cris Freddi, Nikki
Palmer, Billy Robertson,
Martin Ellis and the MATCH
magazine team.

ISBN 978-0-7522-2654-5

Colour origination by
ColourSystems

Printed by L.E.G.O. SpA, Italy

Statistics correct up to
August 14, 2009.

Visit www.panmacmillan.com
to read more about all our
books and to buy them. You
will also find features, author
interviews and news of any
author events, and you can
sign up for e-newsletters so
that you're always first to hear
about our new releases.

CONTENTS

PREMIER LEAGUE »

INCLUDING FOOTBALL LEAGUE (1888-92) & DIVISION ONE (1892-1992)

Chelsea, 2004-05 Premier League champions

Man. United, 2008-09 Premier League champions

FAB FACT!
Liverpool is the most successful city in the top Flight! The Reds have won 18 league titles, while Everton have bagged nine!

PREM WINNERS!

Man. United have bagged 11 titles since the Prem started in 1992-93, but three other clubs have also won the Premier League! **Blackburn** lifted the trophy on the last day of the 1995 season, **Arsenal** finished top in 1998, 2002 and 2004, while **Chelsea** were champions in 2005 and 2006! The Blues also picked up a record 95 points in 2005!

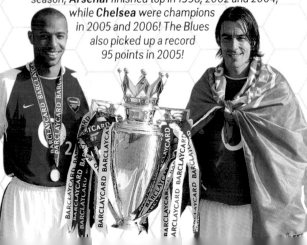

Liverpool won six league titles in the 1980s

MOST TITLES EVER!

Liverpool and **Man. United** are the most successful English clubs of all time! Even though Liverpool have never won the Premier League, the Anfield giants have picked up 18 titles, with their first arriving way back in 1901! Man. United have also won 18 league titles, with their first coming in 1908!

PREM CLUBS!

A massive 43 teams have played in the Prem since the start of the 1992-93 season! The league was made up of 22 clubs in its first season, before being reduced to 20 in 1995-96. Only seven clubs have played in every Prem season so far – **Arsenal, Aston Villa, Chelsea, Everton, Liverpool, Man. United** and **Tottenham!**

BARCLAYS PREMIER LEAGUE
Burnley, 2009-10

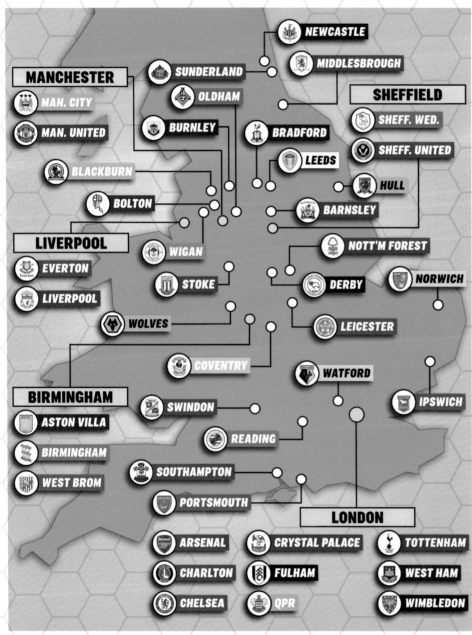

NEWCASTLE
MIDDLESBROUGH
MANCHESTER
SUNDERLAND
OLDHAM
SHEFFIELD
MAN. CITY
MAN. UNITED
BURNLEY
BRADFORD
SHEFF. WED.
BLACKBURN
LEEDS
SHEFF. UNITED
BOLTON
HULL
BARNSLEY
LIVERPOOL
WIGAN
NOTT'M FOREST
EVERTON
STOKE
DERBY
NORWICH
LIVERPOOL
WOLVES
LEICESTER
COVENTRY
WATFORD
BIRMINGHAM
SWINDON
IPSWICH
ASTON VILLA
READING
BIRMINGHAM
SOUTHAMPTON
WEST BROM
PORTSMOUTH
LONDON
ARSENAL
CRYSTAL PALACE
TOTTENHAM
CHARLTON
FULHAM
WEST HAM
CHELSEA
QPR
WIMBLEDON

FOOTY SHORTS!

Liverpool, 1982

Old Trafford

Huddersfield (1924-26), Arsenal (1932-34), Liverpool (1982-84) and Man. United (1999-2001 & 2007-09) have all won three titles in a row!

When Liverpool won their first league title way back in 1901, Anfield could only hold 20,000 fans and goats used to eat grass on the terraces!

The Prem's highest ever attendance was at Old Trafford in 2007, when 76,098 fans watched Man. United beat Blackburn!

TOP FLIGHT CHAMPIONS!

MATCH checks out every winner of the English league title!

Arsenal, 1930

FOOTBALL LEAGUE			
1888-89	Preston	1916-19	No football because of the First World War
1889-90	Preston	1919-20	West Brom
1890-91	Everton	1920-21	Burnley
1891-92	Sunderland	1921-22	Liverpool
LEAGUE DIVISION ONE		1922-23	Liverpool
1892-93	Sunderland	1923-24	Huddersfield
1893-94	Aston Villa	1924-25	Huddersfield
1894-95	Sunderland	1925-26	Huddersfield
1895-96	Aston Villa	1926-27	Newcastle
1896-97	Aston Villa	1927-28	Everton
1897-98	Sheff. United	1928-29	Sheff. Wed.
1898-99	Aston Villa	1929-30	Sheff. Wed.
1899-1900	Aston Villa	1930-31	Arsenal
1900-01	Liverpool	1931-32	Everton
1901-02	Sunderland	1932-33	Arsenal
1902-03	Sheff. Wed.	1933-34	Arsenal
1903-04	Sheff. Wed.	1934-35	Arsenal
1904-05	Newcastle	1935-36	Sunderland
1905-06	Liverpool	1936-37	Man. City
1906-07	Newcastle	1937-38	Arsenal
1907-08	Man. United	1938-39	Everton
1908-09	Newcastle	1940-46	No football because of the Second World War
1909-10	Aston Villa		
1910-11	Man. United	1946-47	Liverpool
1911-12	Blackburn	1947-48	Arsenal
1912-13	Sunderland	1948-49	Portsmouth
1913-14	Blackburn	1949-50	Portsmouth
1914-15	Everton	Continued over >>	

Preston, 1888-89

DID YOU KNOW?

English league footy kicked off on September 8, 1888, when 12 clubs formed the Football League! They were Accrington, Aston Villa, Blackburn, Bolton, Burnley, Derby, Everton, Notts County, Preston, Stoke, West Brom and Wolves!

MOST TITLES BY A PLAYER!

Man. United's legendary midfielder **Ryan Giggs** has won more titles than any other player in Premier League history! Giggsy has played in every Prem season since it started in 1992-93, winning the trophy a massive 11 times!

GIGGSY'S UNITED DEBUT!

Ryan Giggs made his first league appearance against Everton at Old Trafford on March 2, 1991! The Welsh superstar came on as a substitute, but couldn't stop Sir Alex Ferguson's side losing 2-0!

FIRST SENIOR GOAL!

Ryan Giggs scored his first senior goal for The Red Devils just two months after making his debut! He hit the net on his first league start in a 1-0 win against big local rivals **Man. City**!

FAB FACT!
Paul Scholes is only two league titles behind his Man. United team-mate – Scholesy has lifted the trophy nine times!

THE TROPHY!

The Premier League trophy was made by the Royal Jewellers Asprey's of London! The same jeweller looked after the Royal Family's priceless Crown Jewels for over 150 years!

THREE LIONS!
There are two lions on top of the handles! The winning captain represents the third lion when he lifts the trophy at the end of the season!

HEIGHT!
The Prem trophy is almost half the size of Spurs star Aaron Lennon! The flying winger is 165cm tall, while the trophy stands 76cm high!

BLING!
The trophy is made from solid sterling silver! On top of that is a thick layer of silver gilding!

THE BASE!
The bottom of the trophy is made from malachite, which is a stone found in Africa! The green colour symbolises a pitch!

WEIGHT!
You need big muscles to lift this trophy above your head! It weighs a mega 25kg, which is the same size as a fully grown bulldog!

THE LADY!
Before the Premier League began, the Division One winners lifted this ace trophy! It's known as 'The Lady' because of the woman on the lid, and is now given to the winners of the Championship title!

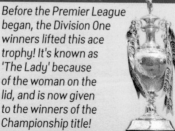

TOP FLIGHT CHAMPIONS!

MATCH checks out every winner of the English league title!

Leeds, 1968-69

LEAGUE DIVISION ONE			
1950-51	Tottenham	1980-81	Aston Villa
1951-52	Man. United	1981-82	Liverpool
1952-53	Arsenal	1982-83	Liverpool
1953-54	Wolves	1983-84	Liverpool
1954-55	Chelsea	1984-85	Everton
1955-56	Man. United	1985-86	Liverpool
1956-57	Man. United	1986-87	Everton
1957-58	Wolves	1987-88	Liverpool
1958-59	Wolves	1988-89	Arsenal
1959-60	Burnley	1989-90	Liverpool
1960-61	Tottenham	1990-91	Arsenal
1961-62	Ipswich	1991-92	Leeds
1962-63	Everton	PREMIER LEAGUE	
1963-64	Liverpool	1992-93	Man. United
1964-65	Man. United	1993-94	Man. United
1965-66	Liverpool	1994-95	Blackburn
1966-67	Man. United	1995-96	Man. United
1967-68	Man. City	1996-97	Man. United
1968-69	Leeds	1997-98	Arsenal
1969-70	Everton	1998-99	Man. United
1970-71	Arsenal	1999-2000	Man. United
1971-72	Derby	2000-01	Man. United
1972-73	Liverpool	2001-02	Arsenal
1973-74	Leeds	2002-03	Man. United
1974-75	Derby	2003-04	Arsenal
1975-76	Liverpool	2004-05	Chelsea
1976-77	Liverpool	2005-06	Chelsea
1977-78	Nott'm Forest	2006-07	Man. United
1978-79	Liverpool	2007-08	Man. United
1979-80	Liverpool	2008-09	Man. United

DID YOU KNOW?

Sheffield Wednesday, who have twice won back-to-back league titles, were originally formed by a cricket club who played their games on Wednesdays!

MOST DOUBLES!

Arsene Wenger & Tony Adams show off Arsenal's silverware

Only five other teams have won the league and FA Cup double since Preston bagged both honours in 1888-89. Man. United (1994, 1996 and 1999) and Arsenal (1971, 1998 and 2002) have each won the double three times. Preston, Aston Villa (1897), Tottenham (1961) and Liverpool (1986) have all done it once!

FAB FACT!
Preston won the first ever English league title without losing a match and the FA Cup without conceding a goal in 1888-89!

MOST TREBLES!

No team has ever won the league title, FA Cup and League Cup in one season. **Man. United** (below) came closest, but lost the League Cup final to Aston Villa in 1994. The Red Devils won a Premier League, FA Cup and Champions League treble in 1999, while **Liverpool** won the league title, League Cup and European Cup in 1984. The Reds also won the FA Cup, League Cup and European Cup Winners' Cup in 2001!

UNBEATEN SEASON!

Arsenal's 'Invincibles'

2003 — 2004

The awesome 2003-04 **Arsenal** team is still the only Prem squad never to lose a match in a whole season. 'The Invincibles' won 26 of their 38 matches and drew the other 12. The only other team to remain unbeaten for an entire season was Preston back in 1888-89, when they won 18 games and bagged four draws!

FEWEST POINTS!

The **Derby** team (left) of 2007-08 will always be remembered for winning just 11 points all season! The Rams won promotion to the top flight through the play-offs the previous season, but picked up just one win during their entire Premier League campaign!

MOST POINTS!

Across a 42-game Premier League season, Man. United's title-winning team of 1994 lifted the silverware with a mega 92 points. As Premier League teams now play 38 games in a season, Chelsea's 95-point haul under Jose Mourinho in 2004-05 is a record. Before the 1980-81 season, teams got two points for a win and Liverpool hold the record with their 68 points in 1978-79!

Frank Lampard wins the title for Chelsea at Bolton in 2005

FOOTY SHORTS!

Thomas sinks Liverpool

The closest top-flight finish was in 1989 when Michael Thomas' late goal at Anfield gave Arsenal the title ahead of Liverpool on goal difference!

Sheffield FC

The oldest football club in the world is Sheffield FC, who were formed in 1857. Notts County, formed in 1864, are the oldest league club!

Hallam FC's stadium

Hallam FC were formed on September 4, 1860 and their Sandygate Road stadium in Sheffield is the oldest ground still in existence!

DERBY WINNERS!

MATCH checks out the stats from England's biggest derby matches!

The Blades battle the Owls

SHEFFIELD DERBY

Matches:	110
United wins:	41
Wednesday wins:	35
Draws:	34

MANCHESTER DERBY

Matches:	140
United wins:	55
City wins:	37
Draws:	48

NORTH LONDON DERBY

Matches:	144
Arsenal wins:	59
Tottenham wins:	45
Draws:	40

MERSEYSIDE DERBY

Matches:	180
Everton wins:	56
Liverpool wins:	68
Draws:	56

TYNE-WEAR DERBY

Matches:	128
Newcastle wins:	49
Sunderland wins:	41
Draws:	40

NORTH-WEST DERBY

Matches:	152
Man. United wins:	58
Liverpool wins:	51
Draws:	43

BIRMINGHAM DERBY

Matches:	106
Aston Villa wins:	43
Birmingham wins:	36
Draws:	27

Villa take on Birmingham

CLASSIC GAME!
LIVERPOOL 4-3 NEWCASTLE

McManaman takes on Lee

APRIL 3, 1996 ★ ANFIELD

WHAT HAPPENED? Newcastle were chasing their first title for 69 years and were 2-1 up at half-time, despite going 1-0 down after just two minutes. Robbie Fowler pulled Liverpool level in the second half, but Faustino Asprilla fired The Magpies back in front. Stan Collymore then broke Newcastle hearts by scoring twice, the winner coming in the 92nd minute. Newcastle eventually lost the title race to Man. United by four points!

Asprilla and Scales in action

David Ginola makes it 2-1 to Newcastle

FAB FACT!
Robbie Fowler netted a late winner as Liverpool beat Newcastle by exactly the same scoreline the following season!

MATCH checks out the greatest games in the history of the English top flight!

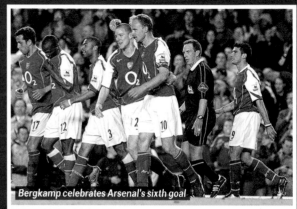

Bergkamp celebrates Arsenal's sixth goal

ARSENAL 7-0 EVERTON

May 11, 2005: Gunners legend Dennis Bergkamp was on fire as his awesome vision destroyed David Moyes' side! Robin van Persie, Robert Pires (2), Patrick Vieira, Edu and Mathieu Flamini were also on target at Highbury!

Beckham taunts the Spurs fans

TOTTENHAM 3-5 MAN. UNITED

September 29, 2001: Spurs fans couldn't believe it when they led 3-0 at half-time against the Prem champs, but they were even more shocked when *David Beckham* completed Man. United's amazing turnaround in the 87th minute!

Beardsley scored 60 goals in 177 games for Liverpool

LIVERPOOL 9-0 CRYSTAL PALACE

September 12, 1989: Palace were on the wrong end of a massive defeat at Anfield the last time Liverpool won the league title! Silky forward *Peter Beardsley* was amongst the scorers as Liverpool went goal crazy!

MOST PREM GOALS IN A SEASON!

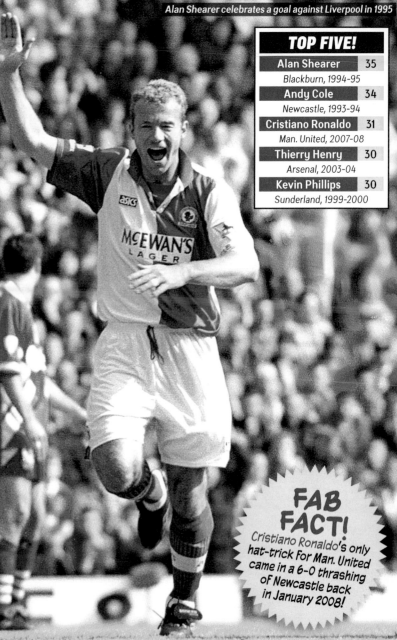

Alan Shearer celebrates a goal against Liverpool in 1995

Former Blackburn goal machine Alan Shearer holds the record for the most strikes in a season! The Rovers star buried 35 goals as Blackburn stormed to the Prem title in the 1994–95 season!

Andy Cole hits the net yet again for Newcastle

FAB FACT!
Cristiano Ronaldo's only hat-trick for Man. United came in a 6-0 thrashing of Newcastle back in January 2008!

MOST GOALS IN A SEASON!

Bill 'Dixie' Dean's record of 60 goals for Everton in 1927-28 is still the highest number of goals in any division! Dean beat the previous record of 59 goals, set the season before by Middlesbrough star **George Camsell**, by scoring seven times in his last two matches!

Dixie Dean in action at Goodison Park

MOST GOALS IN A MATCH!

James saves from Shorey in a 7-4 thriller

Lucky fans at Fratton Park on September 29, 2007 were treated to 11 goals when **Portsmouth** beat **Reading** 7-4! Reading actually drew level at 2-2 early in the second half, and would have also made it 3-3 if Pompey keeper David James hadn't brilliantly saved Nicky Shorey's penalty!

MOST GOALS EVER!

Top flight keepers must have hated one-on-ones with **Jimmy Greaves**! The former Chelsea, Tottenham and West Ham hitman scored a sensational 357 goals in Division One between 1957 and 1970!

Greaves leaves a keeper sprawling

MOST PREM GOALS!

Shearer nets his final goal for Newcastle at Sunderland

TOP FIVE!

Alan Shearer	260
Blackburn & Newcastle	
Andy Cole	187
Newcastle, Man. United, Blackburn, Fulham, Man. City, Portsmouth, Birmingham & Sunderland	
Thierry Henry	174
Arsenal	
Robbie Fowler	163
Liverpool (twice), Leeds, Man. City & Blackburn	
Les Ferdinand	149
QPR, Newcastle, Tottenham, West Ham, Leicester & Bolton	

Ex-Newcastle and Blackburn striker **Alan Shearer** (right) may have hung up his boots in 2006, but his goalscoring record is legendary! The powerhouse hitman buried 260 Prem goals between 1992 and 2006, with his first coming for Blackburn against Crystal Palace and his last for Newcastle at Sunderland from the penalty spot!

FOOTY SHORTS!

Dixie Dean

When Dixie Dean hit 60 goals in 1927-28, he netted a hat-trick in the final game! It included a penalty and a header with five minutes left against Arsenal!

George Camsell

George Camsell and Dixie Dean's net-busting records were both set while English defences were getting used to a new law called 'offside'!

Spurs thrash Everton

The most goals in any top flight match is 14! Aston Villa beat Accrington 12-2 in 1892, while Tottenham won 10-4 against Everton in 1958!

LANDMARK GOALS!

The first ever Football League goal was an own goal, scored by Aston Villa defender Gershom Cox against Wolves on September 8, 1888! Here are some memorable Prem strikes...

Andy Townsend

1ST
Brian Deane for Sheffield United v Man. United
August 15, 1992

100TH
Mark Walters for Liverpool v Ipswich
August 25, 1992

1,000TH
Mike Newell for Blackburn v Nottingham Forest
April 7, 1993

5,000TH
Andy Townsend for Aston Villa v Southampton
December 7, 1996

10,000TH
Les Ferdinand for Tottenham v Fulham
December 15, 2001

15,000TH
Moritz Volz for Fulham v Chelsea
December 30, 2006

Anelka on target against Aston Villa

DID YOU KNOW?

Chelsea striker Nicolas Anelka was the Premier League's top scorer in 2008-09! The France forward netted 19 goals, hitting the net four times in just seven days back in November 2008!

FASTEST EVER GOAL!

Tottenham defender Ledley King netted the Prem's fastest ever goal

The record for the quickest top-flight goal goes to Preston's Bobby Langton – the winger scored after just seven seconds against Man. City on August 25, 1948. The quickest goal in Premier League history was scored by Tottenham's Ledley King after just 10 seconds against Bradford in 2000-01!

FAB FACT!
Bobby Langton's record goal was scored against keeper Frank Swift, who was still bending over to put his cap into the net!

Bendtner strikes after 1.8 seconds

FASTEST GOAL BY A SUBSTITUTE!

Nicklas Bendtner's bullet header against Tottenham in 2007 goes down in history as the quickest strike off the bench! The Denmark goal machine headed home a Cesc Fabregas corner just 1.8 seconds after replacing Emmanuel Eboue!

MOST GOALS IN A MATCH!

Preston's Jimmy Ross and Arsenal striker Ted Drake both netted seven goals in one game. North End star Ross bagged his haul against Stoke in October 1888, while Gunners striker Drake netted seven at Aston Villa in December 1935. It's believed Drake once said that he only had eight shots in that match, hitting the bar with the other one!

Jimmy Ross (wearing the hat)

Ted Drake in action

Ted Drake scored 139 goals for Arsenal

FOOTY SHORTS!

Newcastle legend Shearer

The most goals scored in one Prem match was five by Alan Shearer for Newcastle against Sheffield Wednesday in 1999. Two were penalties!

Penalty king Lee

Back in the 1971-72 season, Francis Lee scored a massive 13 penalties as his Man. City side missed out on the title by just one point!

Schmeichel scores at Everton

Keepers Charlie Williams, Peter Shilton, Steve Sherwood, Brad Friedel, Steve Ogrizovic, Paul Robinson and Peter Schmeichel all scored goals in the top flight!

PREMIER LEAGUE 100 CLUB!

Only 17 players have scored 100 goals in the Premier League! MATCH checks them out...

Jimmy Floyd Hasselbaink

NICOLAS ANELKA (Chelsea)
100TH GOAL: Chelsea v West Ham, 2008
Prem clubs: Arsenal, Liverpool, Man. City, Bolton & Chelsea

ALAN SHEARER (Retired)
100TH GOAL: Blackburn v Tottenham, 1995
Prem clubs: Blackburn & Newcastle

ANDY COLE (Retired)
100TH GOAL: Man. United v Arsenal, 1999
Prem clubs: Newcastle, Man. United, Blackburn, Fulham, Man. City, Portsmouth, Birmingham & Sunderland

THIERRY HENRY (Barcelona)
100TH GOAL: Birmingham v Arsenal, 2003
Prem clubs: Arsenal

ROBBIE FOWLER (North Queensland Fury)
100TH GOAL: Liverpool v Southampton, 1999
Prem clubs: Liverpool (twice), Leeds, Man. City & Blackburn

LES FERDINAND (Retired)
100TH GOAL: Newcastle v Nott'm Forest, 1997
Prem clubs: QPR, Newcastle, Tottenham, West Ham, Leicester & Bolton

TEDDY SHERINGHAM (Retired)
100TH GOAL: Man. United v Southampton, 2000
Prem clubs: Nottingham Forest, Tottenham (twice), Man. United, Portsmouth & West Ham

MICHAEL OWEN (Man. United)
100TH GOAL: West Brom v Liverpool, 2003
Prem clubs: Liverpool, Newcastle & Man. United

JIMMY FLOYD HASSELBAINK (Retired)
100TH GOAL: Chelsea v Wolves, 2004
Prem clubs: Leeds, Chelsea, Middlesbrough & Charlton

DWIGHT YORKE (No club)
100TH GOAL: Derby v Man. United, 2000
Prem clubs: Aston Villa, Man. United, Blackburn, Birmingham & Sunderland

IAN WRIGHT (Retired)
100TH GOAL: Arsenal v West Ham, 1997
Prem clubs: Arsenal & West Ham

DION DUBLIN (Retired)
100TH GOAL: Aston Villa v West Ham, 2002
Prem clubs: Man. United, Coventry & Aston Villa

ROBBIE KEANE (Tottenham)
100TH GOAL: Tottenham v Fulham, 2007
Prem clubs: Coventry, Leeds, Tottenham (twice) & Liverpool

EMILE HESKEY (Aston Villa)
100TH GOAL: Portsmouth v Wigan, 2008
Prem clubs: Leicester, Liverpool, Birmingham, Wigan & Aston Villa

MATT LE TISSIER (Retired)
100TH GOAL: Southampton v Arsenal, 2001
Prem clubs: Southampton

RYAN GIGGS (Man. United)
100TH GOAL: Man. United v Derby, 2007
Prem clubs: Man. United

FRANK LAMPARD (Chelsea)
100TH GOAL: Chelsea v Sunderland, 2008
Prem clubs: West Ham & Chelsea

FASTEST HAT-TRICK!

Fowler celebrates with John Barnes, Jamie Redknapp and Ian Rush

Legendary Liverpool striker Robbie Fowler took just four minutes and 33 seconds to score a top treble against Arsenal in August 1994, making it the fastest ever hat-trick in the Premier League!

FAB FACT!
The Fastest ever Football League hat-tricks were scored in three minutes by Fulham's Graham Leggat in 1963 and Blackburn's Johnny McIntyre in 1922!

MOST HAT-TRICKS!

During his 11 years at Goodison Park, Everton hero **Dixie Dean** netted a top-flight record of 34 hat-tricks! Dean crashed home eight trebles in 1931-32 and seven in 1927-28. The highest in Prem history is 11, set by goal king **Alan Shearer**! He bagged five hat-tricks in the 1995-96 season, against Coventry, Nottingham Forest, West Ham, Bolton and Tottenham!

Shearer nets against West Ham

Jack Balmer hit 111 goals for Liverpool

MOST HAT-TRICKS IN A ROW!

Scoring a treble in one match is tough enough, but three games in a row seems like an impossible task. Wrong! Tottenham's **Frank Osborne** (1925), Leeds' **Tom Jennings** (1926) and Liverpool's **Jack Balmer** (1946) all managed to smash home hat-tricks in three straight games. What an achievement!

LONGEST-RANGE GOALS!

Man. United goalkeeper Ben Foster will want to forget Paul Robinson's 96-yard goal back in 2007! Foster, who was on loan at Watford for the season, saw Robbo's massive free-kick bounce over him and into the net at White Hart Lane! The longest headed goals were both scored by Aston Villa players. Frank Barson ripped the net from 35 yards in 1921, while Peter Aldis did the same thing back in 1952!

Alonso takes aim

In the same season that Paul Robinson scored his wonder goal, Liverpool's Xabi Alonso netted against Newcastle at Anfield from 70 yards out!

Clubs in England were only required to put nets on their goals from 1891, three years after the Football League began!

Foster denies O'Hara

Ben Foster studied Tottenham players taking penalties on his iPod before saving Jamie O'Hara's spot-kick in the 2009 Carling Cup Final!

MOST GOALS SCORED!

These awesome teams couldn't stop ripping the net open!

Alex James & Cliff Bastin, Arsenal

⚽ During the 1930-31 season, nets across the country were ripping to the sound of **Aston Villa** goals as they buried the ball 128 times! Incredibly they only finished as runners-up, seven points behind eventual champions **Arsenal** who scored 127 times!

Quinton Fortune nets for United against Bradford

⚽ The highest number of goals in a Premier League season was set by **Man. United** in 1999-2000! Sir Alex Ferguson's champions lost just three games all season and helped themselves to a record-breaking 97 goals!

MOST GOALS CONCEDED!

Someone should have taught these chumps how to defend!

Swindon concede again at Highbury

⚽ The 1930-31 season was a feast of goals, most of which were leaked by **Blackpool**! The Seasiders' record of 125 goals conceded is still a record to this day, but amazingly they finished one place above the relegation zone!

⚽ The highest number of goals conceded in the Premier League was by **Swindon** in the 1993-94 season! The Robins let in 100 goals and only won five games during their only campaign in the Premier League!

OLD TRAFFORD

SUPER SIZE!
》》Old Trafford is massive! It's the second-biggest ground in England after Wembley! 》》

TOP NICKNAME!
》》Man. United legend Sir Bobby Charlton gave Old Trafford its nickname, The Theatre Of Dreams! 》》

ANCIENT TUNNEL!
》》The Munich Tunnel that sits between the two dugouts is the oldest part of the stadium! 》》

NEW ENTRANCE!
》》The current players' tunnel, in the corner of The Stretford End, has only been used since 1993! 》》

BLOWN UP!
》》Old Trafford's South Stand was destroyed by German bombers during World War Two! 》》

SUPER STADIUMS OF THE WORLD!

CITY	MANCHESTER
OPENED	1910
TEAM	MAN. UNITED
CAPACITY	76,212

GREATEST MATCH EVER!

MAN. UNITED 7-1 ROMA, 2007

Sir Alex Ferguson's side destroyed Roma 7-1 in the quarter-finals of the Champions League! Fergie called it the best ever night of European football at Old Trafford!

LEGENDS!

SIR MATT BUSBY

United's longest-serving boss guided The Red Devils to five league titles, two FA Cups and the European Cup in 1968, ten years after the Munich air disaster killed eight of his players!

ROY KEANE

Keano broke the British transfer record when he joined from Nottingham Forest for £3.75 million, and went on to captain United to nine major trophies in 12 years!

CITY SWITCH!

》》 After Old Trafford was bombed, United had to play at Man City's Maine Road for eight years! 》》

PREM RECORD!

》》 United's 4-1 win over Blackburn in 2007 was watched by 76,098 fans – a Prem record! 》》

TOP BUILDER!

》》 Archie Leitch designed Old Trafford and over 20 other British stadiums, including Villa Park! 》》

MOST WINS!

Tottenham fans must have loved watching their 1960-61 double-winning side! Spurs picked up 31 wins from their 42 matches, which is still the most times a team has ever bagged maximum points in a single season! The highest number of wins in a 38-game Prem season is 29, set by Chelsea in 2004-05! Amazingly, they went on to match their own record just one season later!

FAB FACT!
Man. United have won a massive 1,756 top-flight matches – more than any other club in England!

John White strikes for Spurs against Burnley in 1960

BIGGEST WIN!

Ipswich's 9-0 stuffing at the hands of **Man. United** in 1995 ranks as the biggest victory in Premier League history. But that still falls short of the biggest ever wins in the top flight. **West Brom** won 12-0 against Darwen in 1892, while **Nottingham Forest** beat Leicester Fosse 12-0 back in 1909!

United destroy Ipswich

LONGEST UNBEATEN RUN!

Arsenal's Thierry Henry fires home a penalty against Leicester

The great **Arsenal** squad of 2003 and 2004 played an incredible 49 matches without losing! The Gunners won their last two matches of 2002-03, then remained unbeaten for the entire following season and the first nine games of 2004-05, before eventually losing 2-0 against Man. United at Old Trafford!

BIGGEST COMEBACK!

At 5-0 up at half-time, Everton fans must have thought it was an easy win against **Sheffield Wednesday** in 1904! The Owls had other ideas, though, and battled back in the second half to draw 5-5! The biggest comeback to win the Premier League title was by **Arsenal** in 1997-98! Sir Alex Ferguson's Man. United side were a monster 13 points clear in January, but Arsene Wenger's boys fought back to snatch the title!

Arsenal's class of '98 celebrate their title win

MOST DEFEATS!

Mark Chamberlain, Stoke

Tony Pulis' **Stoke** side must be glad they didn't repeat the terrible form of the 1984-85 Potters team when they returned to the Premier League in 2008-09! The 1984 Stoke side, led by Bill Asprey and Johnny Wilkinson, lost 31 out of their 42 matches! The worst record of losses since the Premier League began is 29 defeats, by **Ipswich** in 1994-95, **Sunderland** in 2005-06 and **Derby** in 2007-08!

FOOTY SHORTS!

The Tyne-Wear derby

Sunderland's 9-1 win at Newcastle in 1908 is the biggest ever away win! Their last five goals came in the final eight minutes!

Newcastle's 0-0 draw at home to Portsmouth in 1931 is believed to be the only league match in which neither side won a corner!

Kevin Bond, Norwich

If you wanted to see some bore draws you had to be a Norwich fan in 1978-79! The Canaries ground out a record 23 draws in 42 matches!

CLEAN SHEET KINGS!

These superstars are the hottest keepers the top flight's ever seen!

Clemence won five league titles at Anfield

⚽ Former England goalkeeper **Ray Clemence** holds the record for the most clean sheets in a top-flight season. The giant shot-stopper kept 28 shut-outs for Liverpool in 1978-79!

⚽ **Edwin van der Sar** will never forget the 2008-09 season. His quality saves meant Man. United kept 14 clean sheets in a row – that's an incredible 1,311 minutes of footy! That beat Petr Cech's previous best of ten in 2004-05!

OWN GOALS!

These muppets loved putting the ball into their own net!

Bobby Stuart, Middlesbrough

⚽ Middlesbrough fans back in 1931 must have hated seeing **Bobby Stuart** with the ball anywhere near his own penalty area! Stuart, who also played for Plymouth, scored five own goals in just one season for Middlesbrough!

Charlton can't believe their luck

⚽ Back in 2003, **Sunderland** leaked three own goals in one match! They set a Prem record against Charlton when striker **Michael Proctor** fired two into his own net in just three minutes!

BIGGEST TRANSFERS!

Real Madrid must have the biggest wallets in the world after splashing the cash on Portugal winger Cristiano Ronaldo in July 2009! The 2008 FIFA World Player Of The Year, who scored 117 goals for Man. United, moved to the Bernabeu for a jaw-dropping £80 million last summer!

Robinho celebrates with Shaun Wright-Phillips

TOP TEN!

Here are the biggest ever transfers involving English clubs!

Cristiano Ronaldo	**£80 million**
Man. United to Real Madrid, July 2009	
Robinho	**£32.5 million**
Real Madrid to Man. City, September 2008	
Andriy Shevchenko	**£30.8 million**
AC Milan to Chelsea, July 2006	
Dimitar Berbatov	**£30.75 million**
Tottenham to Man. United, September 2008	
Rio Ferdinand	**£30 million**
Leeds to Man. United, July 2002	
Juan Sebastian Veron	**£28.1 million**
Lazio to Man. United, July 2001	
Wayne Rooney	**£27 million**
Everton to Man. United, August 2004	
Fernando Torres	**£26.5 million**
Atletico Madrid to Liverpool, July 2007	
Carlos Tevez	**£25.5 million**
Man. United to Man. City, July 2009	
Emmanuel Adebayor	**£25 million**
Arsenal to Man. City, July 2009	

FAB FACT!

Man. City smashed the British transfer record when they signed *Robinho* from Real Madrid for a mega £32.5 million in September 2008!

MOST MATCHES!

Legendary England keeper **Peter Shilton** (left) has appeared in more top-flight games than any other player. Between 1966 and 1991, Shilton starred between the posts an incredible 848 times for Leicester, Stoke, Nottingham Forest, Southampton and Derby. His career didn't finish there, though – Shilts went on to play a total of 1,005 league matches before retiring in 1997!

FAB FACT!
Peter Shilton made his 1,000th appearance at the age of 47 when he kept a clean sheet for Leyton Orient against Brighton in 1996!

CRAZY PLAYER STATS!

MATCH checks out some of the top flight's craziest stats. From 6ft 7ins strikers to 50-year-old wingers – we've seen them all!

TALLEST PLAYER!

Believe it or not, massive hitman **Peter Crouch** isn't the tallest player ever to play at a top-flight ground. At 6ft 7ins tall, awesome England striker Crouchy is exactly the same height as **Kevin Francis** and **Kostas Chalkias**!

Kevin Francis

SHORTEST PLAYER!

Aaron Lennon

Tottenham's **Aaron Lennon** is mega short at 5ft 5ins, but he's not the smallest player ever. That award goes to Chelsea's **Jackie Crawford** and Tottenham's **Fred 'Fanny' Walden**, who were both 5ft 2ins tall when they played in Division One!

OLDEST PLAYER!

One of the greatest English footballers ever to play the game, **Sir Stanley Matthews**, is the oldest star the top flight has ever seen. 'The Wizard Of Dribble' was 50 years and five days old when he pulled on a Stoke shirt against Fulham in February 1965!

Sir Stanley Matthews

YOUNGEST PLAYER!

Matthew Briggs

Matthew Briggs' appearance for Fulham in 2007, aged 16 years and 65 days, makes him the Prem's youngest ever player. But he isn't the youngest ever top-flight star – Sunderland's **Derek Forster** faced Leicester, aged 15 years and 185 days, in 1964!

FOOTY SHORTS!

Alf Common (centre)

Alf Common was England's first £1,000 player. He set the transfer record when he moved from Sunderland to Middlesbrough in 1905!

Trevor Francis

The first £1 million English transfer took place when England striker Trevor Francis moved from Birmingham to Nottingham Forest in 1979!

John Burridge

John Burridge became the Prem's oldest ever player when he appeared in goal for Man. City against QPR in 1995, aged 43 years and 162 days!

MOST RED CARDS!

Vieira (left) sees red against Sunderland

Getting sent off once must be bad enough, but an unwanted record goes to Man. City's Richard Dunne, Everton legend Duncan Ferguson and former Arsenal midfielder Patrick Vieira! They've all picked up eight Premier League red cards!

Ferguson is sent off at Wigan

Another early bath for Dunne

FAB FACT!
Franck Queudrue, Craig Short, David Batty, Slaven Bilic and Vinnie Jones have all been sent for an early bath three times in one season!

FASTEST RED CARD!

Sheffield United's **Keith Gillespie** (left) was given his marching orders against Reading in 2007 when he elbowed Stephen Hunt ten seconds after coming on the pitch! In Arsenal's last ever game at Highbury in 2006, ex-Wigan star **Andreas Johansson** was also sent off just ten seconds after coming off the subs bench. Gutted!

Taxi for Johansson

MOST YELLOW CARDS!

Savage talks his way into the book yet again

Derby midfielder **Robbie Savage** has gone into the ref's notebook more times than any other player in Premier League history! The former Wales international has been shown a yellow card 89 times, while Birmingham's **Lee Bowyer** has had his name taken 84 times and Hull's **George Boateng** has picked up 80 bookings!

BIGGEST FINE!

Tevez & Mascherano turned out to be very expensive signings

West Ham were slammed with a whopping £5.5 million fine by the Premier League in April 2007 – more than double what they paid to sign awesome England goalkeeper Rob Green from Norwich! The Hammers were fined after they broke Premier League rules when they signed Argentina internationals **Carlos Tevez** and **Javier Mascherano**! The fine dwarfed the £1.5 million **Tottenham** had to pay out for financial irregularities in 1994! Spurs were also handed a 12-point league deduction and given a season-long ban from the FA Cup, but the last two penalties were later dropped on appeal!

LONGEST BAN!

The FA banned Man. United's **Enoch 'Knocker' West** (right) for life, along with seven other players, for match-fixing in 1915! The other seven were pardoned after serving in World War One, but West's ban wasn't lifted until 30 years later, when he was 61!

FOOTY SHORTS!

Cantona's kung fu kick

Man. United hero Eric Cantona was banned for nine months after kicking a Crystal Palace fan following his red card at Selhurst Park in 1995!

Ex-Boro boss Bryan Robson

Middlesbrough were deducted three points for postponing a match against Blackburn in 1997 because too many of their players were ill!

Billy Cook

Back in 1925, The FA banned Oldham full-back Billy Cook for 12 months when he refused to leave the pitch after being sent off for persistent fouling!

PFA PLAYERS OF THE YEAR!

Here are the PFA winners from 1973-74 to 2008-09!

Merson & Hughes

YEAR	PLAYER	YOUNG PLAYER
1973-74	Norman Hunter	Kevin Beattie
1974-75	Colin Todd	Mervyn Day
1975-76	Pat Jennings	Peter Barnes
1976-77	Andy Gray	Andy Gray
1977-78	Peter Shilton	Tony Woodcock
1978-79	Liam Brady	Cyrille Regis
1979-80	Terry McDermott	Glenn Hoddle
1980-81	John Wark	Gary Shaw
1981-82	Kevin Keegan	Steve Moran
1982-83	Kenny Dalglish	Ian Rush
1983-84	Ian Rush	Paul Walsh
1984-85	Peter Reid	Mark Hughes
1985-86	Gary Lineker	Tony Cottee
1986-87	Clive Allen	Tony Adams
1987-88	John Barnes	Paul Gascoigne
1988-89	Mark Hughes	Paul Merson
1989-90	David Platt	Matt Le Tissier
1990-91	Mark Hughes	Lee Sharpe
1991-92	Gary Pallister	Ryan Giggs
1992-93	Paul McGrath	Ryan Giggs
1993-94	Eric Cantona	Andy Cole
1994-95	Alan Shearer	Robbie Fowler
1995-96	Les Ferdinand	Robbie Fowler
1996-97	Alan Shearer	David Beckham
1997-98	Dennis Bergkamp	Michael Owen
1998-99	David Ginola	Nicolas Anelka
1999-2000	Roy Keane	Harry Kewell
2000-01	Teddy Sheringham	Steven Gerrard
2001-02	Ruud van Nistelrooy	Craig Bellamy
2002-03	Thierry Henry	Jermaine Jenas
2003-04	Thierry Henry	Scott Parker
2004-05	John Terry	Wayne Rooney
2005-06	Steven Gerrard	Wayne Rooney
2006-07	Cristiano Ronaldo	Cristiano Ronaldo
2007-08	Cristiano Ronaldo	Cesc Fabregas
2008-09	Ryan Giggs	Ashley Young

Young & Giggs

MANAGER OF THE MOST CLUBS!

Big Ron in his Coventry days

Former Man. United boss Ron Atkinson has been in charge of six clubs in the top flight. Big Ron managed West Brom, Man. United, Sheffield Wednesday, Aston Villa, Coventry and Nottingham Forest between 1978 and 1996. Dave Bassett managed five top-flight clubs, and could have made it seven if Crystal Palace (1996) and Barnsley (2000) hadn't lost Championship play-off finals.

Ron Atkinson and Carlton Palmer at Nottingham Forest's City Ground

Atkinson led Aston Villa to second place in the Prem in 1992-93

LONGEST SERVING BOSS!

Legendary Aston Villa gaffer **George Ramsay** (right) was in charge of The Villans for an unbelievable 42 years between 1884 and 1926. In that time, Villa won a massive six league titles and also picked up six FA Cups!

FOOTY SHORTS!

Young Fergie

Sir Alex Ferguson **almost became Arsenal manager in 1986, but decided to take over from Ron Atkinson at Man. United instead!**

Arsene Wenger

Arsene Wenger **is the second longest serving boss in the Prem. He's been in charge of the North London club since 1996!**

Howard Wilkinson

The last English manager to win the top flight was Howard Wilkinson, who led Leeds to their third league title in 1992!

2

FA CUP »

FA CUP »

ALSO KNOWN AS *THE FOOTBALL ASSOCIATION CHALLENGE CUP!*

Aston Villa, 1887

2009 WI

Chelsea came from behind to beat Everton in the 2009 Final

MOST FINALS!

Man. United (below) have appeared in the same amount of FA Cup finals as they've won top-flight titles. The Red Devils have played in the annual showdown a record 18 times, beating **Arsenal** who have appeared in 17 finals. **Liverpool**, **Everton** and **Newcastle** have all played in the final 13 times!

MOST CONSECUTIVE FINALS!

FA Cup success for Arsenal in 2005

Seven different clubs have played in three FA Cup finals in a row, with the most recent being **Arsenal** between 2001 and 2003. The others are **The Wanderers** (1876-78), **Old Etonians** (1881-83), **Blackburn Rovers** (1884-86), **West Brom** (1886-88), **Arsenal** again (1978-80), **Everton** (1984-86) and **Man. United** (1994-96).

CUP WINNERS!

The oldest existing club competition in the world has had 42 winners since it first took place in 1872. **Man. United** have won it a record 11 times, with **Arsenal** second on ten wins, **Tottenham** on eight, **Liverpool** and **Aston Villa** on seven each, and **Newcastle** and **Blackburn** on six!

Man. United, 1963 FA Cup winners

MANCHESTER
- MAN. CITY
- MAN. UNITED

BLACKBURN
- BLACKBURN
- BLACKPOOL
- BLACKBURN OLYMPIC

- PRESTON

LIVERPOOL
- EVERTON
- LIVERPOOL

- BOLTON
- HUDDERSFIELD
- WOLVES

- BURY

- SUNDERLAND
- NEWCASTLE
- MIDDLESBROUGH

- BURNLEY
- BRADFORD
- LEEDS
- BARNSLEY

SHEFFIELD
- SHEFF. WED.
- SHEFF. UNITED
- HULL

- CARDIFF
- COVENTRY
- OXFORD UNIVERSITY

NOTTINGHAM
- DERBY
- NOTTS COUNTY
- NOTT'M FOREST

BIRMINGHAM
- ASTON VILLA
- WEST BROM

- OLD ETONIANS
- OLD CARTHUSIANS
- SOUTHAMPTON
- PORTSMOUTH

- IPSWICH
- ROYAL ENGINEERS

LONDON
- ARSENAL
- CHARLTON
- CHELSEA
- CLAPHAM ROVERS
- TOTTENHAM
- WEST HAM
- WANDERERS
- WIMBLEDON

FOOTY SHORTS!

Preston goalkeeper James Frederick Mitchell became the only man to play in an FA Cup final while wearing glasses back in 1922!

Alf Bond

Alf Bond, who refereed the 1956 Final between Man. City and Birmingham, only had one arm. He also used to run a newsagent's in Fulham!

Fans paid just 5p to watch the first FA Cup Final at the Kennington Oval in London! The most expensive ticket for the 2009 Final was £93!

FA CUP WINNERS!

MATCH checks out every winner of the world-famous cup competition!

Blackburn Rovers, 1884

1871-72	Wanderers	1-0	Royal Engineers
1872-73	Wanderers	2-0	Oxford University
1873-74	Oxford University	2-0	Royal Engineers
1874-75	Royal Engineers	1-1	Old Etonians
Royal Engineers won the replay 2-0			
1875-76	Wanderers	1-1	Old Etonians
Wanderers won the replay 3-0			
1876-77	Wanderers	2-1	Oxford University
Wanderers won after extra-time			
1877-78	Wanderers	3-1	Royal Engineers
1878-79	Old Etonians	1-0	Clapham Rovers
1879-80	Clapham Rovers	1-0	Oxford University
1880-81	Old Carthusians	3-0	Old Etonians
1881-82	Old Etonians	1-0	Blackburn
1882-83	Blackburn Olympic	2-1	Old Etonians
Blackburn Olympic won after extra-time			
1883-84	Blackburn	2-1	Queen's Park
1884-85	Blackburn	2-0	Queen's Park
1885-86	Blackburn	0-0	West Brom
Blackburn won the replay 2-0			
1886-87	Aston Villa	2-0	West Brom
1887-88	West Brom	2-1	Preston
1888-89	Preston	3-0	Wolves
1889-90	Blackburn	6-1	The Wednesday
1890-91	Blackburn	3-1	Notts County
1891-92	West Brom	3-0	Aston Villa
1892-93	Wolves	1-0	Everton
1893-94	Notts County	4-1	Bolton
1894-95	Aston Villa	1-0	West Brom
1895-96	The Wednesday	2-1	Wolves
1896-97	Aston Villa	3-2	Everton
1897-98	Nottingham Forest	3-1	Derby
1898-99	Sheffield United	4-1	Derby
1899-1900	Bury	4-0	Southampton
1900-01	Tottenham	2-2	Sheffield United
Tottenham won the replay 3-1			
1901-02	Sheffield United	1-1	Southampton
Sheffield United won the replay 2-1			
1902-03	Bury	6-0	Derby
1903-04	Man. City	1-0	Bolton
1904-05	Aston Villa	2-0	Newcastle
1905-06	Everton	1-0	Newcastle
1906-07	The Wednesday	2-1	Everton
1907-08	Wolves	3-1	Newcastle
1908-09	Man. United	1-0	Bristol City
1909-10	Newcastle	1-1	Barnsley
Newcastle won the replay 2-0			
1910-11	Bradford	0-0	Newcastle
Bradford won the replay 1-0			
1911-12	Barnsley	0-0	West Brom
Bradford won the replay after extra-time 1-0			
1912-13	Aston Villa	1-0	Sunderland
1913-14	Burnley	1-0	Liverpool
1914-15	Sheffield United	3-0	Chelsea
1916-19	*No FA Cup matches because of the First World War*		

Continued over >>

MOST WINNERS' MEDALS!

Arthur Kinnaird · Roy Keane

MOST FA CUP FINAL APPEARANCES BY A PLAYER!

No player in the modern game has been able to beat **Arthur Kinnaird**'s unbelievable FA Cup final record. Kinnaird, who played in various positions, made nine final appearances in a decade playing for The Wanderers and Old Etonians between 1873-83. The closest any modern player has come to this was **Roy Keane**, who played in seven finals for Nottingham Forest and Man. United!

Sir Alex Ferguson

MOST FA CUP FINAL APPEARANCES BY A MANAGER!

Is there any manager's record that Man. United boss **Sir Alex Ferguson** doesn't hold? Fergie has led The Red Devils to eight FA Cup finals, winning five of them in 1990, 1994, 1996, 1999 and 2004!

FAB FACT!
Paul Bracewell played in Four Cup Finals with Everton and Sunderland, but never got his hands on a winner's medal!

THE FA CUP!

The current version of the FA Cup is the fourth in the competition's 137-year history! Every year, the cup returns to a team of craftsmen at Thomas Lyte Silver who repair the trophy before handing it over to the new winners!

THE LID!
The small sculpture that sits at the very top of the FA Cup is a miniature version of the trophy!

FIRST TROPHY!
The original FA Cup, which was used between 1872 and 1895, was stolen from a Birmingham football shop and melted down to make coins!

KINNAIRD'S CUP!
FA Cup legend Arthur Kinnaird was given the next trophy to keep in 1910! You can now see it at the National Football Museum in Preston!

TODAY'S TROPHY!
The current FA Cup was unveiled in 1992 and was first won by Liverpool. It's a replica of the trophy that was used between 1911 and 1991!

DAMAGE!
The trophy fell off a bus after Chelsea won it in 2007 and was then dropped again by Portsmouth players in 2008!

YOUDAN CUP!
The FA Cup isn't the oldest domestic trophy in world footy! That honour goes to the Youdan Cup, which was first played in Sheffield in 1867!

TROPHY KINGS!
The staff at Thomas Lyte Silver are expert craftsmen! They made the League Cup and golf's Ryder Cup!

FOOTY SHORTS!

The famous FA Cup final song Abide With Me was first sung in 1927. That was also the first final to be broadcast live on BBC Radio!

Norman Whiteside (right)

The youngest final scorer was Norman Whiteside for Man. United in 1983! He was 18 years & 19 days old when he netted against Brighton!

David Seaman

Arsenal legend David Seaman is the oldest ever captain in an FA Cup final! He was 39 years and 240 days old when he lifted the trophy in 2003!

FA CUP FINALS!

MATCH checks out every winner of the world-famous cup competition!

Huddersfield v Preston, 1922

Season	Winner	Score	Runner-up
1919-20	Aston Villa	1-0	Huddersfield
	Aston Villa won after extra-time		
1920-21	Tottenham	1-0	Wolves
1921-22	Huddersfield	1-0	Preston
1922-23	Bolton	2-0	West Ham
1923-24	Newcastle	2-0	Aston Villa
1924-25	Sheffield United	1-0	Cardiff
1925-26	Bolton	1-0	Man. City
1926-27	Cardiff	1-0	Arsenal
1927-28	Blackburn	3-1	Huddersfield
1928-29	Bolton	2-0	Portsmouth
1929-30	Arsenal	2-0	Huddersfield
1930-31	West Brom	2-1	Birmingham
1931-32	Newcastle	2-1	Arsenal
1932-33	Everton	3-0	Man. City
1933-34	Man. City	2-1	Portsmouth
1934-35	Sheff. Wed.	4-2	West Brom
1935-36	Arsenal	1-0	Sheffield United
1936-37	Sunderland	3-1	Preston
1937-38	Preston	1-0	Huddersfield
	Preston won after extra-time		
1938-39	Portsmouth	4-1	Wolves
1940-45	*No FA Cup matches because of the Second World War*		

Continued over >>

Arsenal lift the trophy in 1936

Hughie Ferguson makes history for Cardiff

DID YOU KNOW?
Cardiff became the only non-English team to ever win the FA Cup when they beat Arsenal 1-0 at Wembley in 1927!

CLASSIC GAME!

LIVERPOOL 3 - 3 WEST HAM

LIVERPOOL WIN 3-1 ON PENALTIES

Cisse bags Liverpool's first

MAY 13, 2006 ★ MILLENNIUM STADIUM

WHAT HAPPENED? The last FA Cup final to be played in Cardiff saw West Ham go 2-0 up after 28 minutes, then lead 3-2 with just seconds to play, but it wouldn't be their day. Liverpool captain **Steven Gerrard** unleashed a stunning 40-yard volley in the 90th minute to force extra-time before Reds keeper Pepe Reina saved three spot-kicks in the penalty shoot-out. Gerrard picked up the Man Of The Match award before lifting Liverpool's seventh FA Cup!

Reina saves from Konchesky

Dean Ashton makes it 2-0 to West Ham

THE BEST OF THE REST!

MATCH checks out the greatest games in the history of the FA Cup!

Giggs scores one of the FA Cup's greatest ever goals

MAN. UNITED 2-1 ARSENAL

April 14, 1999: It all kicked off in this FA Cup semi-final replay. Arsenal had a goal wrongly disallowed for offside, Roy Keane was sent off, Dennis Bergkamp missed a penalty and *Ryan Giggs* scored a stunning extra-time winner!

Craig Hignett buries a penalty for Boro

MIDDLESBROUGH 3-3 CHESTERFIELD

April 13, 1997: Third Division Chesterfield thought they were heading to Wembley when Jonathan Howard's shot crashed off the bar and over the line to make it 3-1, but the goal was disallowed. Boro fought back and won the replay!

Nick Pickering celebrates Coventry's winner

COVENTRY 3-2 TOTTENHAM

May 16, 1987: Spurs had never lost an FA Cup final and were red-hot favourites, but underdogs Coventry had other ideas! Keith Houchen's amazing diving header and an own goal from *Gary Mabbutt* saw them pull off a shock victory!

MOST GOALS IN A FINAL!

Stan Mortensen nets the second of his three goals in the 1953 FA Cup Final

Scoring once in an FA Cup final is good enough, but to hit a hat-trick is mind-blowing! Three players have crashed home trebles in the final, but the only one to do it at Wembley was Blackpool striker Stan Mortensen, who scored three in the 1953 final against Bolton. Blackburn winger Billy Townley netted three times against Sheffield Wednesday in 1890, while Jimmy Logan also hit a hat-trick for Notts County against Bolton in 1894!

FAB FACT!
Even though Mortensen scored three of Blackpool's goals in 1953, the match was named the 'Matthews Final' after Sir Stanley Matthews!

MOST GOALS IN A MATCH!

Bournemouth striker **Ted MacDougall**'s boots were on fire against Margate back in the 1970-71 season! The Scotland international, who later played for Man. United and West Ham, scored nine goals in one match against Margate. MacDougall's record beat the previous best set back in 1887, when Preston's legendary striker **Jimmy Ross** bagged eight goals against Hyde during North End's run to the final. Preston's good luck ended there, though, because they were beaten 2-1 by West Brom at Kennington Oval!

Jimmy Ross

FASTEST GOAL!

Louis Saha writes his name into the FA Cup history books

Everton striker **Louis Saha** scored the fastest ever FA Cup final goal in 2009 when he bagged against Chelsea after just 25 seconds of his side's 2-1 defeat! The scorer of the quickest FA Cup goal of all-time is unknown, although West Brom did hit the net after just five seconds against The Druids way back in 1885!

SCORED IN MOST FINALS!

Liverpool superstar **Ian Rush** scored in three different cup finals, in 1986, 1989 and 1992. Rushy's strikes equalled **Arthur Kinnaird**'s record of scoring in the 1873, 1877 and 1878 finals. Kinnaird's goal in 1877 was originally recorded as an own goal, but he had that fact wiped from the record books when he became president of The FA!

Rush nets against Everton in the 1986 final

BIGGEST WIN!

Hyde will want to forget their massive 26-0 defeat at the hands of **Preston** in 1887. North End could have scored even more goals, but they wasted valuable time running to get the ball after every goal because they had no nets!

PRESTON NORTH END FC

BIGGEST COMEBACK!

Man. City fought back from 3-0 down at half-time against Tottenham in a fourth-round replay in February 2004. Incredibly, City had Joey Barton sent off early in the second half but still won 4-3. In a fifth-round replay in 2001, Paul Rideout hit a hat-trick for Tranmere as they also battled back from 3-0 down to beat Southampton 4-3!

Jon Macken celebrates City's winner at White Hart Lane

FOOTY SHORTS!

Due to a shortage of quality materials after the Second World War, the ball burst in both the 1946 and 1947 FA Cup finals!

Gary Mabbutt

Tottenham's Gary Mabbutt, Man. City's Tommy Hutchison and Charlton's Bert Turner have all scored for both teams in an FA Cup final!

Gary Talbot

The fastest FA Cup hat-tricks were scored in three minutes by Chester's Gary Talbot in 1964 and Southend's Billy Best in 1968!

FA CUP WINNERS!

MATCH checks out every FA Cup final from 1946 to 1975!

Newcastle's Joe Harvey lifts the FA Cup in 1951

1945-46	Derby	4-1	Charlton
	Derby won after extra-time		
1946-47	Charlton	1-0	Burnley
	Charlton won after extra-time		
1947-48	Man. United	4-2	Blackpool
1948-49	Wolves	3-1	Leicester
1949-50	Arsenal	2-0	Liverpool
1950-51	Newcastle	2-0	Blackpool
1951-52	Newcastle	1-0	Arsenal
1952-53	Blackpool	4-3	Bolton
1953-54	West Brom	3-2	Preston
1954-55	Newcastle	3-1	Man. City
1955-56	Man. City	3-1	Birmingham
1956-57	Aston Villa	2-1	Man. United
1957-58	Bolton	2-0	Man. United
1958-59	Nottingham Forest	2-1	Luton
1959-60	Wolves	3-0	Blackburn
1960-61	Tottenham	2-0	Leicester
1961-62	Tottenham	3-1	Burnley
1962-63	Man. United	3-1	Leicester
1963-64	West Ham	3-2	Preston
1964-65	Liverpool	2-1	Leeds
	Liverpool won after extra-time		
1965-66	Everton	3-2	Sheff. Wed.
1966-67	Tottenham	2-1	Chelsea
1967-68	West Brom	1-0	Everton
	West Brom won after extra-time		
1968-69	Man. City	1-0	Leicester
1969-70	Chelsea	2-2	Leeds
	Chelsea won the replay 2-1		
1970-71	Arsenal	2-1	Liverpool
	Arsenal won after extra-time		
1971-72	Leeds	1-0	Arsenal
1972-73	Sunderland	1-0	Leeds
1973-74	Liverpool	3-0	Newcastle
1974-75	West Ham	2-0	Fulham

Continued over >>

Bert Trautmann

DID YOU KNOW?

In the 1956 FA Cup final, Man. City keeper Bert Trautmann played on after breaking a bone in his neck in the 75th minute!

HIGHEST ATTENDANCE!

The 1923 final at Wembley drew the largest crowd ever seen at an FA Cup match. The record books say 126,047 people saw Bolton beat West Ham 2-0, but no tickets were sold for the match so it's impossible to count how many made it inside the stadium. Some people reckon the crowd could have been as high as 200,000!

Billie the horse wades through the crowd in 1923

THE WHITE HORSE FINAL!

Bolton's 1923 FA Cup Final victory was the first ever played at Wembley, and there were so many people at the game that fans had to be cleared from the pitch by mounted police. The match has been known as 'The White Horse Final' ever since, because of the famous police horse, Billie, that appeared on the pitch!

FAB FACT!
The FA built a footbridge, known as 'The White Horse Bridge', at the new Wembley stadium in 2006 to celebrate the 1923 Final!

The 1923 FA Cup Final

RED CARDS IN THE FINAL!

Kevin Moran receives his shock red card in 1985

Just before half-time in the 1985 FA Cup Final, referee Peter Willis sent Man. United defender Kevin Moran off after a tackle on Everton midfielder Peter Reid. Moran was the first man to receive a red card in an FA Cup final, with the second not coming until 20 years later in 2005. Arsenal's Jose Antonio Reyes was sent off by ref Rob Styles against Man. United at the Millennium Stadium, but his side still went on to win the cup in a penalty shoot-out!

FASTEST RED CARD!

Swindon's **Ian Culverhouse** was sent off after just 52 seconds of his side's third-round tie at Everton in 1997. His handball led to a penalty, and Swindon lost the game 3-0!

Early bath for Ian Culverhouse

Dave Beasant saves from John Aldridge

VENDEN PAPERS

FIRST PENALTY SAVE!

Wimbledon's **Dave Beasant** became the first goalkeeper to save an FA Cup final penalty in 1988. The Dons captain dived to his left to save Liverpool striker John Aldridge's spot-kick as Wimbledon's Crazy Gang shocked The Reds in one of the biggest cup upsets of all time. The first player to miss a penalty in an FA Cup final was Aston Villa's **Charlie Wallace** (right) against Sunderland way back in 1913!

FOOTY SHORTS!

No fans watched Bradford play Norwich in 1915, because The FA banned fans from stadiums near munitions factories in World War One!

Patrick Vieira
The first penalty shoot-out in an FA Cup final was in 2005, when Arsenal beat Man. United 5-4 after 120 goalless minutes!

Yeovil stun Blackpool in 2000
Yeovil love causing FA Cup upsets! When the Somerset club were a non-league team, they picked up 20 victories against league opponents!

FA CUP FINALS!

MATCH checks out every FA Cup final from 1976 to 2009!

The 'Crazy Gang' go crazy in 1988

Season	Winner	Score	Runner-up
1975-76	Southampton	1-0	Man. United
1976-77	Man. United	2-1	Liverpool
1977-78	Ipswich	1-0	Arsenal
1978-79	Arsenal	3-2	Man. United
1979-80	West Ham	1-0	Arsenal
1980-81	Tottenham	1-1	Man. City
	Tottenham won the replay 3-2		
1981-82	Tottenham	1-1	QPR
	Tottenham won the replay 1-0		
1982-83	Man. United	2-2	Brighton
	Man. United won the replay 4-0		
1983-84	Everton	2-0	Watford
1984-85	Man. United	1-0	Everton
	Man. United won after extra-time		
1985-86	Liverpool	3-1	Everton
1986-87	Coventry	3-2	Tottenham
	Coventry won after extra-time		
1987-88	Wimbledon	1-0	Liverpool
1988-89	Liverpool	3-2	Everton
	Liverpool won after extra-time		
1989-90	Man. United	3-3	Crystal Palace
	Man. United won the replay 1-0		
1990-91	Tottenham	2-1	Nottingham Forest
	Tottenham won after extra-time		
1991-92	Liverpool	2-0	Sunderland
1992-93	Arsenal	1-1	Sheff. Wed.
	Arsenal won the replay 2-1		
1993-94	Man. United	4-0	Chelsea
1994-95	Everton	1-0	Man. United
1995-96	Man. United	1-0	Liverpool
1996-97	Chelsea	2-0	Middlesbrough
1997-98	Arsenal	2-0	Newcastle
1998-99	Man. United	2-0	Newcastle
1999-2000	Chelsea	1-0	Aston Villa
2000-01	Liverpool	2-1	Arsenal
2001-02	Arsenal	2-0	Chelsea
2002-03	Arsenal	1-0	Southampton
2003-04	Man. United	3-0	Millwall
2004-05	Arsenal	0-0	Man. United
	Arsenal won 5-4 on penalties after extra-time		
2005-06	Liverpool	3-3	West Ham
	Liverpool won 3-1 on penalties after extra-time		
2006-07	Chelsea	1-0	Man. United
	Chelsea won after extra-time		
2007-08	Portsmouth	1-0	Cardiff
2008-09	Chelsea	2-1	Everton

Coventry shock Spurs in 1987

WEMBLEY

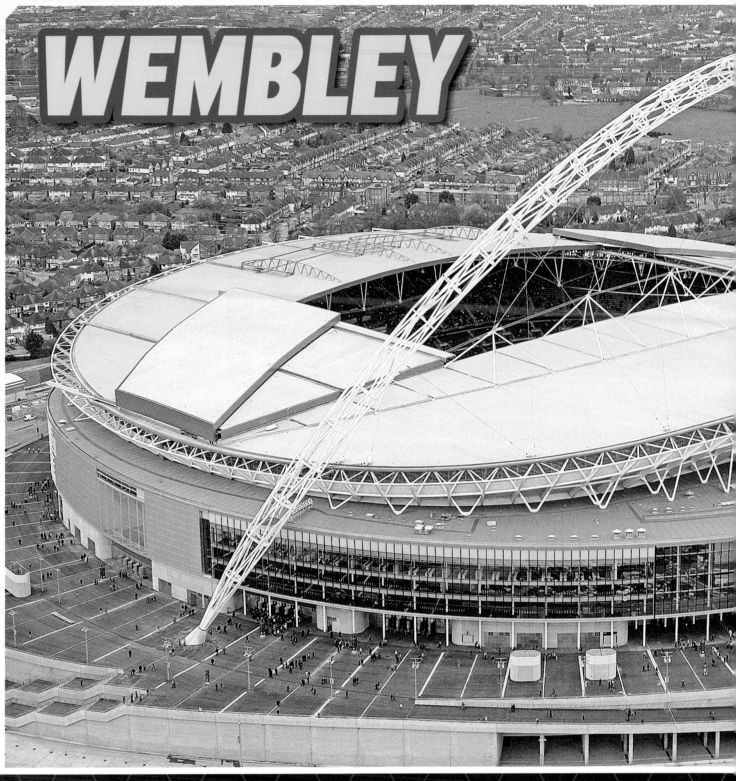

FAB FACTS!

MEGA HIGH!

≫ The new Wembley is four times higher than the old stadium! It can be seen from 13 miles away! ≫

TONS OF TOILETS!

≫ There are 2,618 toilets at Wembley – more than any other sports venue on the planet! ≫

DRY FANS!

≫ All 90,000 seats are covered at Wembley, so fans should stay dry when they watch the match! ≫

GIANT ARCH!

≫ The arch over Wembley is seven metres wide – big enough for a train to burn through! ≫

HUGE SCREENS!

≫ It would take 600 TVs stacked together to match the size of the screens that hang above the pitch! ≫

SUPER STADIUMS OF THE WORLD!

CITY	LONDON
OPENED	2007
TEAM	ENGLAND
CAPACITY	90,000

GREATEST MATCH EVER!

ENGLAND 4-2 WEST GERMANY, 1966

Bobby Moore captained the Three Lions to World Cup glory at Wembley in a classic match! Sir Geoff Hurst is still the only player to hit a hat-trick in the final!

LEGENDS!

GEORGE BEST

Man. United became the first English team to win the European Cup when they beat Benfica 4-1 in 1968! United's legendary winger netted the game's second goal in extra-time!

PAUL GASCOIGNE

Gazza scored one of Wembley's greatest ever goals when England beat rivals Scotland at Euro '96! He flicked the ball over Colin Hendry before burying a class volley!

BIG MONEY!

≫ Wembley cost an incredible £778 million to build! That's as much as 4.8 million Xbox 360s! ≫

HEAVYWEIGHT!

≫ The arch weighs as much as ten jumbo jets or 275 double-decker buses! That's mega heavy! ≫

CRAZY TUBES!

≫ The steel tubes inside the arch are so big that 850 pints of milk could fill each one! ≫

MOST MATCHES AS MANAGER!

Alex Ferguson has won five FA Cups with Man. United

Sir Alex Ferguson holds the record for most finals as a boss, but he falls short of George Ramsay's achievement for the most FA Cup games as a gaffer. Between 1884 and 1926, Aston Villa's legendary manager took charge of his side in an incredible 142 matches. By the end of the 2008-09 season, Fergie had managed Man. United in 104 FA Cup matches!

THE YOUNGEST MANAGER!

Stan Cullis (right) became Wolves boss in 1948 and led his team to an amazing 3-1 FA Cup final win over Leicester in his first season in charge, when he was just 32 years and 187 days old!

FOOTY SHORTS!

Bob Stokoe

In 1973, Sunderland boss Bob Stokoe became the last man to lead a team to FA Cup final glory without having a single international player in his side!

Harry Redknapp

When Harry Redknapp lifted the FA Cup with Portsmouth in 2008, it was his first major honour in over 20 years as a football manager!

Trevor Francis

Trevor Francis (1993) and Bryan Robson (1997) are the only gaffers to have lost the FA Cup and League Cup finals in the same season!

LEAGUE CUP »

LEAGUE CUP »

FAB FACT!
Man. United's Ben Foster became the first keeper for six years to be named Man Of The Match in a League Cup Final after his heroics against Spurs in 2009!

Man. United beat Spurs on penalties to win the 2009 League Cup

MOST FINALS!

Liverpool haven't appeared in the League Cup final since 2005, but they've won the trophy more times than any other club! The Reds played in the final a record ten times between 1978 and 2005, winning four of them on the bounce between 1981 and 1984! Aston Villa, Man. United and Tottenham have all played in seven finals each!

MOST CONSECUTIVE FINALS!

The all-conquering **Liverpool** team of the early 1980s couldn't keep away from the League Cup final. The Reds ran out at Wembley four seasons in a row between 1981 and 1984, and unbelievably won all four of them. That run also included the first ever all-Merseyside League Cup final against Everton in 1984!

CUP WINNERS!

Just 22 clubs have lifted the League Cup since Aston Villa beat Rotherham in the first final back in 1961. During its first six seasons, the finalists played each other home and away to decide who won the trophy, but it changed to a one-off final from 1967. **Liverpool** hold the record with seven League Cup wins, while **Aston Villa** have five. **Chelsea, Tottenham** and **Nottingham Forest** have four each!

Aston Villa lift the League Cup in 1994

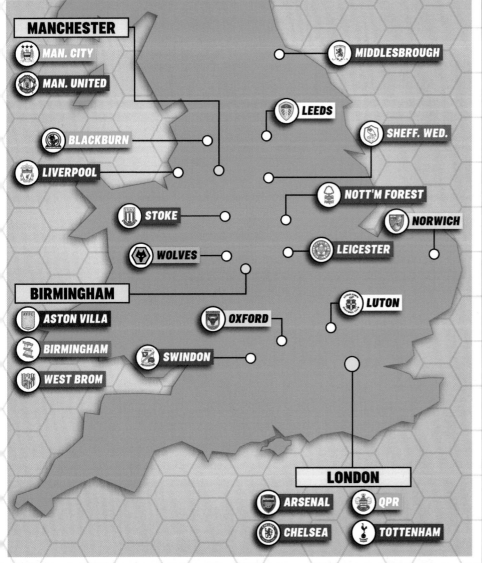

MANCHESTER
- MAN. CITY
- MAN. UNITED

- MIDDLESBROUGH
- LEEDS
- SHEFF. WED.
- BLACKBURN
- LIVERPOOL
- NOTT'M FOREST
- STOKE
- NORWICH
- WOLVES
- LEICESTER

BIRMINGHAM
- ASTON VILLA
- BIRMINGHAM
- WEST BROM
- OXFORD
- LUTON
- SWINDON

LONDON
- ARSENAL
- QPR
- CHELSEA
- TOTTENHAM

FOOTY SHORTS!

Wendy Toms

The first woman to run the line in a League Cup final was Wendy Toms when Leicester beat Tranmere at Wembley in 2000!

Barry Venison

Sunderland's Barry Venison is the youngest ever captain in a League Cup final! He was 20 years old when he wore the armband in 1985!

Armand Traore

Arsenal left-back Armand Traore was just 17 years old when he played against Chelsea in 2007, making him the youngest ever finalist!

LEAGUE CUP FINALS!

MATCH checks out all the finals between 1961 and 1976!

Bobby Tambling nets for Chelsea in 1965

1960-61	Rotherham	2-0	Aston Villa	
	Aston Villa	3-0	Rotherham	
	Aston Villa won 3-2 on aggregate			
1961-62	Rochdale	0-3	Norwich	
	Norwich	1-0	Rochdale	
	Norwich won 4-0 on aggregate			
1962-63	Birmingham	3-1	Aston Villa	
	Aston Villa	0-0	Birmingham	
	Birmingham won 3-1 on aggregate			
1963-64	Stoke	1-1	Leicester	
	Leicester	3-2	Stoke	
	Leicester won 4-3 on aggregate			
1964-65	Chelsea	3-2	Leicester	
	Leicester	0-0	Chelsea	
	Chelsea won 3-2 on aggregate			
1965-66	West Ham	2-1	West Brom	
	West Brom	4-1	West Ham	
	West Brom won 5-3 on aggregate			
1966-67	QPR	3-2	West Brom	
1967-68	Leeds	1-0	Arsenal	
1968-69	Swindon	3-1	Arsenal	
	Swindon won after extra-time			
1969-70	Man. City	2-1	West Brom	
	Man. City won after extra-time			
1970-71	Tottenham	2-1	Aston Villa	
1971-72	Stoke	2-1	Chelsea	
1972-73	Tottenham	1-0	Norwich	
1973-74	Wolves	2-1	Man. City	
1974-75	Aston Villa	1-0	Norwich	
1975-76	Man. City	2-1	Newcastle	

Continued over >>

Trevor Hebberd (centre)

DID YOU KNOW?

Southampton's Trevor Hebberd played in every round of the 1979 League Cup, except the final! The midfielder had to wait until 1986 before winning the final 3-0 with Oxford after scoring the game's opening goal!

MOST WINNERS' MEDALS!

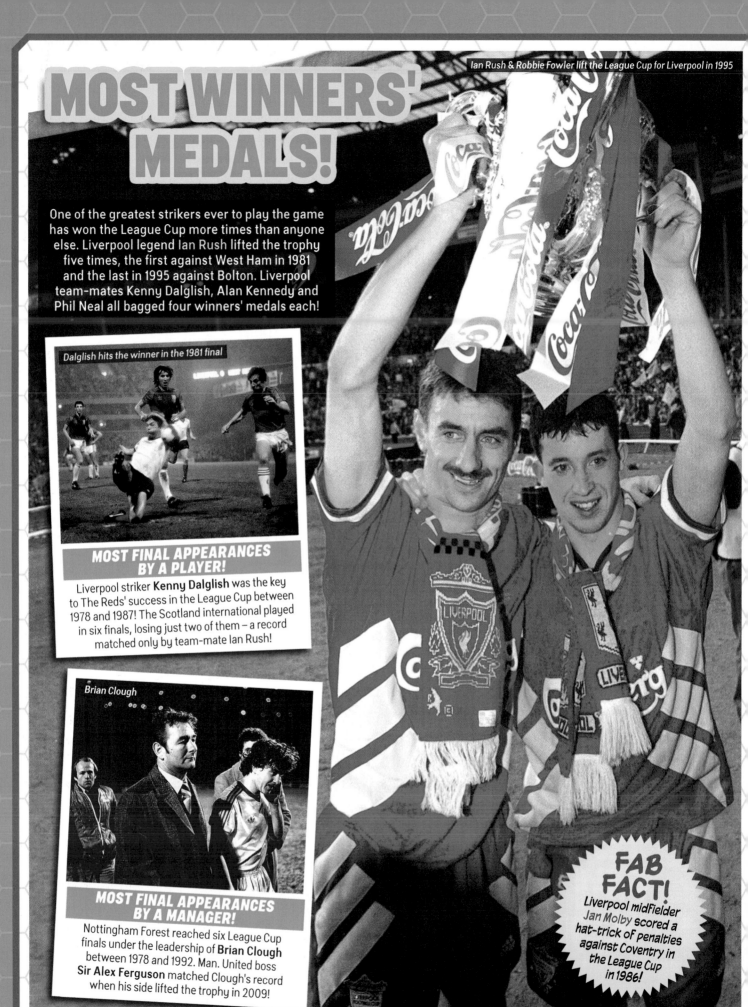

One of the greatest strikers ever to play the game has won the League Cup more times than anyone else. Liverpool legend Ian Rush lifted the trophy five times, the first against West Ham in 1981 and the last in 1995 against Bolton. Liverpool team-mates Kenny Dalglish, Alan Kennedy and Phil Neal all bagged four winners' medals each!

Dalglish hits the winner in the 1981 final

MOST FINAL APPEARANCES BY A PLAYER!

Liverpool striker **Kenny Dalglish** was the key to The Reds' success in the League Cup between 1978 and 1987! The Scotland international played in six finals, losing just two of them – a record matched only by team-mate Ian Rush!

Brian Clough

MOST FINAL APPEARANCES BY A MANAGER!

Nottingham Forest reached six League Cup finals under the leadership of **Brian Clough** between 1978 and 1992. Man. United boss **Sir Alex Ferguson** matched Clough's record when his side lifted the trophy in 2009!

FAB FACT!
Liverpool midfielder Jan Molby scored a hat-trick of penalties against Coventry in the League Cup in 1986!

The Milk Cup

Littlewoods Challenge Cup

MATCH checks out every League Cup final from 1977 to 1992!

Glory for Nottingham Forest in 1989

Season	Team	Score	Team
1976-77	Aston Villa	0-0	Everton

Aston Villa won the second replay 3-2 after a 1-1 draw in the first replay

1977-78	Nottingham Forest	0-0	Liverpool

Nottingham Forest won the replay 1-0

1978-79	Nottingham Forest	3-2	Southampton
1979-80	Nottingham Forest	0-1	Wolves
1980-81	Liverpool	1-1	West Ham

Liverpool won the replay 2-1

MILK CUP

1981-82	Liverpool	3-1	Tottenham

Liverpool won after extra-time

1982-83	Liverpool	2-1	Man. United

Liverpool won after extra-time

1983-84	Liverpool	0-0	Everton

Liverpool won the replay 1-0

1984-85	Norwich	1-0	Sunderland
1985-86	Oxford	3-0	QPR

LITTLEWOODS CHALLENGE CUP

1986-87	Arsenal	2-1	Liverpool
1987-88	Luton	3-2	Arsenal
1988-89	Nottingham Forest	3-1	Luton
1989-90	Nottingham Forest	1-0	Oldham

RUMBLELOWS CUP

1990-91	Sheff. Wed.	1-0	Man. United
1991-92	Man. United	1-0	Nottingham Forest

Continued over >>

It's Norwich City's year in 1985

Rush opens the scoring in the 1987 final

DID YOU KNOW?

When Liverpool were beaten 2-1 in the 1987 Final by Arsenal, it was the first time they'd lost a match in which Ian Rush had scored!

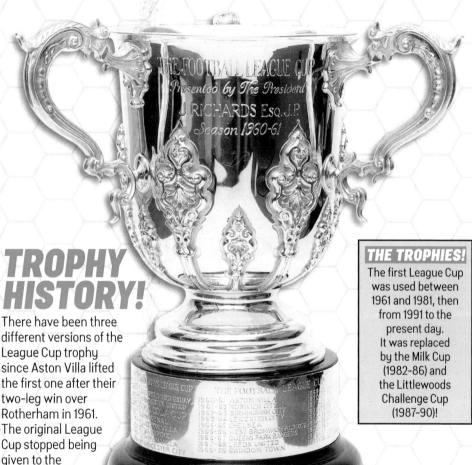

TROPHY HISTORY!

There have been three different versions of the League Cup trophy since Aston Villa lifted the first one after their two-leg win over Rotherham in 1961. The original League Cup stopped being given to the winners after the 1981 final, but was then brought back ten years later!

THE TROPHIES!
The first League Cup was used between 1961 and 1981, then from 1991 to the present day. It was replaced by the Milk Cup (1982-86) and the Littlewoods Challenge Cup (1987-90)!

FOOTY SHORTS!

The Millennium Stadium

The first major English final to be played outside England was the League Cup final in Cardiff in 2001, because Wembley was being rebuilt!

Peter Shilton

At 48 years old, Peter Shilton became the League Cup final's oldest ever player when he was Middlesbrough's back-up keeper against Chelsea in 1998!

Norman Whiteside (left)

Norman Whiteside, aged 17, became the youngest scorer in a League Cup final when he netted for Man. United against Liverpool in 1983!

MOST GOALS IN A FINAL!

Lethal Chelsea goal machine Didier Drogba loves getting on the scoresheet in League Cup finals. The Ivory Coast international has bagged four goals in different finals – once in 2005 and 2008, and twice in 2007. Drogba beat the previous record of three goals, held by Liverpool's Ronnie Whelan and West Brom's Clive Clark!

Drogba sinks Arsenal in the 2007 League Cup Final

MOST GOALS IN A MATCH!

Oldham striker **Frankie Bunn** (left) was on fire against Scarborough in 1989 when he blasted six goals during his side's 7-0 win in the League Cup third round! That beat the five-goal record set by Southampton's **Derek Reeves**, QPR's **Alan Wilks**, Everton's **Bob Latchford** and Coventry's **Cyrille Regis**!

Cyrille Regis

Bob Latchford

FASTEST GOAL!

Bellion beats Almunia at Old Trafford

David Bellion only played five League Cup matches for Man. United between 2003 and 2006, but he still managed to score after just 19 seconds against Arsenal in the 2005 quarter-finals! The fastest goal in a final was volleyed home by Liverpool's **John Arne Riise** against Chelsea after only 45 seconds in 2005!

FASTEST RED CARD!

Former Arsenal defender **Jason Crowe** will probably want to forget his first-team debut in October 1997. Referee Uriah Rennie sent off the current Leeds right-back after he took out Birmingham midfielder Martin O'Connor just 33 seconds after he'd come off the bench to replace Gunners legend Lee Dixon! Crowe only played two more games for Arsenal before joining Portsmouth for £1 million in July 1999!

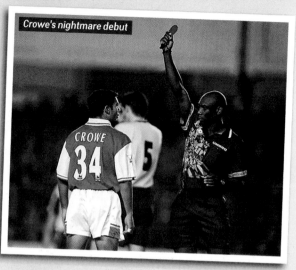
Crowe's nightmare debut

MOST HAT-TRICKS!

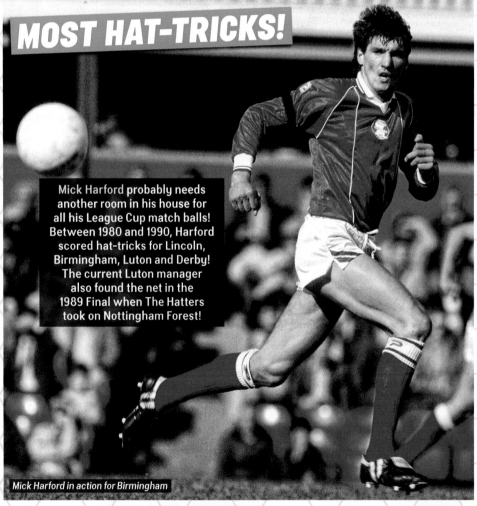

Mick Harford probably needs another room in his house for all his League Cup match balls! Between 1980 and 1990, Harford scored hat-tricks for Lincoln, Birmingham, Luton and Derby! The current Luton manager also found the net in the 1989 Final when The Hatters took on Nottingham Forest!

Mick Harford in action for Birmingham

MATCH checks out all the finals between 1993 and 2009!

Party time for Leicester in 1997

COCA-COLA CUP			
1992-93	Arsenal	2-1	Sheff. Wed.
1993-94	Aston Villa	3-1	Man. United
1994-95	Liverpool	2-1	Bolton
1995-96	Aston Villa	3-0	Leeds
1996-97	Leicester	1-1	Middlesbrough
Leicester won the replay 1-0 after extra-time			
1997-98	Chelsea	2-0	Middlesbrough
Chelsea won after extra-time			
WORTHINGTON CUP			
1998-99	Tottenham	1-0	Leicester
1999-2000	Leicester	2-1	Tranmere
2000-01	Liverpool	1-1	Birmingham
Liverpool won 5-4 on penalties after extra-time			
2001-02	Blackburn	2-1	Tottenham
2002-03	Liverpool	2-0	Man. United
CARLING CUP			
2003-04	Middlesbrough	2-1	Bolton
2004-05	Chelsea	3-2	Liverpool
Chelsea won after extra-time			
2005-06	Man. United	4-0	Wigan
2006-07	Chelsea	2-1	Arsenal
2007-08	Tottenham	2-1	Chelsea
Tottenham won after extra-time			
2008-09	Man. United	0-0	Tottenham
Man. United won 4-1 on penalties after extra-time			

It's Chelsea's year in 2007

Elliott wins the cup for Leicester

DID YOU KNOW?

The 2000 Final between Leicester and Tranmere saw both captains score! Matt Elliott hit a brace for The Foxes, while David Kelly netted for Rovers!

Liverpool v Birmingham

The first League Cup final to be decided on penalties was in 2001 when Liverpool won their shoot-out 5-4 against Birmingham!

George Eastham (right)

George Eastham was 35 years old when he netted to give Stoke the only major trophy in their history in 1972! He's the oldest scorer in a final!

Steve Mildenhall

Goalkeeper Steve Mildenhall scored a free-kick from his own half for Notts County when they beat Mansfield 4-3 in the first round in 2001!

CLASSIC GAME!
LIVERPOOL 3 - 6 ARSENAL

Hyypia nets a consolation goal

JANUARY 9, 2007 ★ ANFIELD

WHAT HAPPENED? Brazil international Julio Baptista only spent one season with Arsenal on loan from Real Madrid, but he guaranteed himself legendary status by scoring four goals in the Carling Cup quarter-final against Liverpool! The Beast tore The Reds apart and even missed a penalty as Liverpool leaked six goals at home for the first time in nearly 77 years! Arsenal's huge win set them on their way to the final, where they lost 2-1 to Chelsea!

Arsenal go goal crazy at Anfield

Jeremie Aliadiere opens the scoring

THE BEST OF THE REST!

MATCH checks out the greatest games in the history of the Carling Cup!

Robbie Keane bags Tottenham's third goal

TOTTENHAM 5-1 ARSENAL

January 21, 2008: Tottenham secured their first win over their massive North London rivals since 1999 to reach the Carling Cup final on an amazing night at White Hart Lane. **Steed Malbranque** completed the rout in the final minute!

Drogba heads home the winner

CHELSEA 2-1 ARSENAL

February 25, 2007: Theo Walcott opened the scoring with his first ever Arsenal goal, but a **Didier Drogba** double won it for Chelsea! Blues captain John Terry was taken to hospital after getting knocked out, so Frank Lampard lifted the cup!

Danny Wilson makes it 2-2

LUTON 3-2 ARSENAL

April 24, 1988: Brian Stein's last-minute goal gave Luton their first major trophy as they battled back from 2-1 down against the holders! Nigel Winterburn had earlier missed a penalty that would have put Arsenal 3-1 up!

MOST GOALS!

Two players hold the record for the most League Cup goals. Between 1962 and 1974, England hero Sir Geoff Hurst scored 49 goals, and helped West Ham reach the final in 1966. Ian Rush, who scored 49 goals for Liverpool and Newcastle between 1981 and 1997, is the only player to equal Hurst's record!

Rush equals Hurst's record at Chesterfield

FAB FACT!

West Ham (against Bury in 1983-84) and Liverpool (against Fulham in 1986-87) both bagged huge 10-0 victories in the League Cup!

MOST GOALS IN A SEASON!

Tottenham striker **Clive Allen** netted 12 League Cup goals to fire his side to the semi-finals in 1986-87. But it wasn't just the League Cup where Allen was deadly that season – he bagged an incredible 49 goals in all competitions for Spurs!

Clive Allen (far left)

LONGEST UNBEATEN RUN!

Andy Gray's strike ends Forest's 25-game unbeaten run in the 1980 League Cup Final

Brian Clough masterminded a 25-game unbeaten run in the League Cup for his Nottingham Forest side between 1977 and 1980. The run was ended by a 1-0 defeat to Wolves in the 1980 final, but Clough almost repeated the record between 1988 and 1990 when Forest went another 22 games unbeaten!

HIGHEST SCORING MATCH!

James Milner celebrates as Villa hammer Wycombe

Fans at **Wycombe**'s Causeway Stadium saw a massive 11 goals in a League Cup second-round match in 2005. The Chairboys went ahead after six minutes, but **Aston Villa** battled back to win a sensational match 8-3. The result matched the 11-goal thriller between **Leyton Orient** and **Chester** in 1962, when Orient won 9-2 in their third-round match at Brisbane Road!

BIGGEST COMEBACK!

In the first League Cup final held at Wembley in 1967, third division side QPR completed an amazing fightback against the holders West Brom. Losing 2-0 at half-time, QPR scored three times in 18 minutes to beat the top-flight club. It was the first time a third division club had won a major trophy and is still the biggest final comeback in League Cup history!

QPR's Mike Keen holds the League Cup aloft in 1967

FOOTY SHORTS!

Graham Roberts

Tottenham's Graham Roberts scored two own goals as his side crashed out 4-1 against Burnley in the fifth round at White Hart Lane in 1983!

Chris Woods

Ex-Nottingham Forest and Norwich keeper Chris Woods kept a record three clean sheets in League Cup finals between 1978 and 1985!

Iyseden Christie

Mansfield's Iyseden Christie scored a four-minute League Cup hat-trick in his side's first-round clash with Stockport in 1997!

CRAZY CROWDS!

MATCH checks out the League Cup's attendance records!

Martin Chivers heads home in 1971

100,000

The 1971 final between **Tottenham** and **Aston Villa** saw the first 100,000 capacity crowd at the old Wembley stadium. Two goals from Martin Chivers saw Spurs win 2-0!

Michael Mifsud celebrates his Old Trafford brace

74,055

The largest crowd outside the League Cup final was recorded at Old Trafford in 2007, when Championship side **Coventry** beat **Man. United** 2-0 thanks to a Michael Mifsud double!

Norwich City's Jimmy Hill, 1963

11,213

Rochdale's Spotland stadium set the record for the lowest attendance at a League Cup final when just 11,213 fans turned up to watch Dale's 3-0 first-leg loss to **Norwich** in 1962!

The Shay

612

The smallest ever attendance for a League Cup match was set at The Shay in September 2000, when **Tranmere** came away 2-1 winners against **Halifax**!

YOUNGEST MANAGER IN A FINAL!

Vialli won five trophies as Chelsea boss

Gianluca Vialli became the youngest boss to lead a team out in a League Cup final in 1998. The former Chelsea gaffer was only 33 years old when The Blues beat Middlesbrough 2-0 at Wembley. The match was one Boro manager Bryan Robson will want to forget — it was his second League Cup final defeat in a row!

THE OLDEST MANAGER!

Sir Alex Ferguson (right) became the oldest boss in League Cup final history when his side beat Tottenham on penalties in March 2009. Ferguson was 67 years old, beating the previous best of 64 set by Liverpool's Bob Paisley in 1983!

FOOTY SHORTS!

Brian Little

Brian Little scored twice for Aston Villa in the 1977 final, including the winner, and was Villa's boss when they lifted the League Cup in 1996!

George Graham

George Graham has led Arsenal and Tottenham to League Cup success. He won it twice with The Gunners (1987 & 1993) and once with Spurs (1999)!

Ron Saunders

Ron Saunders lost the 1973 final with Norwich and the 1974 final with Man. City, but won the trophy twice with Aston Villa (1975 & 1977)!

4

CHAMPIONS LEAGUE »

CHAMPIONS LEAGUE »

INCLUDING EUROPEAN CUP (1955-92) & CHAMPIONS LEAGUE (1992-PRESENT)

FAB FACT!
Barcelona didn't win their First European Cup until 1992, but have now picked up the Famous trophy three times!

Barcelona celebrate their 2-0 win over Man. United in Rome in 2009

MOST FINALS!

Real Madrid haven't played in a final since beating Bayer Leverkusen 2-1 in 2002, but they hold the record for the most appearances in the end-of-season Euro clash. The Spanish giants have played in a massive 12 finals, while **AC Milan** have got there 11 times. Premier League side **Liverpool** are third on the list, having reached the final seven times!

MOST WINNERS' MEDALS!

Francisco Gento (centre) helps Real Madrid win their fifth European Cup in 1960

Real Madrid wing wizard **Francisco Gento** holds the record for the most European Cup final victories as a player. The Spain international lifted the European Cup six times between 1956 and 1966, while AC Milan's **Paolo Maldini** won the trophy five times before retiring at the end the 2008-09 season!

THE TROPHY!

The current **European Champion Clubs' Cup**, as it's officially known, is the sixth version of the trophy. Real Madrid, Ajax, AC Milan, Liverpool and Bayern Munich were allowed to keep the other trophies after winning the cup so many times!

DESIGN!

The original trophy was kept by Real Madrid after they won their sixth final in 1966. The design of the European Cup hasn't changed since Celtic beat Inter Milan 2-1 in 1967!

DESIGNER!

Originally designed by Jürg Stadelmann, the European Cup took 340 hours to make. The UEFA General Secretary Hans Bangerter, who approved the design, wanted a trophy that would appeal to different countries!

HANDLES!

In Spain, the European Cup is called 'La Orejona', which means 'Big Ears', because of the shape of the trophy's massive silver handles!

HEIGHT!

It looks huge, but the European Cup is smaller than the Premier League trophy. It stands at only 62cm tall and cost just £6,000 to make!

WEIGHT!

You'd expect a trophy made of silver to be heavy, but the European Cup is light. While the Prem trophy weighs 25kg, this cup weighs just 7.5kg!

WINNERS!

A mega 21 teams have been crowned European champions since 1956, and each club's name is engraved on the world-famous trophy!

BADGE OF HONOUR!

Since the 2000-01 season, every team that has been allowed to keep the European Cup has worn the UEFA Badge Of Honour (right) on their shirts!

FOOTY SHORTS!

Messi strikes in the final

Barcelona superstar Lionel Messi was the top scorer in the 2008-09 Champions League with a massive nine goals!

Seedorf kisses the trophy

Clarence Seedorf has won the trophy with three different clubs – Ajax (1995), Real Madrid (1998) and AC Milan (2003 & 2007)!

Dino Zoff

Keeper Dino Zoff became the oldest player to appear in a final when he captained Juventus against Hamburg in 1983 at the age of 41!

CHAMPIONS LEAGUE FINALS!

MATCH checks out every winner of the European Cup!

Glory for Celtic's 'Lisbon Lions' in 1967

EUROPEAN CUP			
1955-56	Real Madrid	4-3	Stade de Reims
1956-57	Real Madrid	2-0	Fiorentina
1957-58	Real Madrid	3-2	AC Milan
Real Madrid won after extra-time			
1958-59	Real Madrid	2-0	Stade de Reims
1959-60	Real Madrid	7-3	Eintracht Frankfurt
1960-61	Benfica	3-2	Barcelona
1961-62	Benfica	5-3	Real Madrid
1962-63	AC Milan	2-1	Benfica
1963-64	Inter Milan	3-1	Real Madrid
1964-65	Inter Milan	1-0	Benfica
1965-66	Real Madrid	3-1	Partizan Belgrade
1966-67	Celtic	2-1	Inter Milan
1967-68	Man. United	4-1	Benfica
Man. United won after extra-time			
1968-69	AC Milan	4-1	Ajax
1969-70	Feyenoord	2-1	Celtic
Feyenoord won after extra-time			
1970-71	Ajax	2-0	Panathinaikos
1971-72	Ajax	2-0	Inter Milan
1972-73	Ajax	1-0	Juventus
1973-74	Bayern Munich	1-1	Atletico Madrid
Bayern Munich won the replay 4-0			
1974-75	Bayern Munich	2-0	Leeds
1975-76	Bayern Munich	1-0	St. Etienne
1976-77	Liverpool	3-1	B. Monchengladbach
1977-78	Liverpool	1-0	Club Brugge
1978-79	Nottingham Forest	1-0	Malmo
1979-80	Nottingham Forest	1-0	Hamburg
Continued over >>			

Continued over >>

Real captain Jose Zärraga collects the trophy

DID YOU KNOW?

Real Madrid lifted their fifth European Cup in a row when they stuffed Eintracht Frankfurt 7-3 in the 1960 final. Real's thumping win at Hampden Park is still the highest scoring final ever!

CHAMPIONS LEAGUE WINNERS!

The **Champions League** began in 1955 when the editor of French sports newspaper L'Equipe, Gabriel Hanot, and his work-mate, Jacques Ferran, came up with the idea of a European club tournament! They invited 16 clubs to join the competition and the first match saw Sporting Lisbon and Partizan Belgrade draw 3-3. Spanish giants Real Madrid have since gone on to win it a record nine times, with AC Milan second on seven wins.

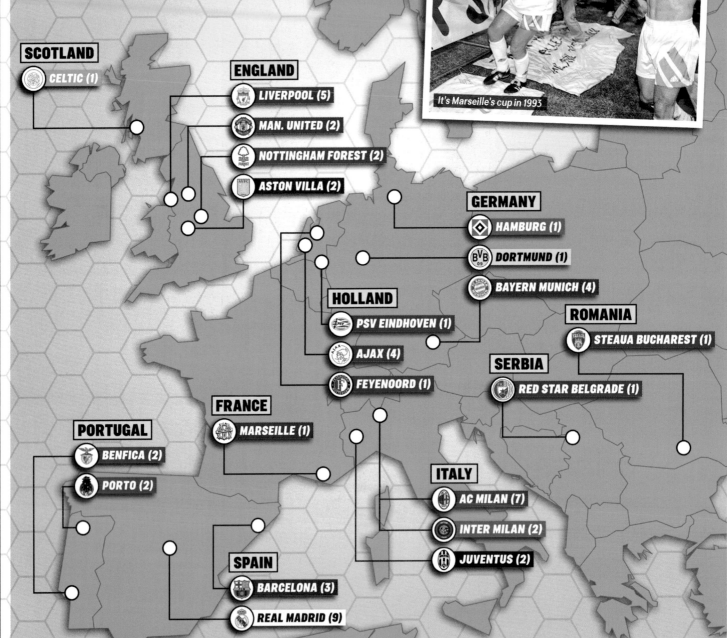

It's Marseille's cup in 1993

SCOTLAND
CELTIC (1)

ENGLAND
LIVERPOOL (5)
MAN. UNITED (2)
NOTTINGHAM FOREST (2)
ASTON VILLA (2)

GERMANY
HAMBURG (1)
DORTMUND (1)
BAYERN MUNICH (4)

HOLLAND
PSV EINDHOVEN (1)
AJAX (4)
FEYENOORD (1)

ROMANIA
STEAUA BUCHAREST (1)

SERBIA
RED STAR BELGRADE (1)

FRANCE
MARSEILLE (1)

PORTUGAL
BENFICA (2)
PORTO (2)

ITALY
AC MILAN (7)
INTER MILAN (2)
JUVENTUS (2)

SPAIN
BARCELONA (3)
REAL MADRID (9)

MOST FINALS BY A MANAGER!

Juventus couldn't get enough of the final under former boss Marcello Lippi. The Italian coach led The Old Lady to four finals, including three back-to-back between 1996 and 1998, before their last appearance in 2003!

Marcello Lippi, 1996

MOST FINALS BY A PLAYER!

Francisco Gento and Paolo Maldini share the record for playing in the highest number of finals. Gento appeared in eight for Real Madrid, and Maldini equalled that record in 2007 when AC Milan beat Liverpool 2-1. Liverpool defender Phil Neal appeared in five finals (1977, 1978, 1981, 1984 and 1985) – a record for any British player!

Phil Neal (right) and Alan Hansen in 1981

FOOTY SHORTS!

Franco Baresi, 1989

Franco Baresi wore the captain's armband a record four times in finals. Baresi led his AC Milan team out in 1989, 1990, 1993 and 1995!

Jens Lehmann sees red

Only two players have been sent off in Champions League finals – Arsenal keeper Jens Lehmann in 2006 and Chelsea striker Didier Drogba in 2008!

Real Madrid v Valencia, 2000

Teams from the same country have appeared in three finals. Real Madrid v Valencia (2000), AC Milan v Juventus (2003) and Man. United v Chelsea (2008).

CHAMPIONS LEAGUE FINALS!

MATCH checks out every winner of the European Cup!

Aston Villa celebrate their 1982 victory

1980-81	Liverpool	1-0	Real Madrid
1981-82	Aston Villa	1-0	Bayern Munich
1982-83	Hamburg	1-0	Juventus
1983-84	Liverpool	1-1	AS Roma
Liverpool won 4-2 on penalties after extra-time			
1984-85	Juventus	1-0	Liverpool
1985-86	Steaua Bucharest	0-0	Barcelona
Steaua Bucharest won 2-0 on penalties after extra-time			
1986-87	Porto	2-1	Bayern Munich
1987-88	PSV Eindhoven	0-0	Benfica
PSV Eindhoven won 6-5 on penalties after extra-time			
1988-89	AC Milan	4-0	Steaua Bucharest
1989-90	AC Milan	1-0	Benfica
1990-91	Red Star Belgrade	0-0	Marseille
Red Star Belgrade won 5-3 on penalties after extra-time			
1991-92	Barcelona	1-0	Sampdoria
Barcelona won after extra-time			
CHAMPIONS LEAGUE			
1992-93	Marseille	1-0	AC Milan
1993-94	AC Milan	4-0	Barcelona
1994-95	Ajax	1-0	AC Milan

Continued over >>

A young Ajax team celebrate in 1995

Alan Kennedy hits the winning penalty in 1984

DID YOU KNOW?

The 1984 final was the first to be decided by a penalty shoot-out. Liverpool overcame Roma 4-2 on spot-kicks after the match had finished 1-1 after extra time!

MOST GOALS!

Real Madrid striker Raul holds the record for the highest number of goals in Champions League history. Between 1995 and 2008, Raul scored 64 goals for the Spanish giants, netting in both the 2000 and 2002 finals. Liverpool midfielder Steven Gerrard has scored more Champions League goals than any British player. The Reds captain, who lifted the trophy in 2005, has netted 28 goals since 2001!

Steven Gerrard strikes against Real Madrid

FAB FACT!

Raul is also Real Madrid's all-time record scorer and has bagged more goals than any other player for the Spanish national team!

MOST GOALS IN A FINAL!

Real Madrid heroes **Alfredo Di Stéfano** and **Ferenc Puskas** (left) share the record for most goals in European Cup finals. Both players hit seven goals, including one penalty, as Real ruled Europe in the 1950s and '60s. The record-breaking pair even scored all of Real Madrid's seven goals against Eintracht Frankfurt in the 1960 final. Di Stéfano netted a hat-trick, while Puskás scored four goals, including a penalty, as Los Blancos won 7-3 in a classic match!

Mike Newell (right)

FASTEST HAT-TRICK!

Blackburn striker **Mike Newell** holds the record for the quickest Champions League treble, after taking just nine minutes to net three goals against Rosenborg in 1995. Red Star Belgrade's **Bora Kostic** holds the European Cup record, after scoring an amazing four-minute hat-trick against Stade Dudelange in 1957!

FASTEST GOAL!

Roy Makaay hits the net after ten seconds

Dutch striker **Roy Makaay** scored the quickest goal in the tournament's history against Real Madrid in 2007. It took the Bayern Munich star just ten seconds to hit the back of the net at the Allianz Arena. AC Milan defender **Paolo Maldini** netted the fastest Champions League final goal after 50 seconds against Liverpool in 2005!

MOST APPEARANCES!

Paolo Maldini captains Milan to glory in 2007

Paolo Maldini holds the record for the most appearances after playing in 141 European Cup matches between 1988 and 2008. Only 13 other players have played 100 or more games in the competition – Alessandro Del Piero, Raul, Roberto Carlos, David Beckham, Oliver Kahn, Luís Figo, Clarence Seedorf, Ryan Giggs, Paul Scholes, Thierry Henry, Gary Neville, Steven Gerrard and Roar Strand.

Celestine Babayaro

Marco Ballotta

Manuel Sanchis lifts the cup

Celestine Babayaro became the youngest man to play in the Champions League when he lined up for Anderlecht at the age of 16 in 1994!

Lazio's Marco Ballotta (43) entered the record books as the oldest player in Champions League history against Real Madrid in 2007!

Manuel Sanchis captained Real Madrid when they won the Champions League in 1998, following his dad who won the 1966 final with the club!

CHAMPIONS LEAGUE FINALS!

MATCH checks out every winner of the European Cup!

Juventus, 1996

Season	Winner	Score	Runner-up
1995-96	Juventus	1-1	Ajax
	Juventus won 4-2 on penalties after extra-time		
1996-97	Borussia Dortmund	3-1	Juventus
1997-98	Real Madrid	1-0	Juventus
1998-99	Man. United	2-1	Bayern Munich
1999-2000	Real Madrid	3-0	Valencia
2000-01	Bayern Munich	1-1	Valencia
	Bayern Munich won 5-4 on penalties after extra-time		
2001-02	Real Madrid	2-1	Bayer Leverkusen
2002-03	AC Milan	0-0	Juventus
	AC Milan won 3-2 on penalties after extra-time		
2003-04	Porto	3-0	Monaco
2004-05	Liverpool	3-3	AC Milan
	Liverpool won 3-2 on penalties after extra-time		
2005-06	Barcelona	2-1	Arsenal
2006-07	AC Milan	2-1	Liverpool
2007-08	Man. United	1-1	Chelsea
	Man. United won 6-5 on penalties after extra-time		
2008-09	Barcelona	2-0	Man. United

John Terry misses a penalty in the 2008 final

Pep Guardiola admires the trophy

DID YOU KNOW?

Pep Guardiola is the youngest ever coach to win the Champions League. The Barcelona boss was just 38 years old when they beat Man. United in last season's final!

CLASSIC GAME!

LIVERPOOL 3-3 AC MILAN

LIVERPOOL WIN 3-2 ON PENALTIES

Gattuso brings down Gerrard

MAY 25, 2005 ★ ATATURK OLYMPIC STADIUM

WHAT HAPPENED? Liverpool lifted their fifth European Cup after the greatest comeback in Champions League history! The Reds were getting thrashed 3-0 at half-time, but three goals in just six second-half minutes by Steven Gerrard, Vladimir Smicer and Xabi Alonso sent the game into extra-time. Liverpool held on for penalties, where goalkeeper Jerzy Dudek saved Andriy Shevchenko's decisive spot-kick to send the trophy back to Anfield!

Smicer bags Liverpool's second

Paolo Maldini opens the scoring after 51 seconds

THE BEST OF THE REST!

MATCH checks out the greatest games in the history of the European Cup!

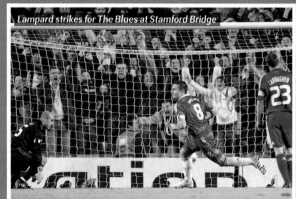

Lampard strikes for The Blues at Stamford Bridge

CHELSEA 4-4 LIVERPOOL

April 14, 2009: Chelsea won the first leg of the all-English quarter-final 3-1, but Liverpool weren't going down without a fight. The Reds twice led the return leg, 2-0 and 4-3, but *Frank Lampard*'s double sent The Blues through!

Keane's header starts United's comeback

JUVENTUS 2-3 MAN. UNITED

April 21, 1999: Despite getting booked early in this semi-final and being suspended for the final, midfielder *Roy Keane* inspired United's fightback! Keane, Dwight Yorke and Andy Cole struck to turn around a two-goal deficit!

Alfredo Di Stefano bags one of his three goals

REAL MADRID 7-3 E. FRANKFURT

May 13, 1960: Glasgow's Hampden Park crowd watched a ten-goal classic as Real Madrid won their fifth straight European Cup! *Alfredo Di Stefano* and *Ferenc Puskas* both netted hat-tricks for a rampant Real side!

BIGGEST WIN!

The first club from Iceland to play in the European Cup suffered the competition's heaviest defeat! KR Reykjavik lost 11-1 on aggregate to Liverpool in 1964, and were then thrashed 12-0 by Dutch side Feyenoord just five years later. The highest aggregate victory in European Cup history was Benfica's 18-0 win against Stade Dudelange in 1965. The Portuguese side won 8-0 in the first leg, then bagged ten more in the return match. Liverpool hold the record for the biggest win since the competition became known as the Champions League – they crushed Besiktas 8-0 in 2007!

FAB FACT!
AC Milan have twice won the European Cup Final by a 4-0 scoreline, against Steaua Bucharest in 1989 and Barcelona in 1994!

MOST GOALS IN A MATCH!

Bayern Munich striker **Gerd Müller** (left) once scored five times in one match against Omonia in 1972! Loads of players have matched Müller's record, but the only Englishman to equal the five-goal haul was Ipswich Town's **Ray Crawford** against Maltese side Floriana way back in 1962!

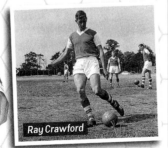

Ray Crawford

MOST GOALS IN A SEASON!

The legendary Altafini gave goalkeepers nightmares

Ruud van Nistelrooy and **Pippo Inzaghi** both hit 12 goals in the 2002-03 Champions League, but it wasn't enough to beat **José Altafini's** amazing record. The deadly striker, who played international footy for Brazil and Italy, netted 14 goals as AC Milan became the first Italian winners of the European Cup in 1963!

LONGEST UNBEATEN RUN!

Man. United set the record for the most Champions League games without defeat during their run to the 2008 and 2009 finals, with their 25-match unbeaten run coming to an end with a 2-0 defeat against Barcelona in Rome in 2009. Sir Alex Ferguson's side beat the previous best of 18 matches, set by themselves between 1997 and 1999, and Dutch giants Ajax between 1994 and 1996!

United's 25-game unbeaten run ends in Rome

MOST CLEAN SHEETS IN A ROW!

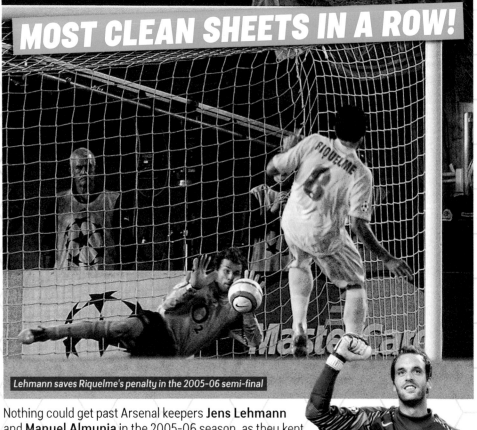
Lehmann saves Riquelme's penalty in the 2005-06 semi-final

Nothing could get past Arsenal keepers **Jens Lehmann** and **Manuel Almunia** in the 2005-06 season, as they kept ten clean sheets between them during Arsenal's run to the final. The pair might have extended their record in the final against Barcelona, but Lehmann was sent off in the first half and Almunia leaked two late goals!

FOOTY SHORTS!

The first ever goal in the European Cup was scored by Sporting Lisbon midfielder João Martins against Partizan Belgrade in September 1955!

Lars Ricken
The fastest goal by a substitute was scored in the 1997 final when Lars Ricken came off the bench and hit the net after only 16 seconds!

Craig Bellamy (right)
Craig Bellamy set the record for the fastest Champo League red card when he was sent off after five minutes against Inter Milan in 2002!

Check out these incredible Champions League crowd stats!

John Hughes equalises for Celtic

135,826

The 1970 European Cup semi-final second leg between **Celtic** and **Leeds** drew the biggest attendance in the competition's history. The huge crowd at Hampden Park saw Celtic win 2-1!

A packed Wembley in 1968

100,000

Wembley hosted England's biggest crowd for a European Cup match in 1968 when **Man. United** beat **Benfica** 4-1 after extra-time to lift the famous trophy for the first time!

Benfica v Barcelona

33,000

Benfica's 3-2 triumph against **Barcelona** in 1961 saw the lowest attendance for a European Cup final. The match was played in Switzerland's Wankdorf Stadium!

Partizan hammer Flora

225

The lowest crowd for a European Cup match, apart from games played behind closed doors, saw **Partizan Belgrade** thrash Estonian side **Flora** 4-1 in the first qualifying round in 1999!

SAN SIRO

SPEEDY BUILDERS!
》 It took 120 builders 13 months to build the San Siro! The original stadium held 35,000 fans! 》

SAINT SIRO!
》 The stadium was named after Saint Syrus Of Pavia, who had a local chapel dedicated to him! 》

LOADS OF PENS!
》 There were 16 penalties in the 2001 Champo League Final – two in normal time and 14 in the shoot-out! 》

SUPER STRIKER!
》 The San Siro is now officially called the Giuseppe Meazza Stadium! He was a top Italy striker! 》

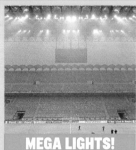

MEGA LIGHTS!
》 There are a massive 256 floodlights covering the roof of the stadium! Each one is 3,500 watts!

SUPER STADIUMS OF THE WORLD!

CITY	MILAN
OPENED	1926
TEAMS	AC MILAN & INTER MILAN
CAPACITY	80,074

GREATEST MATCH EVER!

ARGENTINA 0-1 CAMEROON, 1990

Cameroon stunned the footy world by beating holders Argentina in the opening match of the 1990 World Cup! François Omam-Biyik's header sealed the famous win!

LEGENDS!

PAOLO MALDINI

AC's legendary captain is one of the greatest defenders of all-time! Incredibly, Maldini was still playing at 40 years old and has won the Champions League five times!

JAVIER ZANETTI

Inter's skipper is an all-time superstar! He's awesome at right-back or on the right wing, has played over 500 games for the club and has so much power that he's known as 'The Tractor'!

BANK-BUSTING!

》》 The stadium cost club president Piero Pirelli £3 million to build way back in 1925! 》》

GREAT GIUSEPPE!

》》 Giuseppe Meazza, who the stadium is named after, played for both AC and Inter Milan! 》》

CRAZY CHALK!

》》 A whopping 80kg of chalk is needed to mark out the massive San Siro pitch! 》》

OLDEST MANAGER IN A FINAL!

Raymond Goethals was an incredible 71 years old when he won the Champions League with Marseille in 1993. The Ligue 1 side's 1-0 win against AC Milan meant they became the first French club to lift the trophy, but they were stripped of the title weeks later after being involved in a match-fixing scandal!

Raymond Goethals lifts the trophy with Marseille in 1993

THE YOUNGEST MANAGER!

The youngest ever boss in a European Cup final was English. **Bob Houghton** (left) was just 31 when he led Swedish club Malmo to the 1979 final, but his side lost out to Brian Clough's Nottingham Forest team in Munich!

FOOTY SHORTS!

Fergie at Aberdeen

Sir Alex Ferguson **has** managed a record 173 games in the European Cup, up to and including the 2009 Champions League Final!

Ottmar Hitzfeld

Ottmar Hitzfeld (B. Dortmund & Bayern Munich) and Ernst Happel (Feyenoord & Hamburg) are the only bosses to win the European Cup with two clubs!

Klaus Toppmöller

Klaus Toppmöller's 2001-02 Bayer Leverkusen side were runners-up in the Champions League, the Bundesliga and the German Cup!

5

WORLD CUP»

WORLD CUP »

Fabio Cannavaro lifts the World Cup for Italy in 2006

MOST FINALS!

Brazil and **West Germany** hold the record for the most appearances in the World Cup final, with both countries battling it out to be crowned world champions seven times. Brazil and Germany last appeared in the final in 2002, where Ronaldo scored twice in a 2-0 win for the South Americans. Current holders Italy have played in six finals!

West Germany win the trophy in 1990

MOST MEDALS!

Pele (1958, 1962 and 1970) is the only man with three World Cup winners' medals, but a massive 11 players have won the trophy twice. Italy's **Giovanni Ferrari** and **Giuseppe Meazza** were champs in 1934 and 1938, **Gylmar, Djalma Santos, Nilton Santos, Zito, Garrincha, Didi, Vava** and **Mario Zagallo** lifted the cup for Brazil in 1958 and 1962, while legendary right-back **Cafu** helped the Samba Boys pick up the trophy in both 1994 and 2002!

THE TROPHY!

The current version of the World Cup is the second in the tournament's 79-year history! Designed by Italian artist Silvio Gazzaniga and made in Milan, the current World Cup was first won by West Germany in 1974!

JULES RIMET CUP!

French sculptor Abel Lafleur designed the original trophy for the 1930 World Cup. It was made of silver then gold-plated, stood 35cm high, weighed 3.8kg and was later named after FIFA President Jules Rimet, who created the tournament!

STOLEN IN ENGLAND!

Four months before the 1966 Finals in England, the Jules Rimet Trophy was stolen from a stamp exhibition in Westminster. David Corbett and his dog Pickles later found it lying under a hedge!

TONS OF DESIGNS!

Brazil were allowed to keep the Jules Rimet Trophy after winning it for a third time in 1970. FIFA saw 53 designs for the new World Cup, from seven different countries, before Gazzaniga's version was picked!

HEIGHT!

The current World Cup stands 36cm high, one centimetre taller than the Jules Rimet Cup. "The lines spring out from the base, rising in spirals, stretching out to receive the world," is how Gazzaniga described his design!

WEIGHT!

You don't need massive muscles to lift the World Cup! It only weighs 6.175kg and was first lifted by West Germany captain Franz Beckenbauer after their 2-1 win against Holland in 1974!

WINNERS!

After Brazil were allowed to keep the Jules Rimet Trophy in 1970, it was stolen in Rio de Janeiro and reportedly melted down. FIFA then changed the rules so that no country will ever be able to keep the current World Cup. Winners are given a gold-plated replica instead!

BLING!

The World Cup is made of solid 18-carat gold. Its base is made of malachite, and the name and year of each winner is engraved on the bottom!

FOOTY SHORTS!

England 1-0 Argentina

The biggest TV audience for any England World Cup match was the 450 million who saw their 1-0 win over Argentina in 2002!

Gary Lineker

England striker Gary Lineker won the Golden Boot at the 1986 World Cup in Mexico after smashing home six goals for The Three Lions!

Ray Wilkins

The fastest red card shown to an England player was at the 1986 World Cup when Ray Wilkins was sent off against Morocco after 42 minutes!

WORLD CUP FINALS!

MATCH checks out every winner of the FIFA World Cup!

Argentina in action at World Cup 1930

1930	Uruguay	4-2	Argentina
1934	Italy	2-1	Czechoslovakia
Italy won after extra-time			
1938	Italy	4-2	Hungary
1950	Uruguay	2-1	Brazil
1954	West Germany	3-2	Hungary
1958	Brazil	5-2	Sweden
1962	Brazil	3-1	Czechoslovakia
1966	England	4-2	West Germany
England won after extra-time			
1970	Brazil	4-1	Italy
1974	West Germany	2-1	Holland
1978	Argentina	3-1	Holland
Argentina won after extra-time			
1982	Italy	3-1	West Germany
1986	Argentina	3-2	West Germany
1990	West Germany	1-0	Argentina
1994	Brazil	0-0	Italy
Brazil won 3-2 on penalties after extra-time			
1998	France	3-0	Brazil
2002	Brazil	2-0	Germany
2006	Italy	1-1	France
Italy won 5-3 on penalties after extra-time			

Zidane bags for France in the 1998 final

Hector Castro goes for goal

DID YOU KNOW?

Uruguay striker Hector Castro, who scored in the first World Cup final in 1930, had lost his right hand to an electric saw while working as a carpenter!

WORLD CUP WINNERS!

ENGLAND
1966

WEST GERMANY
1954
1974
1990

FRANCE
1998

ITALY
1934
1938
1982
2006

Argentina captain Daniel Passarella, 1978

BRAZIL
1958
1962
1970
1994
2002

URUGUAY
1930
1950

ARGENTINA
1978
1986

On May 26, 1928 FIFA voted to host an international tournament in 1930, and the **World Cup** was born. The holders of the 1924 and 1928 Olympic titles, Uruguay, were the first hosts and 12 other countries took part – Argentina, Brazil, Bolivia, Chile, Peru, Paraguay, Mexico, USA, Belgium, France, Romania and Yugoslavia. Due to the long journey to South America by boat, many European countries pulled out of the competition. Uruguay won the first title, but Brazil have since gone on to lift the trophy a record five times!

MOST FINALS BY A PLAYER!

Mexico keeper **Antonio Carbajal** and Germany hero **Lothar Matthaus** (left) have both played in a mega five World Cup tournaments. Carbajal from 1950 to 1966 and Matthaus between 1982 and 1998!

Carbajal makes a save in 1966

Parreira with Brazil legend Ronaldo at World Cup 2006

MOST FINALS BY A MANAGER!

Bora Milutinovic couldn't get enough of qualifying for the World Cup. Between 1986 and 2002, he took Mexico, Costa Rica, USA, Nigeria and China to the finals. His record is matched only by **Carlos Alberto Parreira**, who coached Kuwait, United Arab Emirates, Brazil and Saudi Arabia at the World Cup between 1982 and 2006!

YOUNGEST PLAYER!

Norman Whiteside is the youngest scorer in FA Cup and League Cup finals, and also the youngest player ever to appear at a World Cup. The Northern Ireland international was only 17 years old when he played in his first tournament match against Yugoslavia in June 1982. Amazingly, Whiteside was also winning his first cap for his country in the same game!

A teenage Whiteside in 1982

OLDEST PLAYER!

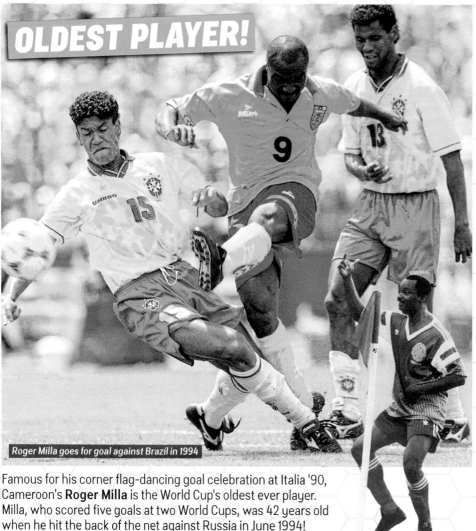
Roger Milla goes for goal against Brazil in 1994

Famous for his corner flag-dancing goal celebration at Italia '90, Cameroon's **Roger Milla** is the World Cup's oldest ever player. Milla, who scored five goals at two World Cups, was 42 years old when he hit the back of the net against Russia in June 1994!

FOOTY SHORTS!

Sir Walter Winterbottom

Sir Walter Winterbottom coached England at four World Cups between 1950 and 1962 – a record for a Three Lions boss!

Peter Shilton

Peter Shilton is the oldest player to pull on an England shirt at the World Cup. Shilts was 40 years old when he played against Italy in 1990!

Pat Jennings

The oldest UK player to play at a World Cup was **Pat Jennings**, who played for Northern Ireland against Brazil in 1986 on his 41st birthday!

MOST WORLD CUP MATCHES!

Tons of great players have starred at the World Cup – check out who holds the appearances record!

Uwe Seeler

Diego Maradona

LOTHAR MATTHAUS 25 matches
Country: West Germany & Germany
First match: West Germany 4-1 Chile, 1982
Last match: Germany 0-3 Croatia, 1998

PAOLO MALDINI 23 matches
Country: Italy
First match: Italy 1-0 Austria, 1990
Last match: South Korea 2-1 Italy, 2002

UWE SEELER 21 matches
Country: West Germany
First match: West Germany 3-1 Argentina, 1958
Last match: West Germany 1-0 Uruguay, 1970

WLADYSLAW ZMUDA 21 matches
Country: Poland
First match: Poland 3-2 Argentina, 1974
Last match: Brazil 4-0 Poland, 1986

DIEGO MARADONA 21 matches
Country: Argentina
First match: Belgium 1-0 Argentina, 1982
Last match: Argentina 2-1 Nigeria, 1994

GRZEGORZ LATO 20 matches
Country: Poland
First match: Poland 3-2 Argentina, 1974
Last match: Poland 3-2 France, 1982

CAFU 20 matches
Country: Brazil
First match: Brazil 1-0 USA, 1994
Last match: France 1-0 Brazil, 2006

Grzegorz Lato

Cafu

Turkey crashed out in the first round in 1954

DID YOU KNOW?

The longest surname in World Cup history is 15 letters long. Lefter Küçükandonyadis scored twice for Turkey at the 1954 tournament!

MOST GOALS IN A FINAL!

Geoff Hurst scores his third goal of the 1966 World Cup Final

England hero **Sir Geoff Hurst** is the only player in World Cup history to score a hat-trick in the final. The Three Lions legend hit his awesome treble as England beat West Germany 4-2 at Wembley in July 1966 to win the World Cup for the only time in their history. Doubts over whether his second goal was over the line still remain today, after it crashed down off the crossbar.

Hurst heads home to make it 1-1

FAB FACT! France striker Just Fontaine netted a record 13 goals in 1958 as Les Bleus reached the World Cup semi-finals!

MOST GOALS IN A MATCH!

Oleg Salenko (left) scored five goals as Russia thrashed Cameroon 6-1 at World Cup 1994 to set the record in his last international appearance. The most goals in a qualifying match stands at 13, scored by Australia's **Archie Thompson** against American Samoa in 2001. He even had a goal disallowed in his country's record-breaking 31-0 victory!

RUS 5 — 31:03 — CMR 1
making soccer history
A WORLD CUP RECORD
WorldCupUSA94

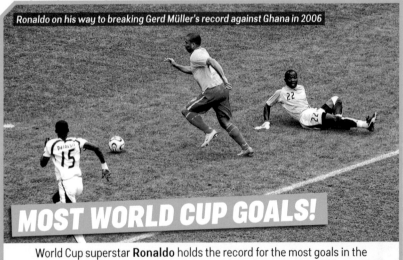

Ronaldo on his way to breaking Gerd Müller's record against Ghana in 2006

MOST WORLD CUP GOALS!

World Cup superstar **Ronaldo** holds the record for the most goals in the tournament's history. The Brazil striker scored 15 goals between 1998 and 2006. West Germany's **Gerd Müller** netted 14 goals between 1970 and 1974, with France hero **Just Fontaine** (13) and Brazil legend **Pele** (12) completing the top four!

FASTEST GOAL!

Turkey fans barely had time to sit down before **Hakan Sükür** scored after 11 seconds against South Korea at World Cup 2002. Sükür's strike beat the previous best of 15 seconds set by Czechoslovakia's **Vaclav Masek** against Mexico in 1962. The record for the quickest goal in a World Cup final is held by Holland's **Johan Neeskens**, who scored after two minutes against West Germany in 1974!

Sükür nets after 11 seconds in the 2002 third-place play-off

FASTEST HAT-TRICK!

Laszlo Kiss

The quickest treble in World Cup history was scored by a substitute. Hungary's Laszlo Kiss came off the bench in the 55th minute against El Salvador in 1982 and scored three times in eight minutes in a 10-1 victory. He's still the only sub to score a hat-trick in a World Cup match. The second-fastest hat-trick was scored in 11 minutes by Argentina goal machine Gabriel Batistuta against Jamaica in 1998!

Batistuta and Argentina on their way to a 5-0 win over Jamaica

FOOTY SHORTS!

Ebbe Sand

The fastest World Cup goal by a substitute was scored by Denmark's Ebbe Sand against Nigeria in 1998 after just 16 seconds!

The Forster brothers

The 1982 World Cup Final saw brothers Karlheinz and Bernd Forster playing alongside each other in defence during West Germany's 3-1 defeat to Italy!

Steven Gerrard misses in 2006

England have never won a World Cup penalty shoot-out, having lost on spot-kicks in 1990, 1998 and 2006. Italy have also lost three shoot-outs!

LANDMARK GOALS!

Check out these memorable strikes from World Cup history!

Marcus Allback scores against England in 2006

1ST
Lucien Laurent for France v Mexico
July 13, 1930

500TH
Bobby Collins for Scotland v Paraguay
June 11, 1958

1,000TH
Rob Rensenbrink for Holland v Scotland
June 11, 1978

2,000TH
Marcus Allback for Sweden v England
June 20, 2006

GOLDEN BOOT WINNERS!

MATCH checks out every winner of the World Cup Golden Boot!

Just Fontaine   *Davor Suker*

Year	Player	Goals
1930	**Guillermo Stabile** *Argentina*	8
1934	**Oldrich Nejedly** *Czechoslovakia*	5
1938	**Leonidas da Silva** *Brazil*	7
1950	**Ademir** *Brazil*	8
1954	**Sandor Kocsis** *Hungary*	11
1958	**Just Fontaine** *France*	13
1962	**Garrincha** *Brazil*	4
	Vava *Brazil*	4
	Leonel Sanchez *Chile*	4
	Drazen Jerkovic *Yugoslavia*	4
	Valentin Ivanov *USSR*	4
	Florian Albert *Hungary*	4
1966	**Eusebio** *Portugal*	8
1970	**Gerd Müller** *West Germany*	10
1974	**Grzegorz Lato** *Poland*	7
1978	**Mario Kempes** *Argentina*	6
1982	**Paolo Rossi** *Italy*	6
1986	**Gary Lineker** *England*	6
1990	**Salvatore Schillaci** *Italy*	6
1994	**Hristo Stoichkov** *Bulgaria*	6
	Oleg Salenko *Russia*	6
1998	**Davor Suker** *Croatia*	6
2002	**Ronaldo** *Brazil*	8
2006	**Miroslav Klose** *Germany*	5

CLASSIC GAME!
ENGLAND 4 - 2 WEST GERMANY
AFTER EXTRA-TIME

Hurst completes his hat-trick

JULY 30, 1966 ★ WEMBLEY STADIUM

WHAT HAPPENED? Sir Geoff Hurst netted a hat-trick in the final against West Germany as England were crowned world champions for the first time. The 98,000 Wembley crowd thought Martin Peters' strike had won it for England when they led 2-1 with seconds remaining, only for Wolfgang Weber's last-gasp goal to force extra-time. But The Three Lions would not be denied and Hurst scored two more dramatic goals to secure the trophy for the hosts!

George Cohen lifts the cup

Germany force extra-time with a last-minute equaliser

FAB FACT!
England's 1966 World Cup winning team contained two brothers, Jack and Bobby Charlton!

THE BEST OF THE REST!

MATCH checks out the greatest games in the history of the World Cup!

Maradona's famous 'Hand Of God' goal

ARGENTINA 2-1 ENGLAND

June 22, 1986: This quarter-final clash was all about Argentina's **Diego Maradona**! He seemed to punch the ball into the net to open the scoring before dribbling from his own half to score one of the greatest goals of all time!

Brazil legend Pele goes for goal

BRAZIL 4-1 ITALY

June 21, 1970: Many people think Brazil's 1970 World Cup winners were the best team in football history, and their performance in the final proved why! They destroyed Italy with goals from **Pele**, **Gérson**, **Jairzinho** and **Carlos Alberto**!

Eusébio inspires Portugal's comeback

PORTUGAL 5-3 NORTH KOREA

July 23, 1966: North Korea stunned the world by taking a three-goal lead in this quarter-final, but Portugal stormed back to book their place in the semis. The great **Eusébio** scored four times in an amazing match at Goodison Park!

BIGGEST WIN!

The biggest victory in World Cup history was in 2001 when Australia crushed American Samoa 31-0 in a qualifier. Yugoslavia recorded the biggest win at a World Cup finals in 1974 when they hammered Zaire 9-0, equalling the same score set by Hungary against South Korea in 1954. The biggest win in a World Cup final goes to Brazil, who beat hosts Sweden 5-2 in 1958 and also hammered Italy 4-1 in 1970!

Yugoslavia 9-0 Zaire

FAB FACT!

Australia broke the world record for the biggest win twice in three days in 2001, thrashing Tonga 22-0 then hammering American Samoa 31-0!

MOST DEFEATS!

Mexico goalkeeper **Antonio Carbajal** lost eight World Cup matches between 1950 and 1962, a record only matched by South Korea defender **Hong Myung-Bo** (left) between 1990 and 2002. **Mexico** lost 22 World Cup games between 1930 and 2006 – more defeats than any other country!

Sweden defeat Mexico 3-0 in 1958

Switzerland keeper Eugene Parlier makes a rare save during his side's 7-5 defeat

HIGHEST SCORING MATCH!

Austria and **Switzerland**'s goalkeepers must have thought about hanging up their gloves after their epic quarter-final battle in 1954. A mind-blowing 12 goals were bagged, making it the highest-scoring match in World Cup history. Austria fought back from 3-0 down in the first half to seal an amazing 7-5 victory!

LONGEST UNBEATEN RUN!

Brazil forgot what it was like to lose a World Cup match between 2002 and 2006! Under Luiz Felipe Scolari and Carlos Alberto Parreira, the Samba Boys won a massive 11 matches before they eventually lost to France in a quarter-final clash in Germany. **Italy** won seven games on the bounce between 1934 and 1938, while **England** bagged six wins on the trot between 1966 and 1970.

The great Ronaldo in action at World Cup 2006

LATEST GOAL!

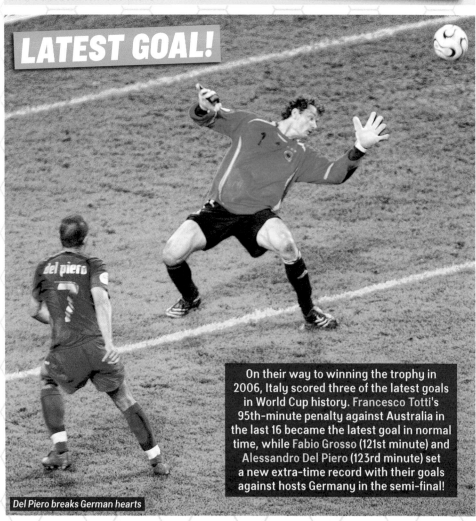

On their way to winning the trophy in 2006, Italy scored three of the latest goals in World Cup history. Francesco Totti's 95th-minute penalty against Australia in the last 16 became the latest goal in normal time, while Fabio Grosso (121st minute) and Alessandro Del Piero (123rd minute) set a new extra-time record with their goals against hosts Germany in the semi-final!

Del Piero breaks German hearts

FOOTY SHORTS!

Bulgaria, 1994

Bulgaria went 17 World Cup games without winning between 1962 and 1994, but ended the run with a 4-0 win over Greece in 1994!

Fabien Barthez

French keeper Fabien Barthez and England shot-stopper Peter Shilton both kept a record ten World Cup clean sheets!

Issa's bad day at the office

South Africa defender Pierre Issa scored two own goals in his country's 3-0 defeat to hosts France at World Cup 1998!

WORLD CUP RELATIVES!

Check out this massive list of players from the same families who've played at the World Cup!

Cesare Maldini

Paolo Maldini

Father		Son
Luis Perez *Mexico 1930*		Mario Perez *Mexico 1970*
Martin Vantolra *Spain 1934*		Jose Vantolra *Mexico 1970*
Domingos da Guia *Brazil 1938*		Ademir da Guia *Brazil 1974*
Roger Rio *France 1934*		Patrice Rio *France 1978*
Vicente Asensi *Spain 1950*		Juan Manuel Asensi *Spain 1978*
Cesare Maldini *Italy 1962*		Paolo Maldini *Italy 1990-2002*
Manuel Sanchis *Spain 1966*		Manuel Sanchis *Spain 1990*
Nicolae Lupescu *Romania 1970*		Ionut Lupescu *Romania 1994*
Jean Djorkaeff *France 1966*		Youri Djorkaeff *France 1998-2002*
Anders Linderoth *Sweden 1978*		Tobias Linderoth *Sweden 2002*
Bum-Kun Cha *South Korea 1986*		Doo-Ri Cha *South Korea 2002*
Pablo Forlan *Uruguay 1974*		Diego Forlan *Uruguay 2002*
Julio Montero *Uruguay 1974*		Paolo Montero *Uruguay 2002*
Wlodzimierz Smolarek *Poland 1982-86*		Ebi Smolarek *Poland 2006*

Jean Djorkaeff

Youri Djorkaeff

France lift the World Cup as hosts in 1998

DID YOU KNOW?

West Germany (1972 and 1974) and France (1998 and 2000) are the only countries to be world and European champs at the same time!

MOST RED CARDS IN A MATCH!

Russian referee Valentin Ivanov (right) went card crazy during the fiery World Cup 2006 battle between Holland and Portugal. The last-16 clash saw four players sent off and 12 yellow cards dished out as Portugal's Maniche stunned the Dutch with the only goal of the game. Both teams finished the match with nine men as Deco, Costinha, Khalid Boulahrouz and Giovanni van Bronckhorst were sent off!

Fernando Clavijo (centre)

OLDEST PLAYER SENT OFF!

July 4 is usually a day of celebration for Americans, but USA defender **Fernando Clavijo** will want to forget Independence Day in 1994. With three minutes remaining of the last-16 match against Brazil, 37-year-old Clavijo became the oldest player in World Cup history to be shown a red card!

Rigobert Song sees red in 1994

YOUNGEST PLAYER SENT OFF!

Cameroon defender **Rigobert Song** was also sent off against Brazil at World Cup '94. The 17-year-old was red carded in the second half of his country's 3-0 defeat to the Samba Boys. The youngest England player to be sent off was **Wayne Rooney** (20) against Portugal in 2006!

FAB FACT!
The fastest red card in a World Cup match was shown to Uruguay's Jose Batista in 1986 when he was sent off after 55 seconds against Scotland!

TALLEST PLAYER!

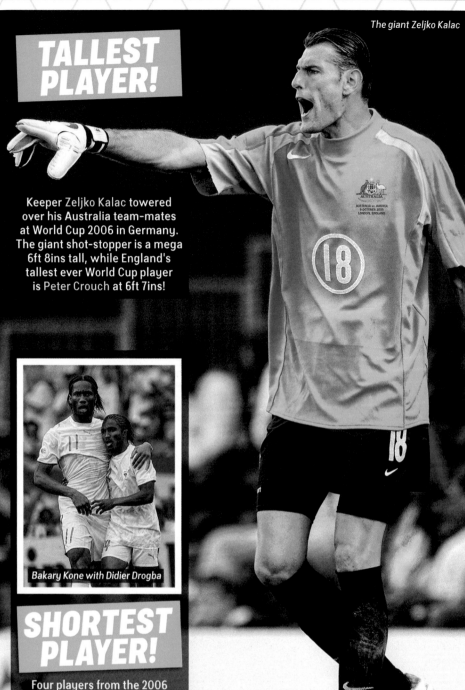

The giant Zeljko Kalac

Keeper Zeljko Kalac towered over his Australia team-mates at World Cup 2006 in Germany. The giant shot-stopper is a mega 6ft 8ins tall, while England's tallest ever World Cup player is Peter Crouch at 6ft 7ins!

Bakary Kone with Didier Drogba

SHORTEST PLAYER!

Four players from the 2006 finals share the record for the World Cup's smallest player. Ecuador's Cristian Lara, Saudi Arabia's Mohammed Al-Shlhoub, Ivory Coast's Bakary Kone and Mexico's Zinha are 5ft 3ins tall!

FOOTY SHORTS!

World Cup fever in 2002

The 2002 World Cup Final between Brazil and Germany was watched by approximately 1.1 billion people around the globe!

Arie Haan (right)

The longest-range goal in World Cup history was scored by Holland's Arie Haan from 40 yards against Italy in 1978!

Zinedine Zidane

Vava (1958 & 1962) Pele (1958 & 1970), Geoff Hurst (1966) and Zinedine Zidane (1998 & 2006) have all scored three goals in World Cup finals!

WORLD CUP ATTENDANCES!

Check out this list of awesome World Cup attendance records!

Brazil v Uruguay, 1950

173,850
The Maracana hosted the World Cup's biggest ever crowd as **Brazil** were stunned 2-1 at home by **Uruguay** in 1950. Some people think the crowd could have been as big as 205,000!

98,270
The biggest crowd to watch a World Cup match outside Brazil and Mexico City was at Wembley, where nearly 100,000 fans watched **England** beat **France** 2-0 in 1966!

45,124
The lowest crowd for a World Cup final was in 1938 when **Italy** beat **Hungary** 4-2 in Paris to win the trophy for the second tournament in a row!

100
A tiny crowd of just 100 fans turned up to watch **Jordan** draw 1-1 with **Uzbekistan** in a World Cup qualifying game in Amman in May 2001!

20
There were more players on the pitch than in the crowd when **Turkmenistan** beat **Taiwan** 1-0 in May 2001. The match, played on a neutral venue in Amman in Jordan, holds the record for the smallest World Cup crowd!

Miguel Angel Nadal (left) is sent off

DID YOU KNOW?
The 2008 Wimbledon men's singles champ Rafael Nadal had an uncle who played at the World Cup. Miguel Angel Nadal was sent off in his first finals match against South Korea in 1994!

MARACANA

FAB FACTS!

MASTER BUILDERS!
>> It took builders less than two years to build the Maracana for the first game of the 1950 World Cup! >>

BOG OFF!
>> There was no chance of going to the toilet when the Maracana was first built – it didn't have any! >>

WATER FACT!
>> The stadium is named after a local river that flows through the Maracana district of Rio de Janeiro! >>

RECORD CROWD!
>> It only holds 95,000 fans today, but 199,854 people watched the 1950 World Cup Final! >>

ENGLISH OFFICIAL!
>> The 1950 World Cup Final referee was English! George Reader was 53 – the final's oldest official! >>

SUPER STADIUMS OF THE WORLD!

CITY	RIO DE JANEIRO
OPENED	1950
TEAMS	FLAMENGO, FLUMINENSE & BRAZIL
CAPACITY	95,000

GREATEST MATCH EVER!

URUGUAY 2-1 BRAZIL, 1950

Brazil were expected to easily win the 1950 World Cup on home soil, but Uruguay came from one goal down to win the final 2-1! It's one of the biggest upsets ever!

LEGENDS!

PELE

The Brazil international scored his 1,000th goal at the Maracana in front of a massive crowd of 125,000 adoring fans! Pele tucked the ball home from the penalty spot!

ZICO

Zico's one of the greatest Brazil players of all time and scored loads of quality goals at the Maracana! The attacking midfielder netted 52 times in just 72 matches for his country!

UP FOR THE CUP!

≫ Man. United played their FIFA Club World Cup matches at the Maracana stadium back in 2000! ≫

PLAYER PRINTS!

≫ Footy legends Kaka and Pele have their footprints in the Maracana's cool 'Soccer Walk Of Fame'! ≫

WORLD CUP FINAL!

≫ The Maracana will host the World Cup final for the second time in its history in 2014! ≫

MOST MATCHES AS MANAGER!

Glory for Helmut Schön and West Germany in 1974

West Germany boss Helmut Schön's record for the most World Cup games as a coach still stands over 30 years after he set it. Between 1966 and 1978, Schön managed 25 matches as his side became one of the toughest opponents in world footy. In his time as coach, Schön was a runner-up in 1966, then finished third in 1970 before lifting the World Cup in 1974. His final tournament wasn't so good, though – West Germany were knocked out in the second round!

MOST FINALS AS MANAGER!

Italy's **Vittorio Pozzo** (1934 & 1938), West Germany's **Franz Beckenbauer** (1986 & 1990), Argentina's **Carlos Bilardo** (1986 & 1990), Brazil's **Mario Zagallo** (1970 & 1998) and West Germany's **Helmut Schön** (1966 & 1974) have all reached the final twice!

FOOTY SHORTS!

World Cup 1930

The only man to coach a team and referee a match in a World Cup tournament was Bolivia's Ulises Saucedo in 1930!

Franz Beckenbauer, 1990

West Germany legend Franz Beckenbauer is the only man to win the World Cup as a captain (1974) and as a coach (1990)!

Tommy Svensson

In 1994, Tommy Svensson became the sixth Sweden coach to play a World Cup match against Brazil without winning!

6

EUROPEAN CHAMPIONSHIP »

EUROPEAN CHAMPIONSHIP »

Spain celebrate their 1-0 win over Germany in the Euro 2008 Final

MOST GOALS!

France captain **Michel Platini** (left) scored a record nine goals at Euro 1984. Platini, who was European Footballer Of The Year at the time, netted nine goals, including two hat-tricks and another goal in the final against Spain. Just behind Platini in the goalscoring charts is England's **Alan Shearer**, who hit seven goals, five in 1996 and two at Euro 2000!

Alan Shearer at Euro '96

MOST MEDALS!

West Germany beat Belgium to win the Euro title in 1980

Germany are the most successful side in European Championship history. They've reached the final a record six times, winning in 1972, 1980 and 1996. The **USSR** have played in four Euro finals, **Spain** have reached three, while **France, Italy, Czech Republic** and **Yugoslavia** have made two each!

THE TROPHY!

The current trophy is the second in European Championship history, after it was redesigned in time for Euro 2008. The new trophy is higher and heavier than the original, which was lifted for the last time by Greece captain Theo Zagorakis in 2004!

TROPHY MAKER!
Pierre Delaunay was given the job of making the original European Championship trophy. The goldsmith then sold it to well-known Paris jewellers Arthus-Bertrand in 1960!

HENRI DELAUNAY TROPHY!

The European Championship trophy is also known as the Henri Delaunay Trophy. Delaunay (right) was a former president of the French Football Federation, who came up with the idea of a competition for Europe's top footy nations!

EURO 2008 REDESIGN!
For Euro 2008, the trophy's marble plinth and a figure performing a keepy-uppy on the back were removed. The trophy was given a silver base and made bigger to make it more stable!

HEIGHT!
The trophy is now 60cm high, 18cm taller than the original. English silversmiths Asprey's Of London made it ahead of the last European Championship in Austria and Switzerland!

WEIGHT!

To reflect the scale and size of the tournament, the new trophy is much heavier. It now weighs 8kg, 2kg more than the original, and was first lifted by Spain's Iker Casillas (right) in 2008!

WINNERS!
Since the removal of the original marble plinth, the names of each winning country have also moved. They're now engraved on the back of the Euro trophy!

BLING!
The upper part of the new Henri Delaunay trophy is based on the original and is made of sterling silver. The makers, Asprey's Of London, also designed the current Premier League trophy!

FOOTY SHORTS!

Denmark take the 1992 title

Paul Gascoigne at Euro '96

USSR win the trophy in 1960

Unlike the World Cup, no player has ever picked up two European Championship titles since the tournament started back in 1960!

England have twice reached the semi-finals at the Euros. The Three Lions lost 1-0 to Yugoslavia in 1968 and 6-5 on penalties to Germany in 1996!

At the first Euro Championship in 1960, countries played each other home and away until the semi-finals, then a host was chosen from the last four!

EURO CHAMPIONSHIP WINNERS!

MATCH checks out every winner of the European Championship title since the tournament started in 1960!

Italy claim the silverware in 1968

Year	Winner	Score	Runner-up
1960	USSR	2-1	Yugoslavia
	USSR won after extra-time		
1964	Spain	2-1	USSR
1968	Italy	1-1	Yugoslavia
	Italy won the replay 2-0		
1972	West Germany	3-0	USSR
1976	Czechoslovakia	2-2	West Germany
	Czechoslovakia won 5-3 on penalties after extra-time		
1980	West Germany	2-1	Belgium
1984	France	2-0	Spain
1988	Holland	2-0	USSR
1992	Denmark	2-0	Germany
1996	Germany	2-1	Czech Republic
	Germany won with a golden goal in extra-time		
2000	France	2-1	Italy
	France won with a golden goal in extra-time		
2004	Greece	1-0	Portugal
2008	Spain	1-0	Germany

Greece celebrate their shock Euro 2004 title

UEFA Euro 2004 GREECE CHAMPIONS

Oliver Bierhoff's golden goal in the Euro '96 final

DID YOU KNOW?
The golden goal rule was first used in England at Euro '96. The new rule handed victory to the first team to score a goal in extra-time!

EURO WINNERS!

The idea for a **European Championship** began in 1927 when Henri Delaunay proposed the idea to FIFA, but it wasn't until 1957 that Delaunay's son, Pierre, saw his dad's plan become reality. The first European Nations' Cup, as it was then known, saw 16 countries take part after Czechoslovakia knocked out the Republic Of Ireland in a play-off qualifier. Austria, Bulgaria, Denmark, East Germany, Greece, Hungary, Norway, Poland, Portugal, Romania, Spain and Turkey were all knocked out in the early rounds, leaving France, USSR, Yugoslavia and Czechoslovakia to compete in the final tournament in France!

Czechoslovakia claim the 1976 title

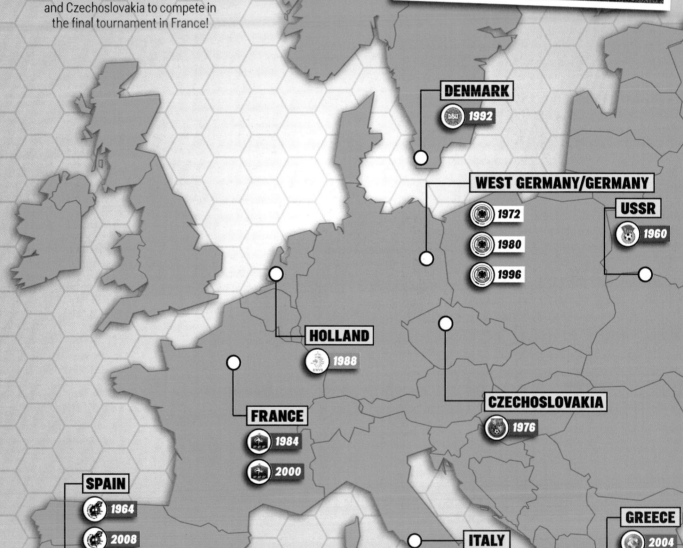

DENMARK
1992

WEST GERMANY/GERMANY
1972
1980
1996

USSR
1960

HOLLAND
1988

FRANCE
1984
2000

CZECHOSLOVAKIA
1976

SPAIN
1964
2008

ITALY
1968

GREECE
2004

YOUNGEST PLAYER!

Belgium midfielder Enzo Scifo became the youngest player ever to appear at the Euros when he lined up against Yugoslavia in 1984, aged just 18 years and 155 days. The youngest player to appear in a European Championship final is Cristiano Ronaldo, who was 19 when he faced Greece in 2004!

Enzo Scifo on the ball

Lothar Matthaus

OLDEST PLAYER!

Playing in his 150th and last international for Germany in 2000, international legend Lothar Matthaus (39) became the oldest footy star to appear at the Euros. The oldest player to appear in a final is Germany keeper Jens Lehmann, who was 38 years old when he received a runners-up medal after losing to Spain at Euro 2008!

FOOTY SHORTS!

Wayne Rooney

Peter Shilton

Alan Shearer, 2000

Wayne Rooney (18) became the youngest player to pull on an England shirt in a European Championship match against France at Euro 2004!

England goalkeeper Peter Shilton picked up his 100th cap during England's crushing 3-1 defeat to Holland at Euro 1988!

England have never won their opening match at the European Championship, losing four games and drawing three!

MOST MATCHES!

MATCH checks out which superstars have played the most European Championship matches!

Lilian Thuram

Edwin van der Sar

LILIAN THURAM 16 matches
Country: France
First match: France 1-0 Romania, 1996
Last match: Holland 4-1 France, 2008

EDWIN VAN DER SAR 16 matches
Country: Holland
First match: Holland 0-0 Scotland, 1996
Last match: Russia 3-1 Holland, 2008

ZINEDINE ZIDANE 14 matches
Country: France
First match: France 1-0 Romania, 1996
Last match: Greece 1-0 France, 2004

KAREL POBORSKY 14 matches
Country: Czech Republic
First match: Germany 2-0 Czech Republic, 1996
Last match: Greece 1-0 Czech Republic, 2004

LUIS FIGO 14 matches
Country: Portugal
First match: Denmark 1-1 Portugal, 1996
Last match: Greece 1-0 Portugal, 2004

NUNO GOMES 14 matches
Country: Portugal
First match: Portugal 3-2 England, 2000
Last match: Germany 3-2 Portugal, 2008

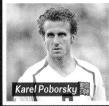
Karel Poborsky

Luis Figo

Vladimir Smicer

DID YOU KNOW?

Vladimir Smicer, whose goal put the Czech Republic into the quarter-finals in 1996, flew back to Prague to get married straight after the game. He returned two days later to play in his country's quarter-final win over Portugal!

MOST GOALS IN A FINAL!

No player has ever scored a hat-trick in the final, but three German stars have netted a brace. West Germany superstar Gerd Müller busted the net twice against the USSR in 1972, before Horst Hrubesch also hit two goals against Belgium in 1980. Oliver Bierhoff then won the trophy for Germany with his double against the Czech Republic in the 1996 final!

Oliver Bierhoff is Germany's match-winner in the Euro '96 Final

Gerd Müller strikes again

Horst Hrubesch hits the winner in the 1980 final

MOST GOALS IN A MATCH!

No player has scored four goals in one European Championship match, but tons of goal machines have netted hat-tricks. The most devastating of all was France legend Michel Platini, who scored a treble against Belgium in 1984, then followed it up with another hat-trick three days later against Yugoslavia. The other hat-trick heroes are Holland pair **Patrick Kluivert** (2000) and **Marco van Basten** (1988), West Germany stars **Dieter Müller** (1976) and **Klaus Allofs** (1980), Spain's **David Villa** (2008) and Portugal wing wizard **Sérgio Conceiçao**, who hit a treble at Euro 2000!

FASTEST GOAL IN A FINAL!

Jesús Maria Pereda (far left) scores his record-breaking goal

USSR's legendary keeper Lev Yashin had to pick the ball out of the net just six minutes into the 1964 final. The Bernabeu erupted when Spain striker **Jesús María Pereda** ripped the net with a quality goal following a defensive blunder. The USSR equalised two minutes later, but Spain eventually won 2-1!

FASTEST GOAL!

Russia's **Dmitri Kirichenko** hit the net just 71 seconds into a group match against Greece in 2004. Kirichenko's goal after one minute and 11 seconds is a European Championship record. The quickest Euro goal by an England player was scored by **Alan Shearer**, who netted after just two minutes against Germany in the Euro '96 semi-finals. It wasn't to be England's night, though, because Germany battled back to win the match 6-5 in a penalty shoot-out!

Kirichenko jumps for joy after his goal against Greece in 2004

FASTEST HAT-TRICK!

Yugoslavia hold the unfortunate record of having the quickest treble scored against them. On his way to becoming the top scorer at Euro 1984, France hero Michel Platini took only 17 minutes to hit a hat-trick in a 3-2 win. Holland's Patrick Kluivert scored the second-quickest treble in just 30 minutes at Euro 2000, also against Yugoslavia!

Michel Platini tears Yugoslavia apart

FOOTY SHORTS!

Zidane crushes England

The latest goal scored against England in normal time was by France's Zinedine Zidane at Euro 2004, when he sunk The Three Lions in the 93rd minute!

Rooney makes history

Wayne Rooney became the youngest England player to score at the Euros when he netted against Switzerland at the age of 18 in 2004!

– Jermain Defoe (right)

England and Tottenham striker Jermain Defoe was either on the bench or subbed off in every one of his first 34 international matches!

LANDMARK GOALS!

Check out these memorable strikes from Euro Championship history!

Xavi scores for Spain against Russia in 2008

1ST
Milan Galic for Yugoslavia v France
June 6, 1960

100TH
Alain Giresse for France v Belgium
June 16, 1984

500TH
Xavi for Spain v Russia
June 26, 2008

GOLDEN BOOT WINNERS!

MATCH checks out every European Championship Golden Boot winner!

Tomas Brolin

Milan Baros

Year	Player	Goals
1960	**François Heutte** *France*	2
	Valentin Ivanov *USSR*	2
	Viktor Ponedelnik *USSR*	2
	Slava Metreveli *USSR*	2
	Milan Galic *Yugoslavia*	2
	Drazen Jerkovic *Yugoslavia*	2
1964	**Jesús Maria Pereda** *Spain*	2
	Ferenc Bene *Hungary*	2
	Dezso Novak *Hungary*	2
1968	**Dragan Dzajic** *Yugoslavia*	2
1972	**Gerd Müller** *West Germany*	4
1976	**Dieter Müller** *West Germany*	4
1980	**Klaus Allofs** *West Germany*	3
1984	**Michel Platini** *France*	9
1988	**Marco van Basten** *Holland*	5
1992	**Henrik Larsen** *Denmark*	3
	Karlheinz Riedle *West Germany*	3
	Dennis Bergkamp *Holland*	3
	Tomas Brolin *Sweden*	3
1996	**Alan Shearer** *England*	5
2000	**Patrick Kluivert** *Holland*	5
	Savo Milosevic *Yugoslavia*	5
2004	**Milan Baros** *Czech Republic*	5
2008	**David Villa** *Spain*	4

CLASSIC GAME!
ENGLAND 4 - 1 HOLLAND

Bergkamp takes on Southgate

JUNE 18, 1996 ★ WEMBLEY STADIUM

WHAT HAPPENED? A Dutch side led by Guus Hiddink and starring Dennis Bergkamp, Clarence Seedorf and Edwin van der Sar was taught a footy lesson as England boss Terry Venables masterminded an incredible result at Euro '96. Hosts England turned on the style as they raced into a 4-0 lead, with strike partners Alan Shearer and Teddy Sheringham scoring twice, before Patrick Kluivert slotted home a late consolation for Holland!

Kluivert scores for Holland

Teddy Sheringham grabs his second goal

THE BEST OF THE REST!

MATCH checks out the greatest games in European Championship history!

Vladimir Smicer wins a thriller at Euro 2004

CZECH REPUBLIC 3-2 HOLLAND

June 19, 2004: Holland were cruising to victory after going 2-0 up, but the Czechs battled back for a famous win. Goals from Jan Koller and Milan Baros pulled the tie level, before **Vladimir Smicer** hit a dramatic late winner!

Gaizka Mendieta slides home a cool penalty

SPAIN 4-3 YUGOSLAVIA

June 21, 2000: Spain looked to be going out of the tournament after Slobodan Komljenovic's strike put ten-man Yugoslavia 3-2 ahead, but **Gaizka Mendieta** and Alfonso struck in stoppage-time to turn it all around!

John Jensen opens the scoring after 18 minutes

DENMARK 2-0 GERMANY

June 26, 1992: Goalkeeper Peter Schmeichel and his Danish team-mates shocked the footy world by beating hot favourites Germany in the Euro '92 Final. Goals from **John Jensen** and Kim Vilfort stunned the world champions!

BIGGEST WIN!

There were loads of crazy games at Euro 1984. France's 5-0 victory against Belgium and Denmark's win by the same scoreline against Yugoslavia are the biggest in Euro Championship history. The biggest win in a qualifier was set in September 2006 when Germany cruised to a 13-0 win against San Marino. Lukas Podolski hit four goals, while Bastian Schweinsteiger, Miroslav Klose and Thomas Hitzlsperger all netted twice!

Lukas Podolski scores one of his four goals against San Marino

Michel Platini has plenty to smile about scoring France's fifth goal against Belgium

FAB FACT!
Spain needed to beat Malta by just 11 goals to qualify for Euro 1984, and they managed to do it by pulling off an amazing 12-1 victory!

MOST DEFEATS!

Man. United legend **Peter Schmeichel** (left) has lost more European Championship games than any other player. Despite winning the title in 1992, Schmeichel lost seven matches at the finals between 1988 and 2000. In total, **Denmark** lost 12 Euro Championship matches between 1964 and 2004 – more than any European country!

Davor Suker strikes against Denmark

Yugoslavia in action at the 1960 European Championship

HIGHEST SCORING MATCH!

The nine goals scored by **Yugoslavia** and **France** back in July 1960 is still the European Championship's biggest goal fest. France, who were playing at home, were winning 4-2 with 15 minutes to play before Yugoslavia netted three goals in three minutes to win 5-4!

LONGEST UNBEATEN RUN!

European giants **Italy**, **Holland** and **West Germany** all hold the record for the most games without losing. Not counting matches lost on penalties, all three countries went ten games without losing, with Holland being the last team to equal the record last in 1996. Holland achieved the amazing run of results between 1988 and 1996, while West Germany took 12 years, between 1972 and 1984!

Holland's Dennis Bergkamp runs with the ball at Euro '92

LONGEST LOSING RUN!

Andrey Arshavin and Yuri Zhirkov had a quality Euro 2008 with Russia, but their run to the semi-finals broke a rubbish run of results. Between 1992 and 2004, Russia played a massive nine matches without winning. England's worst record was at the 1988 finals, when they lost all three group matches against the Republic of Ireland, Holland and the USSR!

Scotland 3-0 Russia, 1992

FOOTY SHORTS!

Gazza sinks Scotland

England went seven matches without a win at the Euros between 1988 and 1996. The run ended with a 2-0 win over rivals Scotland at Euro '96!

Kubilay Türkyilmaz

Switzerland have scored 16 European Championship goals against England, and every one of them was netted by a different player!

Eidur Gudjohnsen (centre)

Striker Eidur Gudjohnsen (2004) and his dad Arnór Gudjohnsen (1982) have both starred for Iceland in games against England!

LATEST GOALS!

MATCH checks out the greatest last-gasp Euro strikes!

Semih Senturk celebrates

120 + 2 MINUTES

In the quarter-finals of Euro 2008, Turkey's *Semih Senturk* scored an incredible late equaliser just seconds after Croatia's Ivan Klasnic had struck in the last minute of extra-time. Turkey went on to win the penalty shoot-out 3-1!

90 + 5 MINUTES

Spain's *Alfonso* netted the latest ever European Championship goal in normal time in a 4-3 win against Yugoslavia in 2000. Spain knew they had to beat Yugoslavia to reach the quarter-finals, and turned the match around after being 3-2 down in stoppage-time!

90 + 4 MINUTES

Portugal left it late in a group win against Romania at Euro 2004. Substitute *Costinha* headed the only goal after 94 minutes during Portugal's run to the semi-finals!

90 + 3 MINUTES

Austria's ancient striker *Ivica Vastic* found the net after 93 minutes against Poland at Euro 2008. Vastic's goal, scored when he was 38 years old, was Austria's first in any Euro finals. They'd qualified as joint hosts with Switzerland!

CLEAN SHEET KINGS!

These No.1s are the best keepers in the history of the Euros!

Edwin van der Sar   *Dino Zoff*

⚽ Man. United's **Edwin van der Sar** has been the most successful keeper at the Euros. Between his debut in 1996 and defeat against Russia at Euro 2008, the Holland star kept ten clean sheets. Van der Sar kept five shut-outs in a row at Euro '96 and Euro 2000!

⚽ Van der Sar's amazing record beat the previous best set by Italy keeper **Dino Zoff**. Zoff played 464 minutes between the 1968 and 1980 finals without conceding a goal. The Italy No.1 also won the title with his country in 1968!

YOUNGEST SCORER!

At Euro 2004, the record for the tournament's youngest scorer was broken twice in four days. England's Wayne Rooney was just 18 years and 237 days old when he scored twice against Switzerland in a 3-0 victory on June 17. Swiss striker Johan Vonlanthen (right), who was 18 years and 141 days old, then scored against France in a 3-1 defeat on June 21!

Ivica Vastic scores against Poland at Euro 2008

OLDEST SCORER!

Austria's **Ivica Vastic** is the oldest goal grabber in European Championship history. The striker was 38 years and 257 days old when his late penalty at Euro 2008 bagged the joint hosts a 1-1 draw in a group match against Poland!

FAB FACT!

Yugoslavia striker Dragan Stojkovic was the tournament's youngest scorer until 2004, after his 1984 penalty against France at the age of 19!

TALLEST PLAYER!

Lanky Sweden international Andreas Isaksson is the tallest goalkeeper in Euros history at 6ft 6ins, but he just falls short of the overall record. That goes to Czech Republic star Jan Koller. The giant striker, who scored three goals at the last two Euros, stands a whopping 6ft 7ins tall!

Alain Giresse

SHORTEST PLAYER!

Alain Giresse, who was part of the France team that won Euro 1984, is the tournament's smallest ever player. Giresse was just 5ft 4ins tall when he played alongside Michel Platini in the middle of Les Bleus' midfield. Allan Simonsen was just one inch taller when he played in the same tournament for Denmark!

Jan Koller scored 55 goals in 90 games for the Czech Republic

FOOTY SHORTS!

Latal gets an early bath

Czech Republic bad boy Radoslav Latal was shown two red cards at the Euros – against Portugal at Euro '96 and Holland at Euro 2000!

Kezman sees red

Yugoslavia substitute Mateja Kezman was shown a red card after only 44 seconds against Norway at Euro 2000!

Yvon Le Roux

French defender Yvon Le Roux is the only player to be sent off in a European Championship final. He saw red in his side's 2-0 win over Spain in 1984!

MEGA MATCHES!

MATCH checks out the craziest crowds in Euros history!

Martin Peters strikes for England in 1968

134,461
The biggest ever crowd was in a Euro qualifier between **England** and **Scotland** at Glasgow's Hampden Park. World Cup hero Martin Peters scored in a 1-1 draw back in February 1968!

85,000
The largest crowd for a Euros final was in 1968. **Italy**'s 1-1 draw against **Yugoslavia** at the Stadio Olimpico in Rome is still a record to this day!

17,966
The smallest ever crowd for a Euros final was in 1960, when the **USSR** won the title in Paris with a 2-1 win against **Yugoslavia** after extra-time!

1,659
The **USSR**'s 1-0 win against **Hungary** in 1972 drew the smallest crowd for a finals match. The game was played in Brussels at the same time as the other semi-final, which featured hosts Belgium and was live on TV!

50
Back in August 1995, hardly anyone turned up for the goalless draw between **Azerbaijan** and **Slovakia**, because Azerbaijan had been forced to play the qualifier in Trabzon, Turkey!

A packed Wembley stadium in 1996

DID YOU KNOW?

Over 76,000 fans turned up at Wembley to watch all three of England's group matches at Euro '96!

NOU CAMP

WORLD-CLASS!
》》 The Nou Camp hosted the first match of the 1982 World Cup, when Belgium beat holders Argentina! 》》

COOL NAME!
》》 Nou Camp means 'new ground'! It replaced Barça's old Camp des Les Corts when it opened in 1957! 》》

HOLY STADIUM!
》》 Barça's awesome stadium has a chapel next to the changing rooms! How mad is that? 》》

TOP ATTRACTION!
》》 Over 1.2 million people visit the club museum each year! It's the most popular museum in Catalonia! 》》

SLAM DUNK!
》》 Next to the Nou Camp is the club's sports hall, the Palau Blaugrana! It's used for basketball matches!

SUPER STADIUMS OF THE WORLD!

CITY	BARCELONA
OPENED	1957
TEAM	BARCELONA
CAPACITY	98,772

GREATEST MATCH EVER!

MAN. UNITED 2-1 BAYERN MUNICH, 1999

Last-gasp goals from Teddy Sheringham and Ole Gunnar Solskjaer won the treble for United as they came from a goal down to win the Champions League final!

LEGENDS!

SAMUEL ETO'O

It took Eto'o just 67 games to score 50 goals for Barça after joining from Real Mallorca! The speedy striker also netted in the 2006 and 2009 Champo League finals!

LIONEL MESSI

Barça's silky forward is one of the hottest players on the planet! Leo loves burning past defenders with his deadly dribbling and scores loads of awesome goals!

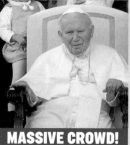

MASSIVE CROWD!

≫ Back in 1982, 120,000 people attended a mass with Pope John Paul II at the Nou Camp! ≫

CLUB ANTHEM!

≫ The club's anthem 'El Cant del Barça' is sung by the fans before every Barça home match! ≫

LOADSA MONEY!

≫ The Nou Camp cost a staggering £1.5 billion to build – the same price as 262 billion Mars Bars! ≫

OLDEST MANAGER!

Otto Baric set the record as the European Championship's oldest manager when he took charge of Croatia at Euro 2004, aged 71. But it turned out to be a forgettable tournament, as his side were knocked out in the group stage. The oldest gaffer to appear in a final was Spain's Luis Aragones at Euro 2008 – he was 69 years old!

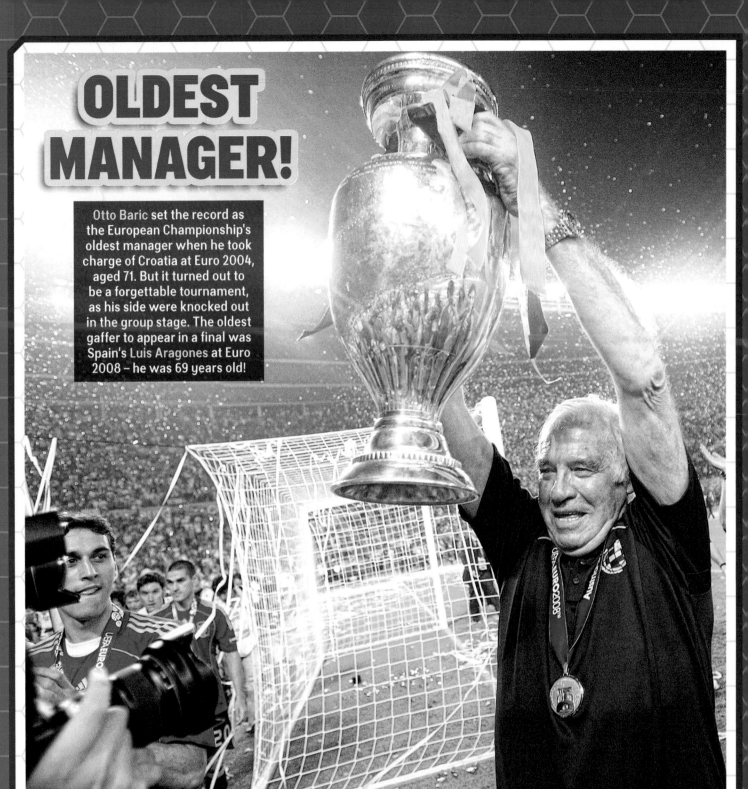

Luis Aragones celebrates Spain's 1-0 win over Germany in the Euro 2008 Final

THE YOUNGEST MANAGER!

Poul Petersen set a record way back in 1964 that still hasn't been broken. The Denmark boss was just 31 years old when he took his team to the semi-finals, where they lost 3-0 to the USSR! **Graham Taylor** (left) became the youngest England boss at a Euro Championship in 1992 when he was 47 years old!

FOOTY SHORTS!

Misery for Darius Vassell

When Sven-Goran Eriksson's England team lost on penalties against Portugal at Euro 2004, 23.9 million people watched the match in Britain!

Guus Hiddink

Rinus Michels (1992), Guus Hiddink (1996) and Frank Rijkaard (2000) all saw their Holland teams knocked out of the Euros on penalties!

Berti Vogts

Germany coach Berti Vogts took charge of a record 11 European Championship matches between 1992 and 1996!

7

CLUB-BY-CLUB »

ACCRINGTON STANLEY

★ COCA-COLA LEAGUE 2 ★

FAB FACT!
When Accrington won the Northern Premier League in 2003, they scored 97 goals and ended the season with a jaw-dropping 100 points!

CLUB STATS!

Stadium: The Fraser Eagle Stadium

Capacity: 5,057

Formed: 1968

Nickname: Reds

Manager: John Coleman

Captain: Peter Cavanagh

Record signing: Ian Craney from Swansea, £85,000

Biggest win: 10-1 v Lincoln United, 1991

Biggest defeat: 9-1 v Runcorn, 1985

Highest attendance: 4,368 v Colchester, 2004

Home kit: Red shirts, shorts and socks

Away kit: Yellow shirts, shorts and socks

Honours:
Blue Square Premier (2006),
Northern Premier League (2003),
Northern Premier Division One (2000),
Lancashire Combination (1974 & 1978),
Cheshire County Division Two (1981)

John Coleman

CLUB HISTORY!

An Accrington team played in the first five seasons of the Football League before they resigned, but they weren't associated with the club we know today. A team called Stanley Villa, who formed in 1891 at the Stanley Arms pub, took the name Accrington in 1893 to become Accrington Stanley, but they were forced to resign from the Football League due to money problems midway through the 1961-62 season. Re-forming in 1968, Stanley eventually won promotion back to the league, winning the Conference by 11 points back in 2006!

Financial troubles in 1962

⚽ Boss John Coleman has been in charge of the Reds for over ten years, making him the longest-serving manager in Accrington Stanley's history!

⚽ Accrington Stanley were formed by a group of men who lived on Stanley Street in the town. It's believed they met in a pub called The Stanley Arms!

⚽ One of Accrington's legends is striker Brett Ormerod. He scored 32 league goals in 52 matches before going on to star for Blackpool and Southampton!

CHAMPIONS 2008
BLUE SQ PREMIER
ALDERSHOT TOWN

FAB FACT! Aldershot became the first winners of a Football League play-off tie when they beat Wolves 3-0 over two legs in 1987!

CLUB STATS!

Stadium:
The EBB Stadium at the Recreation Ground

Capacity: *7,500*

Formed: *1992*

Nickname: *The Shots*

Manager: *Gary Waddock*

Captain: *Anthony Charles*

Record signing: *Marvin Morgan from Woking, Undisclosed*

Biggest win: *9-1 v Andover, 2000*

Biggest defeat: *10-1 v Southend, 1990*

Highest attendance: *19,138 v Carlisle, 1970*

Home kit: *Red shirts with blue trim, red shorts and socks*

Away kit: *Yellow shirts, shorts and socks*

Honours:
Blue Square Premier League (2008), Isthmian League Third Division (1993), Ryman League First Division (1998), Ryman League Premier Division (2003)

Gary Waddock in action for QPR in 1982

CLUB HISTORY!

Massive debts caused the original Aldershot team to go bust after its final match against Cardiff in March 1992, but just days later a new Shots side was born. Aldershot's next 11 seasons were spent in the Isthmian Leagues, before they were eventually promoted to the Conference in 2003. Five years later they became a league club again when they were crowned Conference champions with 101 points. The Shots' first match back in League 2 was a historic 1-0 win over Accrington Stanley on August 9, 2008!

⚽ Aldershot boss Gary Waddock used to play in midfield for QPR. The Shots gaffer even played in the 1982 FA Cup Final, but lost to Tottenham after a replay!

⚽ Jason Chewins stopped playing for Aldershot in 2004, but the tough-tackling left-back's 489 appearances remains a club record to this day!

⚽ Aldershot Town's 101 points in the 2007-08 season is a Conference record. They held off Cambridge and Torquay to claim the title by 15 points!

Waddock celebrates promotion

ARSENAL
★ BARCLAYS PREMIER LEAGUE ★

FAB FACT!
Arsenal have spent a massive 90 years in the English top flight! They were promoted in 1919 and haven't been relegated since!

Theo Walcott

Andrey Arshavin celebrates one of his four goals at Anfield in 2009

CLUB HISTORY!

Workers at the Woolwich Arsenal Armament Factory founded The Gunners as Dial Square in 1886, named after the sundial that sat above the door of the factory. Their first kit was redcurrant, which they wore again in 2005-06, their last season at Highbury.

The Gunners moved into their former ground in 1913 after they were relegated to the Championship, but the club hit back after the arrival of boss Herbert Chapman in 1925, winning the top flight in 1931 and 1933, and the FA Cup in 1930. Three more titles and an FA Cup followed under George Allison and Joe Shaw in the 1930s.

After World War Two, Arsenal were champions again in 1948 and 1953, and under former club physio Bertie Mee they became only the fourth side to win the league and cup double in 1970-71.

Arsenal turned to George Graham in 1986, who won three titles before he was sacked in 1995. A year later Arsene Wenger arrived.

The French tactician won the double twice in five seasons (1998 and 2002), led 'The Invincibles' to the title in 2004 and took the North London giants to the 2006 Champions League Final!

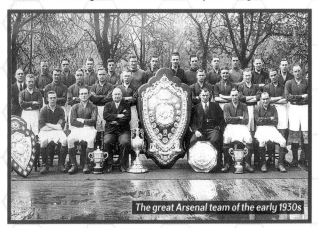

The great Arsenal team of the early 1930s

⚽ Arsenal have played in every Premier League season since it began in 1992-93. The Gunners won the title in 1998, 2002 and 2004. Their lowest finish was 12th in 1995!

⚽ Andrey Arshavin is the only player in Prem history to score four goals in one match and still not win. Arshavin netted all of Arsenal's goals in their 4-4 draw with Liverpool in 2009!

⚽ Gilberto Silva scored Arsenal's first goal at the Emirates Stadium in August 2006. His late equaliser bagged a 1-1 draw against Aston Villa on the opening day of the season!

The Emirates Stadium

CLUB STATS!

Stadium: The Emirates

Capacity: 60,361

Formed: 1886

Nickname: The Gunners

Manager: Arsene Wenger

Captain: Cesc Fabregas

Record signing: Andrey Arshavin from Zenit St. Petersburg, £15 million

Biggest win: 12-0 v Loughborough, 1900

Biggest defeat: 8-0 v Loughborough, 1896

Highest attendance: 73,707 v Lens, 1998 (at Wembley)

Home kit: Red and white shirts and socks, white shorts

Away kit: Blue shirts, shorts and socks

Honours: English League title (13), European Cup Winners' Cup (1), Fairs Cup (1), FA Cup (10), League Cup (2)

Robin van Persie

CLUB LEGENDS!

MATCH checks out the club's greatest players!

THIERRY HENRY

The France international is the greatest goalscorer in Arsenal's history. In just 254 Prem appearances, Henry scored an amazing 174 goals!

TONY ADAMS

Arsene Wenger called Adams a 'professor of defence' as the solid centre-back led his team to ten trophies in a 14-year spell as club captain!

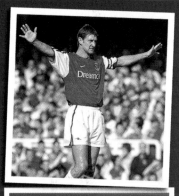

DAVID SEAMAN

Seaman played 564 games and won eight trophies with Arsenal, lifting the FA Cup as captain in his final game for The Gunners in 2003!

ASTON VILLA

FAB FACT!
An amazing 67 Villa stars, including Ashley Young and Emile Heskey, have played for England. That's more than any other English club!

Ashley Young

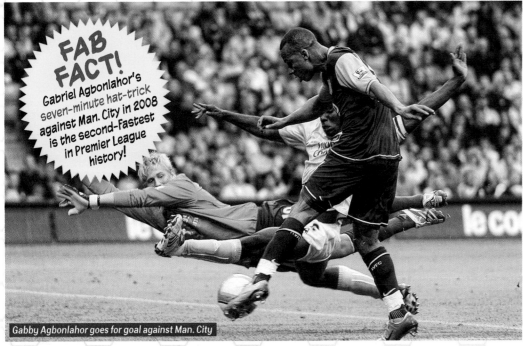

Gabby Agbonlahor goes for goal against Man. City

CLUB HISTORY!

Four members of the Villa Cross Wesleyan Chapel cricket team are said to have met under a gaslight to form Aston Villa in 1874. After winning the FA Cup in 1887, Villa were one of the founding 12 teams of the Football League in 1888. They had won five league titles and three FA Cups, including a league and cup double, by 1900.

By 1936 Villa's success had dried up and they were relegated to the Championship in 1959, bouncing back as champions just a season later. But it didn't last, and by 1970 they were in League 1.

In 1974, Villa's legendary boss Ron Saunders took over and led the club back to the top flight. They shocked the rest of the league to win the title in 1981, then beat giants Bayern Munich to lift the European Cup in 1982 thanks to Peter Withe's 67th-minute strike.

Aston Villa became one of the founders of the Premier League in 1992-93 and have been there ever since, winning the League Cup in 1994, under Ron Atkinson, and again in 1996, under Brian Little.

Since the arrival of Martin O'Neill, Villa have threatened to break into the Prem's 'Big Four', finishing sixth in both 2008 and 2009!

Villa's 1897 double-winning team

⚽ Aston Villa's first match after they were formed in 1874 was against Aston Brook St. Mary's rugby team. They agreed to play rugby in the first half and football in the second half!

⚽ Conservative party leader David Cameron, Hollywood legend Tom Hanks, Prince William, Harry Potter star Oliver Phelps and rocker Ozzy Osbourne are all massive fans of The Villans!

⚽ Aston Villa boss Martin O'Neill loves criminology and started training to be a lawyer when he was younger, but gave up his degree to sign for Nottingham Forest in 1971!

Villa Park

CLUB STATS!

Stadium: Villa Park
Capacity: 42,640
Formed: 1874
Nickname: The Villans
Manager: Martin O'Neill
Captain: Martin Petrov
Record signing: Stewart Downing from Middlesbrough, £12 million
Biggest win: 13-0 v Wednesbury Old Athletic, 1886
Biggest defeat: 8-1 v Blackburn, 1889
Highest attendance: 76,588 v Derby, 1946
Home kit: Claret and blue shirts, white shorts, blue socks
Away kit: White shirts and socks, blue shorts
Honours: English League title (7), Championship (2), League 1 (1), Champions League (1), European Super Cup (1), FA Cup (7), League Cup (5)

James Milner

CLUB LEGENDS!

MATCH checks out the club's greatest players!

MARTIN LAURSEN

Injury brought an early end to the former captain's career, but the classy centre-back will be remembered for his quality defending in 84 Prem games!

PAUL McGRATH

Villa spent a bargain £400,000 on the Ireland centre-back, who won the PFA Player Of The Year award after leading Villa to second place in 1992-93!

PETER WITHE

A club-record buy in 1980 after turning down Everton, Withe won the league in his first season and scored the winner in the 1982 European Cup Final!

BARNET
★ COCA-COLA LEAGUE 2 ★

FAB FACT!
Barnet assistant manager *Gary Breen* scored For the Republic OF Ireland at the 2002 World Cup!

CLUB STATS!

Stadium: *Underhill Stadium*

Capacity: *5,568*

Formed: *1888*

Nickname: *The Bees*

Manager: *Ian Hendon*

Captain: *Kenny Gillett*

Record signing: *Gary Heald from Peterborough, £130,000*

Biggest win: *7-0 v Blackpool, 2000*

Biggest defeat: *9-1 v Peterborough, 1998*

Highest attendance: *11,026 v Wycombe, 1952*

Home kit: *Gold and black striped shirts, black shorts and socks*

Away kit: *White shirts, amber shorts and socks*

Honours:
Blue Square Premier League (1991 & 2005), Southern League Division 1 (1966), Southern League Division 1 South (1977)

Marlon King in action for Barnet in 2000

CLUB HISTORY!

Originally called Woodville, Barnet were formed in 1888, and were known as The Hillmen. Early opponents included Thames Ironworks, who later became West Ham. Barnet played amateur footy until they became one of 21 teams to form the first Conference season in 1979-80. After finishing second three times (1987, 1988 and 1990), they returned to the league in 1991, winning promotion in their second season after finishing third. Barnet slipped back to the Conference in 2001, but returned in 2005!

⚽ The red and white crossed swords on the club's badge represent a famous battle that took place near Barnet in 1471 during the War of the Roses!

⚽ Former Bees include Birmingham keeper Maik Taylor, Jamaica striker Marlon King and TV pundit Mark Lawrenson, who played just two games for Barnet!

⚽ Barnet's Underhill Stadium is well known for its crazy pitch, which slopes north to south. It used to be even worse before the club improved it in the late 1980s!

Underhill

BARNSLEY

★ COCA-COLA CHAMPIONSHIP ★

FAB FACT!
Barnsley lost the 1910 FA Cup Final to Newcastle, but bounced back to lift the trophy by beating West Brom two years later!

CLUB STATS!

Stadium: *Oakwell*

Capacity: *23,176*

Formed: *1887*

Nickname: *The Tykes*

Manager: *Simon Davey*

Captain: *Stephen Foster*

Record signing: *Georgi Hristov from Partizan Belgrade, £1.5 million*

Biggest win: *9-0 v Loughborough, 1899*

Biggest defeat: *9-0 v Notts County, 1927*

Highest attendance: *40,255 v Stoke, 1936*

Home kit: *Red shirts, white shorts, red socks*

Away kit: *Black shirts, shorts and socks*

Honours:
Division Three North (1934, 1939 & 1955), FA Cup (1912)

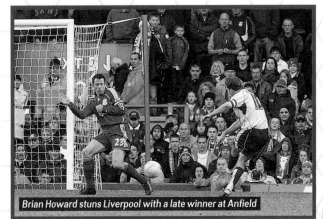
Brian Howard stuns Liverpool with a late winner at Anfield

CLUB HISTORY!

Formed by Reverend Tiverton Preedy in 1887, the Oakwell club were originally called Barnsley St. Peters after the church where Preedy worked.
In 1912, Harry Tufnell entered the Barnsley history books when he scored the only goal in their FA Cup final replay against top-flight side West Brom. It's still the only time the club has ever lifted the trophy. Following their only Prem season in 1998, Barnsley slipped into League 1, returning to the Championship in 2006 after beating Swansea on penalties in the play-off final!

⚽ Barnsley had an amazing FA Cup run in 2007-08. Simon Davey masterminded victories against Liverpool and Chelsea, before losing to Cardiff in the semi-finals!

⚽ The Tykes managed to stay in the Championship with victory on the final day of last season. Barnsley beat Plymouth 2-1 at Home Park and sent Norwich down!

⚽ Reuben Noble-Lazarus set a Football League record in 2008-09 as the youngest ever player. The striker was only 15 when he came off the bench against Ipswich!

Barnsley's 1912 FA Cup winners

FAB FACT!
St. Andrew's was used as a rifle range in World War One, and the Kop's roof was destroyed by German planes during World War Two!

Marcus Bent celebrates

Cameron Jerome goes for goal

CLUB HISTORY!

Birmingham were founded in 1875 by cricketers from Holy Church in Bordesley Green, taking the name Small Heath Alliance. The club then decided to turn professional a decade later.

Their original name was replaced by Birmingham City in 1905, a year before the club switched to St. Andrew's. The first player to score at the new ground, Benny Green, was awarded a piano.

From 1920-35 the club's all-time record goalscorer, Joe Bradford, netted 267 goals in 445 appearances, including an equaliser in the 1931 FA Cup Final when Blues lost 2-1 to West Brom.

Following World War Two, Blues became the first English team to play in the Inter-Cities Fairs Cup when they drew 0-0 with Inter Milan in 1956. They reached the 1960 final, but lost to Barcelona. Three years later they beat rivals Aston Villa to lift the League Cup.

The 1970s saw top-flight footy at St. Andrew's, but by 1989 they were in League 1. Two Johnstone's Paint Trophy victories in the 1990s earned some silverware before Steve Bruce achieved Prem promotion, a feat repeated by Alex McLeish in 2008-09!

Birmingham's 1905-06 squad photo

⚽ The first £1 million transfer in British football saw striker Trevor Francis leave Birmingham for Nottingham Forest in February 1979. Francis returned as manager in 1996!

⚽ Birmingham made a blistering start to the 2008-09 season, winning five of their first six matches in the Championship before losing 1-0 to Blackpool. They finished in second spot!

⚽ In the FA Cup third round in 2007, Birmingham crushed Newcastle 5-1 at St. James' Park. It was the first time in 93 years The Magpies had leaked five goals in an FA Cup match!

St. Andrew's

CLUB STATS!

Stadium: St. Andrew's
Capacity: 30,079
Formed: 1875
Nickname: Blues
Manager: Alex McLeish
Captain: Damien Johnson
Record signing: Christian Benitez from Santos Laguna, £8.5 million
Biggest win: 12-0 v Walsall Town Swifts (1892) and Doncaster (1903)
Biggest defeat: 9-1 v Blackburn (1895) and Sheffield Wednesday (1930)
Highest attendance: 66,844 v Everton, 1939
Home kit: Blue and white shirts, white shorts, blue socks
Away kit: Black shirts with gold and white trim, black shorts and socks
Honours: Championship (4), League 1 (1), League Cup (1), Johnstone's Paint Trophy (2)

Damien Johnson

CLUB LEGENDS!

MATCH checks out the club's greatest players!

MAIK TAYLOR

The awesome keeper has been pure class since joining in 2003, making 185 league appearances and earning tons of caps as Northern Ireland's No.1!

SEBASTIAN LARSSON

Blues fans have loved the Sweden midfielder since he arrived in 2006. Premier League keepers will hate his long-range rockets in the 2009-10 season!

TREVOR FRANCIS

The ex-England striker made his debut at just 16 years old in 1970 and went on to score 133 goals in 328 matches before his big move to Nottingham Forest!

FAB FACT!
The left-hand side of Blackburn's shirts has been blue since 1934, but Rovers did wear blue on the right-hand side in earlier seasons!

El Hadji Diouf and Benni McCarthy

Morten Gamst Pedersen celebrates against Portsmouth

CLUB HISTORY!

A meeting at Blackburn's St. Leger Hotel on Bonfire Night in 1875 resulted in the club being founded by John Lewis and Arthur Constantine, ex-students of Shrewsbury public school.

In 1882 Rovers reached their first FA Cup final, only to lose 1-0 to twice-winners Old Etonians. Then came three straight FA Cup wins from 1884-86, before they joined the Football League in 1888.

They won league titles in 1912 and 1914, and the 1928 FA Cup, but were relegated in 1936 and didn't return to the top flight until 1958.

After bouncing between League 1 and the Championship in the 1970s, the club was mounting serious play-off challenges to the top flight by the late 1980s, before Jack Walker bought the club.

Walker's millions saw the arrival of striker Alan Shearer in 1992 for a British transfer record £3.5 million, and thanks to Shearer's goals the Premier League title came to Ewood Park in 1995.

Silverware returned to Blackburn under Graeme Souness in 2002 when he led them to League Cup glory, and Sam Allardyce will be looking to guide Rovers up the table in the 2009-10 season!

Blackburn's 1928 FA Cup winners

⚽ Blackburn are the only club apart from Man. United, Chelsea and Arsenal to win the Premier League. They pipped United to the title by just one point on the last day of the 1994-95 season!

⚽ Club captain Ryan Nelsen scored his first league goal for Blackburn in 2009. The New Zealand international headed home Rovers' second goal in a 2-0 win against Wigan in April!

⚽ Ewood Park is one of the oldest grounds in English football. The ancient stadium was first opened in 1882, when it was used for football, athletics and greyhound racing!

Ewood Park

CLUB STATS!

Stadium: Ewood Park

Capacity: 31,154

Formed: 1875

Nickname: Rovers

Manager: Sam Allardyce

Captain: Ryan Nelsen

Record signing: Andy Cole from Man. United, £8 million

Biggest win: 11-0 v Rossendale, 1884

Biggest defeat: 8-0 v Arsenal, 1933

Highest attendance: 62,522 v Bolton, 1929

Home kit: Blue and white halved shirts, white shorts, blue socks

Away kit: White shirts, red shorts and socks

Honours: English League title (3), Championship (1), League 1 (1), FA Cup (6), League Cup (1)

David Dunn fires a shot at goal

BRAD FRIEDEL

The towering goalkeeper played 287 league games for Blackburn. The former USA international even scored in a 3-2 defeat to Charlton in February 2004!

ALAN SHEARER

In a four-season spell at Ewood Park, Shearer was on fire as he netted 112 league goals in 138 appearances before joining Newcastle for £15 million!

TUGAY

The legendary playmaker hung up his boots at the end of 2008-09, but will always be remembered for his ace passing and long-range net-busters!

BLACKPOOL
★ COCA-COLA CHAMPIONSHIP ★

FAB FACT!
Blackpool First started wearing *tangerine* shirts in 1923-24 after a club director refereed an international game between Holland and Belgium!

Keith Southern

Blackpool celebrate in the 2007 League 1 Play-off Final

CLUB LEGENDS!

MATCH checks out the club's greatest players!

SIR STANLEY MATTHEWS

The England winger signed for £11,500 in 1947, won the FA Cup when he was 38 years old and bagged the first ever European Footballer Of The Year award!

CLUB HISTORY!

The Lancashire club was formed at the Stanley Arms Hotel in 1887 after a dispute among players from Blackpool St. Johns FC. They joined the League for the 1896-97 season, before a merger with South Shore allowed the club to move into Bloomfield Road.

Following World War One, Blackpool were a Championship side before winning promotion in 1930 and staying in the top flight for three seasons. After World War Two, they became unstoppable.

With Sir Stanley Matthews and Stan Mortensen in great form, Joe Smith's side reached three FA Cup finals, winning in 1953, and finished second in the league in 1956, 11 points behind Man. United.

By 1967 Blackpool were back in the Championship, slipping into League 2 in 1981. The club experienced the highs and lows of the new play-off system, losing on penalties to Torquay in 1991, before beating Scunthorpe on spot-kicks the following season.

Even Sam Allardyce couldn't achieve promotion from League 1 in the 1990s – that was left to Robbie Williams and Keigan Parker, who both scored in the 2007 Play-off Final against Yeovil!

Bloomfield Road

CLUB STATS!

Stadium: Bloomfield Road
Capacity: 9,731
Formed: 1887
Nickname: The Seasiders
Manager: Ian Holloway
Captain: Rob Edwards
Record signing: Stephen McPhee from Hull, £300,000
Biggest win: 7-0 v Reading (1928) and Preston (1948)
Biggest defeat: 10-1 v Small Heath Alliance (1901) and Huddersfield (1930)
Highest attendance: 38,098 v Wolves, 1955
Home kit: Tangerine shirts and socks, white shorts
Away kit: White shirts and socks, tangerine shorts
Honours: Championship (1), FA Cup (1), Johnstone's Paint Trophy (2)

STAN MORTENSEN

Blackpool's incredible striker survived a plane crash in World War Two and went on to score 197 goals in 14 years with the Lancashire club!

The Matthews Cup Final, 1953

⚽ Blackpool's FA Cup win in 1953 is known as 'The Matthews Final', after Sir Stanley Matthews' awesome performance, and despite his team-mate Stan Mortensen hitting a hat-trick!

⚽ Blackpool is Ian Holloway's fifth club as a manager. He started out at Bristol Rovers before taking over Championship sides Leicester, QPR and Plymouth!

⚽ The Seasiders won two Johnstone's Paint Trophy finals in three seasons, against Cambridge (2002) and Southend (2004). John Murphy took 74 seconds to net against The Shrimpers!

Rob Edwards scores against Derby

JIMMY ARMFIELD

Now a Radio 5 Live pundit, Armfield was club captain for a decade and played his entire career at Blackpool, making 626 appearances from 1954 to 1971!

BOLTON WANDERERS
★ BARCLAYS PREMIER LEAGUE ★

FAB FACT!
At 6ft 6ins tall, Bolton defender Zat Knight, who arrived at The Reebok from Aston Villa in July 2009, is the Prem's lankiest defender!

Matt Taylor celebrates

Gary Cahill scores at Upton Park

CLUB HISTORY!

Bolton were one of the original 12 founding members of the Football League in 1888, having been set up 14 years before by the vicar of Christ Church Sunday school in Bolton, who wanted to create an outdoor sports club in the town.

Bolton reached five FA Cup finals between 1894 and 1929, winning it three times. One of those games was the 'White Horse Final' in 1923 – the first to be played at Wembley. David Jack and Jack Smith scored the only goals of the game against West Ham.

Bolton spent 29 seasons in the English top flight after winning promotion from Division Two in 1935, and picked up another FA Cup in 1958 – the last time they lifted a major trophy.

The Trotters had slipped into League 2 by 1987, but under Bruce Rioch they won an epic play-off final 4-3 against Reading in 1995 to reach the Premier League.

A sixth-place finish in 2005 saw Sam Allardyce's side play UEFA Cup footy at the Reebok for the first time, and they even reached the last 16 in 2008 only to get knocked out by Sporting Lisbon!

Bolton show off the FA Cup in 1923

⚽ Bruce Rioch's Bolton side became known as cup giant-killers in the early 1990s, after picking up impressive FA Cup victories over Liverpool, Arsenal, Aston Villa and Everton!

⚽ Defender Sebastien Puygrenier scored Bolton's 4,000th top-flight goal on his Trotters debut against Tottenham in a 3-2 win at the Reebok Stadium in January 2009!

⚽ Bolton boss Gary Megson played for nine different clubs as a midfielder between 1977 and 1995. He returned to manage two of them – Norwich and Nottingham Forest!

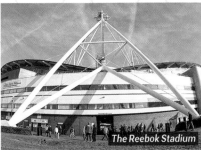

The Reebok Stadium

CLUB STATS!

Stadium: The Reebok Stadium

Capacity: 28,101

Formed: 1874

Nickname: The Trotters

Manager: Gary Megson

Captain: Kevin Davies

Record signing: Johan Elmander from Toulouse, £11 million

Biggest win: 13-0 v Sheffield United, 1890

Biggest defeat: 9-1 v Preston, 1887

Highest attendance: 69,912 v Man. City, 1933

Home kit: White shirts and socks, blue shorts

Away kit: Blue shirts and socks, white shorts

Honours: Championship (3), League 1 (1), FA Cup (4)

Ricardo Gardner

CLUB LEGENDS!

MATCH checks out the club's greatest players!

NAT LOFTHOUSE

A Bolton striker for his whole career from 1946 to 1960, the 1958 FA Cup Final captain made 452 league appearances and scored an amazing 285 goals!

JUSSI JAASKELAINEN

Bolton's awesome shot-stopper has played over 427 matches since joining from Finnish club VPS Vassa in 1997 for a bargain £100,000!

KEVIN DAVIES

After taking over the captain's armband when Kevin Nolan moved to Newcastle, Bolton's tough striker scored 12 Prem goals in the 2008-09 season!

BOURNEMOUTH
★ COCA-COLA LEAGUE 2 ★

FAB FACT!
One of the reasons Bournemouth are known as the Cherries could be that their Dean Court stadium was built by a cherry orchard!

CLUB STATS!

Stadium:
The Fitness First Stadium at Dean Court

Capacity: 10,375

Formed: 1899

Nickname: Cherries

Manager: Eddie Howe

Captain: Danny Hollands

Record signing: Gavin Peacock from Gillingham, £210,000

Biggest win: 11-0 v Margate, 1971

Biggest defeat: 9-0 Lincoln, 1982

Highest attendance:
28,799 v Man. United, 1957

Home kit: Red and black shirts, black and red shorts, black socks

Away kit: Black and red shirts, black and red shorts, black socks

Honours:
League 1 (1987),
Johnstone's Paint Trophy (1984)

Milton Graham strikes against Man. United in 1984

CLUB HISTORY!

AFC Bournemouth rose from the ashes of Boscombe St. Johns Institute Football Club. Despite only winning two trophies in their history, Bournemouth looked to be heading to Wembley for the 1957 FA Cup Final after beating Wolves and Spurs, but they lost 2-1 to Man. United in the sixth round.
In 1983 the club appointed Harry Redknapp as manager and he guided them to the League 1 title with a record 97 points in 1987. Due to massive debts, the club started 2008-09 on minus 17 points, but 12 wins in their last 23 matches saw them stay up!

The 1957 FA Cup run

⚽ Bournemouth caused an FA Cup giantkilling in 1984 when they beat holders Man. United 2-0 in the third round. Harry Redknapp was Cherries boss at the time!

⚽ Before changing their name in 1971, the Cherries were known as 'Bournemouth and Boscombe Athletic'. That must be one of the longest names in footy history!

⚽ Harry Redknapp isn't the only current Prem boss who was a gaffer at Dean Court. Stoke's Tony Pulis took over from Redknapp before leaving the club in 1994!

BRADFORD CITY
★ COCA-COLA LEAGUE 2 ★

FAB FACT!
Manager *Stuart McCall* scored twice in the 1989 FA Cup Final for Everton, but The Toffees lost 3-2 to Liverpool after extra-time!

CLUB STATS!

Stadium: *Coral Windows Stadium*

Capacity: *25,136*

Formed: *1903*

Nickname: *The Bantams*

Manager: *Stuart McCall*

Captain: *Peter Thorne*

Record signing: *David Hopkin from Leeds, £2.5 million*

Biggest win: *11-1 v Rotherham, 1928*

Biggest defeat: *9-1 v Colchester, 1961*

Highest attendance: *39,146 v Burnley, 1911*

Home kit: *Claret with amber trim shirts, shorts and socks*

Away kit: *Black shirts, shorts and socks*

Honours:
*Championship (1908),
League 1 (1985),
Division Three North (1929),
FA Cup (1911)*

Chris Kamara celebrates promotion at Wembley in 1996

CLUB HISTORY!

Five years after joining the Football League in 1903, Bradford were promoted to the top flight. Three years later in 1911 they won the FA Cup after a replay against Newcastle. After winning Division Three North in 1929, Bradford had to wait 56 years to bag another title, but the final day of the 1985 season saw one of the worst disasters in English football when a fire at Valley Parade killed 56 fans. Paul Jewell took over from Chris Kamara and won promotion to the Prem in 1999, where they spent two seasons before slipping back down the leagues!

FA Cup winners, 1911

⚽ Sky Sports pundit Chris Kamara was Bradford manager from 1995 to 1998. Kamo led the club to play-off glory against Notts County in 1996!

⚽ Former Everton goalkeeper Neville Southall set a club record when he played in a 2-1 defeat against Leeds in 2000. The Wales legend was 41 years old!

⚽ Bradford's first season in the Prem in 1999-2000 ended in dramatic fashion, when David Wetherall's goal in the final game against Liverpool kept them up!

BRENTFORD
★ COCA-COLA LEAGUE 1 ★

CHAMPIONS 2009 BRENTFORD F.C.

FAB FACT!
You can see Griffin Park when landing at Heathrow Airport, so companies pay to use the roof of Brentford's stadium for advertising!

CLUB STATS!

Stadium: Griffin Park
Capacity: 12,400
Formed: 1889
Nickname: The Bees
Manager: Andy Scott
Captain: Kevin O'Connor
Record signing: Hermann Hreidarsson from Crystal Palace, £750,000
Biggest win: 9-0 v Wrexham, 1963
Biggest defeat: 7-0 v Swansea, 1924
Highest attendance: 38,678 v Leicester, 1949
Home kit: Red and white striped shirts, black shorts, red and black socks
Away kit: Sky blue shirts, blue shorts and socks
Honours:
Championship (1935),
League 1 (1992),
League 2 (1963, 1999 & 2009),
Division Three South (1933)

Brentford in action at the Millennium Stadium in 2001

CLUB HISTORY!

Brentford FC was formed in 1889 by a rowing club who wanted a sport to play during the winter. Their first kit was a disgusting mixture of pink, claret and light blue hoops. Fans used to shout 'Buck up B's!' at home games, which the newspapers thought was 'Buck up Bees!' The nickname stuck. Under manager Harry Curtis, Brentford finished in the top six of Division One three seasons in a row between 1936 and 1938. Griffin Park has since seen lower league footy, but they made the sixth round of the FA Cup in 1989 and won League 2 in 2009!

⚽ When Brentford sealed the League 2 title in 2008-09, they became the second team after Doncaster to win the bottom division three times!

⚽ Together with Bristol City, Bristol Rovers, Carlisle, Stockport and Southend, Brentford have lost the Johnstone's Paint Trophy final twice!

⚽ When he's not recording music, the frontman of indie band Hard-Fi, Richard Archer, goes to Griffin Park to watch The Bees. He's a massive a Brentford fan!

Brentford's Gerry McAloon, 1938

BRIGHTON & HOVE ALBION
★ COCA-COLA LEAGUE 1 ★

FAB FACT!
Man. City and England star *Gareth Barry* used to play for Brighton's youth team before moving to Aston Villa in 1997!

CLUB STATS!

Stadium: *Withdean Stadium*

Capacity: *8,850*

Formed: *1901*

Nickname: *The Seagulls*

Manager: *Russell Slade*

Captain: *Nicky Forster*

Record signing: *Andy Ritchie from Man. United, £500,000*

Biggest win: *10-1 v Wisbech, 1965*

Biggest defeat: *9-0 v Middlesbrough, 1958*

Highest attendance: *36,747 v Fulham, 1958 (at the Goldstone Ground)*

Home kit: *Blue and white striped shirts, white shorts and socks*

Away kit: *Red and black striped shirts, black shorts, red socks*

Honours:
*League 1 (1965 & 2002),
League 2 (2001),
Division Three South (1958),
Community Shield (1910)*

Brighton's Gordon Smith scores in the 1983 FA Cup Final

CLUB HISTORY!

Formed in the early 20th Century, The Seagulls were Southern League champions when they beat Aston Villa to win the Community Shield 1-0 in 1910. Brighton had climbed to the top flight by the start of the 1979-80 season and in 1983 they almost beat Man. United in the FA Cup final, but Gordon Smith's last-gasp shot was saved and they lost the replay. They won back-to-back promotions in 2001 and 2002, and knocked Man. City out of the 2009 League Cup, but haven't been able to escape the lower leagues in recent years!

Brighton v Arsenal, 1980

⚽ Tons of Prem stars have worn Brighton's blue and white stripes, including Wolves star Chris Iwelumo, Aston Villa's Steve Sidwell and Fulham's Bobby Zamora!

⚽ Brighton had a crazy season in 1982-83. They reached the FA Cup final, where they lost to Man. United, and were relegated from the top flight after finishing bottom!

⚽ Norman 'Fatboy Slim' Cook is one of the most famous Brighton fans ever. The DJ's record label, Skint Records, has sponsored the team's shirts since 1999!

BRISTOL CITY
★ COCA-COLA CHAMPIONSHIP ★

Nicky Maynard

FAB FACT!
The Robins have beaten local rivals *Bristol Rovers* 34 times in their 88 league meetings, with 30 draws between the two sides!

FAB FACT!
The club's official anthem 'One For The Bristol City' by The Wurzels reached No.66 in the charts when it was released back in 2007!

CONGRATULATIONS ON PROMOTION
Nationwide

The Robins claim promotion in 1998

CLUB HISTORY!

The Robins turned professional in 1897 when Bristol South End changed their name after a meeting in Bedminster. The club's first boss, Sam Hollis, was given £40 to spend on players.

Runners-up to Newcastle in their first top-flight season in 1907, Bristol City reached the FA Cup final two years later, only to lose 1-0 to fellow debutants Man. United. Relegation followed in 1911, starting an exile from the top flight which lasted 65 years.

The club suffered back-to-back relegations in the early '80s and were declared bankrupt in 1982. They put it behind them, though, and by the end of the decade won promotion to the Championship.

In January 1994, Bristol City shocked Liverpool with a 1-0 win in the FA Cup third round, but the league was a different story. City slipped out the Championship in 1995 and didn't return until 2007 in Gary Johnson's second season in charge.

After just missing out on Premier League football in 2008, City suffered a slump in form. Only a decent second half to the 2009 season stopped the club sliding back into League 1!

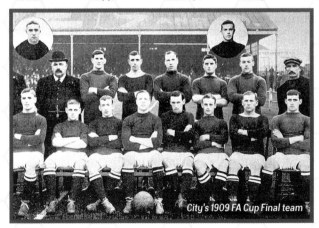

City's 1909 FA Cup Final team

⚽ Bristol City were just 90 minutes away from the Premier League in 2007-08, but a great volley from Dean Windass sealed a 1-0 win for Hull in the Championship play-off final!

⚽ Famous footy gaffers David Moyes and Steve McClaren both played for Bristol City in the 1980s. McClaren was part of the side that reached the League Cup semi-finals in 1989!

⚽ Ex-striker Ade Akinbiyi is the club's record signing and record sale. After joining for £1.2 million in May 1998, he left just one year later for £3 million after 25 goals in 53 games!

Ashton Gate

CLUB STATS!

Stadium: Ashton Gate
Capacity: 21,804
Formed: 1894
Nickname: Robins
Manager: Gary Johnson
Captain: Louis Carey
Record signing: Ade Akinbiyi from Gillingham, £1.2 million
Biggest win: 11-0 v Chichester, 1960
Biggest defeat: 9-0 v Coventry, 1934
Highest attendance: 43,335 v Preston, 1935
Home kit: Red shirts, white shorts and socks
Away kit: Black shirts, shorts and socks
Honours: Championship (1), Division Three South (3), Johnstone's Paint Trophy (2), Welsh Cup (1), Anglo-Scottish Cup (1)

Louis Carey

CLUB LEGENDS!

MATCH checks out the club's greatest players!

JOHN ATYEO

From 1951-66, Atyeo scored 351 goals in 645 matches, setting a club record that's never been broken. Despite all his games for City, he was never booked!

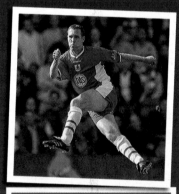

BRIAN TINNION

'Tinman' became a City hero after scoring a last-gasp penalty against Bristol Rovers in his first match. He also hit the winner at Anfield in the 1994 FA Cup!

SCOTT MURRAY

The flying Scotland winger was a big fans' favourite at Ashton Gate. His 30-yard lob over Boro keeper Mark Schwarzer in the 2007 FA Cup was a classic!

BURNLEY

★ BARCLAYS PREMIER LEAGUE ★

FAB FACT!
Turf Moor is thought to be the first ground visited by a member of the Royal Family. Prince Albert watched a Burnley match in October 1886!

Wade Elliott

PLAY OFF WINNERS 2009

COCA-COLA CHAMPIONSHIP PLAY OFF WINNERS 2009
BURNLEY

Burnley clinch promotion to the Premier League in 2009

FAB FACT!
The Clarets were invited to move to Turf Moor by Burnley cricket club in the 1880s. The cricket team still play next to the ground!

CLUB HISTORY!

May 1882 marked the beginning of Burnley FC when the club switched from playing rugby to football. Six years later they were playing in the Football League, finishing in ninth place.

They won the second division in 1898, claiming the title by three points, and went on to lift the FA Cup against Liverpool just months before the outbreak of World War One in 1914.

The top-flight title arrived in 1921 as Burnley were unbeaten in 30 matches, a record which stood until Arsenal's 'Invincible' season in 2003-04. By 1930, The Clarets were back in the Championship.

An FA Cup final appearance in 1947 was the start of Burnley's revival as they won the title in 1960, were runners-up in 1962 and came third in 1966. But by 1985 they were in League 2, avoiding the drop in 1987 by beating Leyton Orient 2-1 on the final day.

Five years later and Burnley were promoted, with play-off success in 1994 before they arrived in the Championship after finishing second in League 1 in 2000. Less than two seasons after Owen Coyle's appointment, Burnley reached the Premier League!

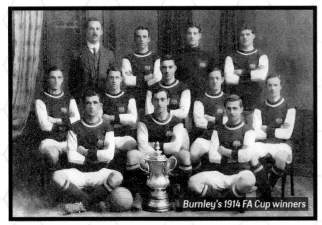
Burnley's 1914 FA Cup winners

⚽ Burnley's 1-0 victory against Sheffield United in the 2008-09 Championship Play-off Final saw the Lancashire club reach the English top flight for the first time in 33 years!

⚽ Burnley played in green kits at the start of the 20th Century. Legend has it the green shirts were unlucky, so the club switched to their current claret and blue strip in 1910!

⚽ The Clarets have won all four English divisions, the FA Cup and the Community Shield. They almost reached the 2009 League Cup Final, but lost 6-4 to Tottenham in the semi-finals!

Turf Moor

CLUB STATS!

Stadium: Turf Moor
Capacity: 21,973
Formed: 1882
Nickname: The Clarets
Manager: Owen Coyle
Captain: Steven Caldwell
Record signing: Steven Fletcher from Hibernian, £3 million
Biggest win: 9-0 v Darwen (1892), Crystal Palace (1909), New Brighton (1957) and Penrith (1984)
Biggest defeat: 10-0 v Aston Villa (1925) and Sheffield United (1929)
Highest attendance: 54,775 v Huddersfield, 1924
Home kit: Claret and blue shirts and socks, white shorts
Away kit: White shirts and socks, black shorts
Honours: English League title (2), Championship (2), League 1 (1), League 2 (1), FA Cup (1)

Steven Caldwell celebrates against Preston

ROBBIE BLAKE

Currently in his second spell at Turf Moor, Burnley's classy forward has made 211 league appearances for the club and scored 59 goals!

TOMMY CUMMINGS

Burnley's former captain played 434 league matches for the club, putting him fifth on their all-time appearance list. He won the title with The Clarets in 1959-60!

BRIAN MILLER

Quality Burnley defender Miller played 379 games for the club over 11 years and had two spells as manager, leading The Clarets to the League 1 title in 1981-82!

BRISTOL ROVERS
★ COCA-COLA LEAGUE 1 ★

FAB FACT!
Bristol Rovers fans are known as Gasheads, because of a gasworks that was built near the club's old Eastville Stadium!

CLUB STATS!

Stadium: The Memorial Stadium

Capacity: 11,916

Formed: 1883

Nickname: The Pirates

Manager: Paul Trollope

Captain: Stuart Campbell

Record signing: Andy Tillson from QPR, £375,000

Biggest win: 7-0 v Brighton, 1952

Biggest defeat: 12-0 v Luton, 1936

Highest attendance:
11,530 v Bristol City, 2007

Home kit: Blue and white quarter shirts, blue shorts, blue and white socks

Away kit: Yellow shirts, green shorts, yellow and green socks

Honours:
League 1 (1990),
Division Three South (1953),
Southern League Division One (1905)

The 2007 Johnstone's Paint Trophy run ends with defeat in the final

CLUB HISTORY!

Bristol Rovers were known as the Black Arabs when they were formed in 1883, after the team's black shirts and a rugby club called the Arabs who played nearby. It took another 16 years before The Pirates became known as Bristol Rovers in 1899. The club has never played top-flight footy – the closest they got was in 1956 when they missed out on promotion by four points. In 2002, Rovers finished one place above relegation to the Conference and reached the Johnstone's Paint Trophy final in 2007, where they lost 3-2 to Doncaster!

⚽ Bristol Rovers didn't concede a goal on their way to the 2007 Johnstone's Paint Trophy Final, but then went a goal down against Doncaster after 45 seconds!

⚽ Rovers beat Sheffield United to win the Watney Cup back in 1972, an old pre-season tournament between the two top-scoring teams in all four divisions!

⚽ Bristol Rovers fans should check out the British comedy film Hot Fuzz, because Nick Frost's character can be seen wearing a Pirates shirt in the movie!

Brian Godfrey lifts the Watney Cup

BURTON ALBION
★ COCA-COLA LEAGUE 2 ★

FAB FACT! Before Albion were formed, the Staffordshire town had clubs called Burton Swifts, Burton Town, Burton United and Burton Wanderers!

CLUB STATS!

Stadium: The Pirelli Stadium
Capacity: 6,912
Formed: 1950
Nickname: Brewers
Manager: Paul Peschisolido
Captain: Darren Stride
Record signing: Russell Penn from Kidderminster, £20,000
Biggest win: 12-1 v Coalville Town, 1954
Biggest defeat: 10-0 v Barnet, 1970
Highest attendance: 22,492 v Leicester, 1985 (at the Baseball Ground)
Home kit: Yellow shirts, black shorts and socks
Away kit: White shirts with blue trim, blue shorts and socks
Honours:
Blue Square Premier (2009),
Unibond League (2002)

Burton fans cheer on their team at Old Trafford in the FA Cup

⚽ Super skipper Darren Stride has been at Burton all his career, holds the club record for most appearances and is the Brewers' third highest goalscorer of all time!

⚽ Over 11,000 Burton fans made the trip to Old Trafford for the FA Cup third round replay against Man. United in 2006. It's the largest ever away crowd at the ground!

⚽ At one stage in 2008-09, Burton were 19 points clear at the top of the Conference. Albion were eventually crowned champions, but only by two points!

CLUB HISTORY!

The town of Burton went ten years without a football club before Albion were formed at a public meeting in 1950. Crystal Palace gaffer Neil Warnock was at the club before leaving to join Scarborough in 1986, but no Burton boss can match the record set by Nigel Clough. During his 11-year spell as player-manager, Clough, the son of Nottingham Forest legend Brian, won the club's first title in 52 years and twice reached the semi-finals of the FA Trophy. Clough's success alerted bigger clubs and he moved to Derby in January!

Nigel Clough

FAB FACT!
Riverside AFC, which became Cardiff City, had one of the worst kits ever. In the early 20th Century they wore amber and brown shirts!

Ross McCormack

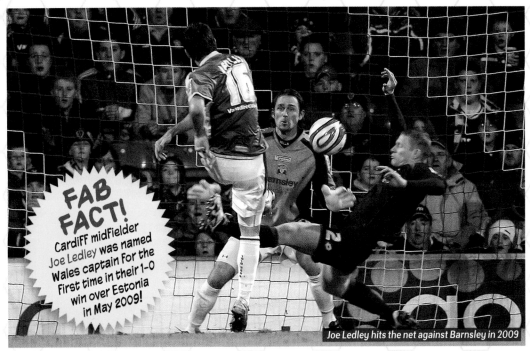

Joe Ledley hits the net against Barnsley in 2009

CLUB HISTORY!

Bartley Wilson was the man who brought football to the Welsh capital when he decided to give his cricket team something to do in the winter. Riverside AFC was born, becoming Cardiff in 1908.

Ten years after moving to Ninian Park in 1910, The Bluebirds joined the Football League. The 1920s were a great time to be a Cardiff fan, as the club finished runners-up to Huddersfield in 1924 and reached the 1925 and 1927 FA Cup Finals. After slipping down to Division Three South before World War Two, Cardiff were promoted when football resumed in 1946-47.

As winners of the Welsh Cup, City were allowed to enter the European Cup Winners' Cup after the war and reached as far as the semi-finals in 1968, before losing narrowly to Hamburg.

After a long period in the Championship, Cardiff hit rock bottom in 1996 as they escaped relegation from League 2 by five points. The Bluebirds have since taken off under Dave Jones and have become one of the most feared clubs in the Championship. They reached the 2008 FA Cup Final, but lost out 1-0 to Portsmouth.

Cardiff's 1927 FA Cup winners

⚽ After 99 years at Ninian Park, Cardiff moved to their brand new Cardiff City Stadium in 2009. The Bluebirds went down 3-0 to Ipswich in their last league game at Ninian Park!

⚽ Cardiff are the only club from outside England to win the FA Cup. The Welsh side beat Arsenal 1-0 thanks to Hughie Ferguson's second-half goal in the 1927 final!

⚽ For the first time in ten seasons, Cardiff and mega rivals Swansea battled it out in the Championship in 2008-09. Both league fixtures ended in hard-fought 2-2 draws!

Cardiff City Stadium

CLUB STATS!

Stadium: Cardiff City Stadium

Capacity: 26,828

Formed: 1899

Nickname: The Bluebirds

Manager: Dave Jones

Captain: Mark Hudson

Record signing: Michael Chopra from Sunderland, £3 million

Biggest win: 9-2 v Thames, 1932

Biggest defeat: 11-2 v Sheffield United, 1926

Highest attendance: 57,893 v Arsenal, 1953 (at Ninian Park)

Home kit: Blue and yellow shirts, white shorts and socks

Away kit: Yellow shirts, shorts and socks

Honours: Division Three South (1), League 2 (1), FA Cup (1), Community Shield (1), Welsh Cup (22)

Stephen McPhail

CLUB LEGENDS!

MATCH checks out the club's greatest players!

BILLY HARDY

Manager Fred Stewart paid just £25 for Hardy in 1911. The Cardiff legend went on to play 585 matches, starring in his last game at the age of 41 in 1932!

ROBERT EARNSHAW

The speedy striker entered the Cardiff City history books in 2003 when his 35 league goals broke Stan Richards' 56-year-old record!

ROGER JOHNSON

Before moving to Birmingham in June 2009, Johnson became a Ninian Park hero with his rock-solid tackling at the heart of Cardiff's defence!

BURY

★ COCA-COLA LEAGUE 2 ★

FAB FACT! The 2009-10 season marks Bury's 125th anniversary! The team's home and away kits are replicas of those worn in 1887-88!

CLUB STATS!

Stadium: Gigg Lane
Capacity: 11,669
Formed: 1885
Nickname: Shakers
Manager: Alan Knill
Captain: Paul Scott
Record signing: Chris Swailes from Ipswich and Darren Bullock from Swindon, both £200,000
Biggest win: 12-1 v Stockton, 1897
Biggest defeat: 10-0 v Blackburn, 1887
Highest attendance: 35,000 v Bolton, 1960
Home kit: Brown and sky blue halved shirts, white shorts and brown socks
Away kit: Red and white striped shirts, blue shorts and socks
Honours:
Championship (1895),
League 1 (1961 & 1997),
FA Cup (1900 & 1903)

David Nugent hits the net against Tranmere in 2002

CLUB HISTORY!

A meeting between two Bury footy clubs – the Unitarians and Wesleyans – in 1885 formed the team we now know as Bury FC. They remained unbeaten in 1895, winning the old second division title in the process, then went on to beat Southampton in the 1900 FA Cup Final. They won the cup again in 1903 without conceding a goal, beating Derby 6-0 in 1903 – the final's biggest ever score. Former Bury defender Alan Knill took over from Chris Brass as boss in February 2008, and led them to fourth spot and the play-offs in his first full season in charge!

⚽ Bury almost reached the 2009 League 2 Play-off Final, but Shrewsbury equalised with two minutes of the semi-final second leg left. The Shrews won on penalties!

⚽ The League 2 side were thrown out of the FA Cup in 2006 and replaced by Chester because they used an ineligible player in their second-round replay!

⚽ Former England striker David Nugent used to play at Gigg Lane. Nugent scored 18 goals in 88 league games between 2002 and 2005 before moving to Preston!

The 1900 FA Cup-winning team

CARLISLE UNITED

★ COCA-COLA LEAGUE 1 ★

CLUB STATS!

Stadium: Brunton Park

Capacity: 16,982

Formed: 1903

Nickname: Cumbrians

Manager: Greg Abbott

Captain: Paul Thirlwell

Record signing: Joe Garner from Blackburn, £140,000

Biggest win: 8-0 v Hartlepool, 1928

Biggest defeat: 11-1 v Hull, 1939

Highest attendance: 27,500 v Birmingham (1957) and v Middlesbrough (1970)

Home kit: Blue shirts with red and white trim, white shorts and socks

Away kit: Black shirts with red trim, black shorts and socks

Honours:
League 1 (1965),
League 2 (1995 & 2006),
Johnstone's Paint Trophy (1997)

Keeper Jimmy Glass saves Carlisle from relegation in 1999

CLUB HISTORY!

Carlisle United were founded way back in 1904 when Shaddongate United decided to change their team name. Early matches were played at Millholme Bank before the team moved to Brunton Park in 1909, losing 2-0 to Newcastle in their first match at the new ground. The club reached the old Division One in 1974, but finished bottom, and by 1987-88 they were back in the bottom division. Carlisle have since reached four Johnstone's Paint Trophy finals, but their only win was on penalties in 1997 against Colchester!

⚽ Carlisle survived a League 1 relegation scrap at the end of the 2008-09 season. A 2-0 win against Millwall in the last match meant Northampton went down instead!

⚽ Carlisle reached the League Cup semi-finals back in 1969-70, where the Cumbrians lost to eventual runners-up West Brom over two legs!

⚽ The Cumbrians' finish to the 1998-99 season was incredible. Needing a win against Plymouth, keeper Jimmy Glass scored a 94th-minute goal to seal a 2-1 win!

Carlisle v Chelsea, 1974

FAB FACT!
Charlton made a club record £16.5 million when they sold England goal machine Darren Bent to Tottenham back in May 2007!

Lloyd Sam

Clive Mendonca on his way to a hat-trick in the 1998 Championship Play-off Final

CLUB HISTORY!

Charlton can trace their footballing roots back to June 9, 1905 when they were formed by a group of teenagers on East Street, near where London's Thames Barrier now stands.

The Valley dates back to 1919 when a pitch was dug out of an old sand and chalk pit by an army of volunteers, and by 1921 Charlton were playing league football in Division Three South.

Under manager Jimmy Seed, Charlton became a dominant force before World War Two, winning back-to-back promotions from League 1 and ensuring they didn't finish outside the top four in the top flight between 1937 and 1939.

After the war, Charlton reached two FA Cup finals, winning 1-0 in 1947, but by the 1970s they were back in League 1 and money problems caused the club to leave The Valley in 1985.

Groundsharing with Crystal Palace and West Ham, The Addicks clawed their way back up the leagues and returned to The Valley in 1992. Charlton spent seven seasons in the top flight after their 2000 promotion, before being relegated back down to League 1!

The Valley

CLUB STATS!

Stadium: The Valley
Capacity: 27,111
Formed: 1905
Nickname: The Addicks
Manager: Phil Parkinson
Captain: Nicky Bailey
Record signing: Darren Bent from Ipswich, £2.5 million
Biggest win: 8-1 v Middlesbrough, 1953
Biggest defeat: 7-0 v Burton Albion, 1956
Highest attendance: 75,031 v Aston Villa, 1938
Home kit: Red shirts, white shorts and socks
Away kit: White shirts, black shorts and socks
Honours: Championship (1), Division Three South (2), FA Cup (1)

Charlton v Huddersfield, 1957

⚽ The Addicks were losing 5-1 to Huddersfield with 28 minutes left back in 1957, before Johnny Summers scored five goals, including a six-minute hat-trick, as Charlton won 7-6!

⚽ Charlton won one of the greatest ever play-off finals against Sunderland in 1998. Clive Mendonca netted a hat-trick in a 4-4 draw, before The Addicks won 7-6 on penalties!

⚽ Legendary boss Alan Curbishley was in charge of Charlton for 15 years. Curbs was gaffer for 729 games, one less than another of The Addicks' great bosses, Jimmy Seed!

Nicky Bailey

CLUB LEGENDS!

MATCH checks out the club's greatest players!

SAM BARTRAM

Charlton's super shot-stopper still holds the record for the club's most league appearances – an incredible 579 games between 1934 and 1956!

DEREK HALES

In two spells at the club in the 1970s and 1980s, the striker known by fans as 'Killer' scored 168 goals, the highest ever total by an Addicks player!

MARK KINSELLA

The legendary Charlton captain led The Addicks to the Championship title during his six-year stay at The Valley between 1996 and 2002!

CHELSEA
★ BARCLAYS PREMIER LEAGUE ★

FAB FACT!
Ex-Chelsea midfielder Roberto di Matteo scored after just 42 seconds in his side's 2-0 FA Cup Final win over Middlesbrough in 1997!

Nicolas Anelka

Didier Drogba scores yet another goal for Chelsea

CLUB HISTORY!

March 14, 1905, in a pub opposite Stamford Bridge known as The Butcher's Hook, saw the formation of Chelsea. Two months later The Blues were elected to the Football League and signing big stars, such as 22-stone keeper William 'Fatty' Foulke.

Chelsea reached the 1915 Cup Final but lost 3-0 to Sheffield United. The match later became known as the 'Khaki Cup Final', because of the large number of fans in military uniform.

After World War Two, Ted Drake led Chelsea to the top-flight title in 1955, Tommy Docherty won the League Cup in 1965 and Dave Sexton clinched the FA Cup and European Cup Winners' Cup.

The Blues were nearly relegated to League 1 in the 1980s, before clawing their way back to the Premier League. Then after playing some great football in the late 1990s, they added another FA Cup, League Cup and Cup Winners' Cup to their trophy cabinet.

Under former manager Jose Mourinho, Chelsea picked up back-to-back Prem titles in 2005 and 2006, while Avram Grant and Guus Hiddink just missed out on Champions League glory!

Stamford Bridge

CLUB STATS!

Stadium: Stamford Bridge
Capacity: 41,841
Formed: 1905
Nickname: The Blues
Manager: Carlo Ancelotti
Captain: John Terry
Record signing: Andriy Shevchenko from AC Milan, £29.5 million
Biggest win: 13-0 v Jeunesse Hautcharage, 1971
Biggest defeat: 8-1 v Wolves, 1953
Highest attendance: 82,905 v Arsenal, 1935
Home kit: Blue shirts and shorts, white socks
Away kit: Blue shirts, shorts and socks with neon yellow trim
Honours: English League title (3), Championship (2), European Cup Winners' Cup (2), European Super Cup (1), FA Cup (5), League Cup (4), Community Shield (4)

The FA Cup gets a bath in 1970

⚽ A strike from top scorer Nicolas Anelka gave Chelsea a 1-0 win at Aston Villa in February 2009 and recorded their first Premier League victory at Villa Park since 1998-99!

⚽ Super skipper John Terry made his 400th appearance for Chelsea against local rivals Fulham in May 2009. It was a memorable day for the England captain as Chelsea won 3-1!

⚽ Chelsea became the first team to stop La Liga champions Barcelona scoring at the Nou Camp in 2008-09. The Blues bagged a 0-0 draw in the Champions League semi-final first leg!

Petr Cech in action against Fulham

CLUB LEGENDS!

MATCH checks out the club's greatest players!

JOHN TERRY

Apart from a loan spell at Nottingham Forest in 2000, club captain JT has spent his entire career at Chelsea, winning seven major trophies!

FRANK LAMPARD

Lamps has scored more goals from midfield than any other Blues player and played a record 164 league games in a row between 2001 and 2005!

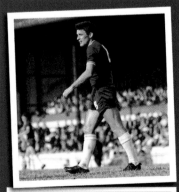

BOBBY TAMBLING

After making his debut aged 17 against West Ham in 1959, Tambling went on to score a club record 202 goals in 370 games for The Blues!

CHELTENHAM TOWN

★ COCA-COLA LEAGUE 2 ★

CLUB STATS!

Stadium: Whaddon Road

Capacity: 7,136

Formed: 1887

Nickname: The Robins

Manager: Martin Allen

Captain: John Finnigan

Record signing: Grant McCann from West Ham and Brian Wilson from Stoke, £50,000

Biggest win: 12-0 v Chippenham, 1935

Biggest defeat: 7-0 v Crystal Palace, 2002

Highest attendance: 10,389 v Blackpool, 1934 (at the Cheltenham Athletic Ground)

Home kit: Red shirts with white trim, red shorts and socks

Away kit: Yellow shirts with red trim, yellow shorts and socks

Honours:
Blue Square Premier (1999),
Southern League (1985),
The FA Trophy (1998)

Martin 'Mad Dog' Allen barking out orders

CLUB HISTORY!

Despite being formed in 1887 by Albert Close White, Cheltenham only won promotion to the Football League in 1999 after finishing as Conference champions under the guidance of manager Steve Cotterill. The ex-Robins boss also won promotion to League 1 in 2002, the highest division Cheltenham have ever played in. After Cotterill left for Stoke, relegation followed in 2003, before they beat Grimsby 1-0 in the 2006 League 2 Play-off Final. However, the club kicked off the 2009-10 season back in the bottom division!

⚽ Carlisle love to pick their managers from the same family. Current boss Martin Allen is the son of Dennis Allen, who was Robins gaffer back in the 1970s!

⚽ Before becoming a Sky Sports commentator, Andy Gray played for Cheltenham. It was the last club he played for before hanging up his boots!

⚽ Cheltenham survived the drop from League 1 in the last match of 2007-08. Needing to beat promotion-chasers Doncaster, The Robins pulled off a 2-1 victory to stay up!

Steve Cotterill

CHESTERFIELD
★ COCA-COLA LEAGUE 2 ★

FAB FACT!
Bolton captain Kevin Davies played for Chesterfield between 1994 and 1997, slamming in 30 goals before moving to Southampton!

CLUB STATS!

Stadium: The Recreation Ground
Capacity: 8,504
Formed: 1866
Nickname: Spireites
Manager: John Sheridan
Captain: Robert Page
Record signing: Jason Lee from Watford, £250,000
Biggest win: 10-0 v Glossop NE, 1903
Biggest defeat: 10-0 v Gillingham, 1987
Highest attendance: 30,968 v Newcastle, 1939
Home kit: Blue shirts, white shorts and socks
Away kit: Red shirts, shorts and socks
Honours:
League 2 (1970 & 1985),
Division Three North (1931 & 1936),
Anglo-Scottish Cup (1981)

The controversial 1997 FA Cup semi-final against Middlesbrough

CLUB HISTORY!

Chesterfield are the third oldest current Football League club. Formed in 1866, only Nottingham Forest and Notts County have been around longer than the Saltergate side. As a founding member of the old Division Three North, Chesterfield have since spent all of their Football League life in the lower divisions. Their highest finish was fourth in the Championship in 1947, missing out on a place in the top flight by just eight points. The club will move out of Saltergate at the end of the 2009-10 season into their awesome new £13 million stadium!

⚽ Chesterfield almost reached the 1997 FA Cup Final, but Jon Howard's goal was disallowed when the Spireites were 2-1 up. Middlesbrough drew 3-3 and won the replay!

⚽ England's World Cup-winning keeper Gordon Banks once played for Chesterfield. He earned £17-a-week before moving to Leicester for just £6,000 in 1959!

⚽ The 2009-10 season marks Chesterfield's last campaign at Saltergate. After 139 years, the club is moving to a 10,500 all-seater stadium on Whittington Moor!

Play-off glory at Wembley in 1995

COVENTRY CITY

★ COCA-COLA CHAMPIONSHIP ★

FAB FACT!
In 1978 Coventry wore one of the worst away kits ever. Their brown shirts made a limited-edition comeback against Watford in 2008!

Clinton Morrison

Robbie Keane joins Coventry in 1999

CLUB HISTORY!

The Sky Blues were formed by Willie Stanley, an employee of a Coventry cycle factory called Singers.

The club's first season in the Football League in 1919-20 was instantly forgettable, as they lost 5-0 to Spurs on the opening day of the campaign and didn't win again until Christmas Day.

Under new boss Harry Storer, Coventry were in awesome form in the 1930s, winning promotion back to the Championship and just missing out on the top flight before World War Two broke out.

Jimmy Hill's arrival in 1961 sparked a revival for the lower league club as they eventually returned to the top flight in 1967 and played in Europe after finishing sixth in 1970.

By the 1980s the club was struggling, avoiding relegation on the last day of the season three times, before George Curtis and John Sillett led Coventry to FA Cup success in 1987.

Coventry struggled in the early Premier League years and by 2001 were relegated back to the Championship, where they've been battling it out for a return to the top flight ever since!

The Sky Blues stun Tottenham at Wembley to win the 1987 FA Cup

⚽ After playing just 31 matches for Coventry and scoring 12 goals, Republic Of Ireland striker Robbie Keane was sold to Serie A giants Inter Milan for a club record £13 million!

⚽ Coventry's impressive Ricoh Arena, which they moved to in 2005, will be one of the venues that hosts Rugby World Cup matches when it comes to England in 2015!

⚽ Coventry's classic 3-2 FA Cup victory in 1987 against an all-star Tottenham side was their first ever final. The Sky Blues battled back after going a goal down in the second minute!

Ricoh Arena

CLUB STATS!

Stadium: Ricoh Arena
Capacity: 32,609
Formed: 1883
Nickname: Sky Blues
Manager: Chris Coleman
Captain: Stephen Wright
Record signing: Craig Bellamy from Norwich, £6.5 million
Biggest win: 9-0 v Bristol City, 1934
Biggest defeat: 10-2 v Norwich, 1930
Highest attendance: 51,455 v Wolves, 1967 (at Highfield Road)
Home kit: Sky blue shirts and socks, navy blue shorts
Away kit: Black shirts, shorts and socks with gold trim
Honours:
Championship (1), League 1 (1), Division Three South (1), FA Cup (1)

Stephen Wright fights for the ball

CLUB LEGENDS!

MATCH checks out the club's greatest players!

DION DUBLIN

After his £1.95 million move in 1994, Dublin won the Premier League Golden Boot in 1998 and fired home 68 goals in his four years at Highfield Road!

STEVE OGRIZOVIC

'Oggy' was a legendary shot-stopper who made 241 consecutive appearances after joining from Shrewsbury. He's now the club's keeper coach!

LLOYD McGRATH

McGrath suffered a broken leg, three dislocated shoulders, fractured cheekbones, plus eye and knee injuries at City, but still won the FA Cup in 1987!

COLCHESTER UNITED

★ COCA-COLA LEAGUE 1 ★

FAB FACT!
The U's played at their old Layer Road stadium for 71 years before moving to a new ground ahead of the 2008-09 season!

CLUB STATS!

Stadium:
Weston Homes Community Stadium

Capacity: 10,000

Formed: 1937

Nickname: The U's

Manager: Paul Lambert

Captain: Dean Hammond

Record signing: Steven Gillespie from Cheltenham, £400,000

Biggest win: 9-1 v Bradford (1961) and Leamington (2005)

Biggest defeat: 8-0 v Leyton Orient (1988)

Highest attendance: 19,072 v Reading, 1948 (at Layer Road)

Home kit: Blue and white striped shirts, blue shorts, blue and white socks

Away kit: Yellow shirts, shorts and socks

Honours:
Blue Square Premier (1992),
Southern Football League (1939),
The FA Trophy (1992)

Teddy Sheringham in action against QPR

CLUB HISTORY!

Colchester United played their first ever match against Bath City in September 1937, six months after Colchester Town shut. After being allowed to copy Huddersfield's blue and white striped kit, The U's began life in the Southern League before earning promotion to the Football League in 1950. Colchester suffered relegation back to non-league football in 1990, but after a league and cup double they bounced back. The U's then won promotion to the Championship in 2006, ending in tenth spot – their highest ever league finish!

The U's upset Leeds in 1971

⚽ Ex-Man. United, Tottenham and England striker Teddy Sheringham joined Colchester for his last season as a player in 2007. He made over 700 appearances in his career!

⚽ Colchester's biggest rivals are Essex neighbours Southend. In 60 league games against the Shrimpers, The U's have won 21 matches, drawn 14 and lost 25!

⚽ Colchester caused one of the biggest FA Cup upsets of all time back in 1971. The U's, who were in League 2 at the time, beat top-flight giants Leeds 3-2 in the fifth round!

CREWE ALEXANDRA

★ COCA-COLA LEAGUE 2 ★

FAB FACT!
Ex-Crewe keeper *Mark Smith* received one of the fastest ever red cards when he was sent off after 19 seconds against Darlington in 1994!

CLUB STATS!

Stadium: The Alexandra Stadium

Capacity: 10,046

Formed: 1877

Nickname: Railwaymen

Manager: Gudjon Thordarson

Captain: Billy Jones

Record signing: Rodney Jack from Torquay, £650,000

Biggest win: 8-0 v Rotherham (1932), Hartlepool (1995) and Doncaster (2002)

Biggest defeat: 13-2 v Tottenham, 1960

Highest attendance: 20,000 v Tottenham, 1960

Home kit: Red shirts, white shorts and red socks

Away kit: Blue shirts with yellow trim, blue shorts and socks

Honours: Welsh Cup (1936 & 1937)

Crewe legend Dario Gradi

CLUB HISTORY!

Crewe's name is said to have been taken from Princess Alexandra, the wife of King Edward VII who ruled England from 1901-10. Formed in 1877, the biggest achievement in Crewe's early years came in 1888 when they reached the FA Cup semi-finals, but after relegation in 1896, they didn't become a Football League club again until 1921. The club's first ever promotion came 40 years later, and in 1983 Dario Gradi took charge of his first match as boss. Crewe dropped back into League 2 for the first time in 15 years in the 2008-09 season!

⚽ Apart from a short spell in 2003 while he underwent heart surgery, legendary Crewe boss Dario Gradi managed the Railwaymen for over 24 years!

⚽ Current gaffer Gudjon Thordarson used to be the manager of Iceland. He almost guided his country to Euro 2000, but they just missed out on qualification!

⚽ West Ham striker Dean Ashton used to play for Crewe. The powerful striker scored 61 league goals in just 158 appearances before moving to Norwich in 2005!

Crewe v Tottenham, 1960

CRYSTAL PALACE
★ COCA-COLA CHAMPIONSHIP ★

FAB FACT!
Before moving to Spurs, John Bostock became Palace's youngest ever player when he came off the bench against Watford in 2007, aged 15!

Clint Hill strikes against Watford in the 2008-09 FA Cup

Ian Wright comes off the bench to score twice in the 1990 FA Cup Final

CLUB HISTORY!

An amateur Crystal Palace side existed from 1861, but the club as we know it today was formed in 1905 at the world-famous glass Crystal Palace building that was built for the 1851 Great Exhibition.

After playing at Herne Hill and then The Nest, Palace moved to Selhurst Park in 1924. In 1930-31 Peter Simpson scored 46 goals in 42 games, including six in one match against Exeter as Palace finished runners-up in Division Three South.

A four-season stay in the top flight ended in 1973, by which time they were called The Eagles after a change to their badge. In 1976 Peter Taylor became the first Palace player to score for England.

Terry Venables took over in 1977 and led his 'Team of the Eighties' to two promotions in three seasons, but they were back in the Championship by 1981 after finishing bottom.

After eight seasons, Palace were back in the top flight, losing the FA Cup final and finishing a club-best third in 1991, but over the following seasons bounced between the top two tiers. Under Neil Warnock they just missed out on the play-off final in 2008!

Selhurst Park

CLUB STATS!

Stadium: Selhurst Park
Capacity: 26,297
Formed: 1905
Nickname: The Eagles
Manager: Neil Warnock
Captain: Shaun Derry
Record signing: Valerien Ismael from RC Strasbourg, £2.75 million
Biggest win: 9-0 v Barrow, 1959
Biggest defeat: 9-0 v Burnley (1909) and Liverpool (1990)
Highest attendance: 51,482 v Burnley, 1979
Home kit: Red and blue striped shirts, blue shorts and socks
Away kit: White and blue shirts, white shorts and socks
Honours: Championship (2), Division Three South (1), Zenith Data Systems Cup (1)

Terry Venables and his 'Team Of The '80s' in training

⚽ The 1989-90 season will be remembered for Palace's 9-0 league defeat at the hands of Liverpool, but they got their revenge in the FA Cup semi-final with a 4-3 win after extra-time!

⚽ Crystal Palace's only FA Cup final appearance was a classic. The Eagles drew 3-3 with Man. United after battling back from 2-1 down in 1990, before losing the Wembley replay 1-0!

⚽ After Hungarian international Gabor Kiraly joined Burnley, Palace keeper Julian Speroni made the No.1 spot his own and was named the club's Player Of The Year in 2008 and 2009!

Shaun Derry

CLUB LEGENDS!

MATCH checks out the club's greatest players!

DOUGIE FREEDMAN

Palace's super striker scored an 11-minute hat-trick in his first season and never looked back. In two spells at the club, Dougie smashed in 95 league goals!

JIM CANNON

A legendary defender, Cannon was voted Palace's Player Of The Year three times and made a record 663 appearances in 16 years at Selhurst Park!

GEOFF THOMAS

The former electrician joined Palace from Crewe in 1987! He captained The Eagles in the 1990 FA Cup Final and played 249 games for the club!

DAGENHAM & REDBRIDGE

★ COCA-COLA LEAGUE 2 ★

FAB FACT!
Dagenham & Redbridge skipper Anwar Uddin is the first ever British Asian player to captain a team in the top four divisions!

CLUB STATS!

Stadium: *Victoria Road*

Capacity: *6,087*

Formed: *1992*

Nickname: *The Daggers*

Manager: *John Still*

Captain: *Anwar Uddin*

Record signing: *Paul Cobb from Purfleet, £15,000*

Biggest win: *8-1 v Woking, 1994*

Biggest defeat: *9-0 v Hereford, 2004*

Highest attendance: *5,949 v Ipswich, 2002*

Home kit: *Red and blue striped shirts, white shorts and red socks*

Away kit: *Yellow shirts, shorts and socks*

Honours:
*Blue Square Premier (2007),
Ryman League Premier Division (2000)*

Dagenham suffer play-off heartbreak against Doncaster in 2003

⚽ Dagenham & Redbridge were on the brink of the League 2 play-offs in 2009, but they ended a point short after a 2-1 defeat to Shrewsbury in the final match!

⚽ The Daggers' first ever season saw them finish third in the Blue Square Premier and lose a 5-4 thriller to Leyton Orient in the first round of the FA Cup!

⚽ Ex-Daggers stars Craig Mackail-Smith & Shane Blackett set a club record when they moved to Championship side Peterborough in 2007. They cost £125,000 each!

CLUB HISTORY!

Dagenham & Redbridge were formed only 17 years ago when Dagenham merged with Redbridge Forest in 1992. Forest themselves had been formed from three clubs – Ilford, Leytonstone and Walthamstow Avenue. In 2002, The Daggers just missed out on promotion to the Football League on goal difference, and the following year suffered a 3-2 defeat in the Blue Square Premier Play-off final against Doncaster. Their dream of promotion finally came true in 2007, when a 2-1 win against Aldershot bagged the title and a place in League 2!

The 1997 FA Trophy Final, Wembley

DARLINGTON
★ COCA-COLA LEAGUE 2 ★

FAB FACT!
After going through the turnstiles at Darlington's old ground Feethams, fans had to walk around a cricket pitch to get to the stands!

CLUB STATS!

Stadium: Darlington Arena

Capacity: 27,000

Formed: 1883

Nickname: The Quakers

Manager: Colin Todd

Captain: Steve Foster

Record signing: Julian Joachim from Boston and Pawel Abbott from Swansea, £100,000

Biggest win: 9-2 v Lincoln, 1928

Biggest defeat: 10-0 v Doncaster, 1964

Highest attendance: 21,023 v Bolton, 1960 (at Feethams)

Home kit: Black and white hooped shirts, black shorts and socks

Away kit: Red shirts, white shorts, red socks

Honours:
League 2 (1991),
Blue Square Premier (1990),
Division Three North (1925)

Darlington take on Newcastle in a pre-season friendly in 2009

CLUB HISTORY!

Darlington FC was formed at Darlington Grammar School in 1883, and in the 1910-11 FA Cup they played 11 games in eight rounds to reach the last 16, an achievement the club didn't manage to repeat until 1958. Darlington have spent only two seasons in the Championship, bagging their highest ever finish of 15th in 1926, but they did reach the last eight of the League Cup in 1968 before losing 5-4 to Derby County. The club reached Wembley play-off finals in both 1996 and 2000, and managed top eight finishes in 2005, 2006 and 2008!

⚽ Darlington's assistant player-manager Dean Windass has played for ten different clubs in his career, including North-East neighbours Middlesbrough!

⚽ The Quakers have been playing in League 2 since way back in 1992. They missed out on promotion twice after losing the play-off final in 1996 and 2000!

⚽ Despite getting knocked out of the 1999-2000 FA Cup, Darlington won a 'losers' lottery' to replace Man. United, who were playing in the FIFA Club World Championship!

Darlington reach Wembley, 2000

FAB FACT!
Derby almost reached the European Cup Final in 1973, but were knocked out after a 3-1 defeat to Juventus in the semi-Finals!

Przemyslaw Kazmierczak

Brian Clough and Peter Taylor celebrate Derby's 1972 league title win

CLUB HISTORY!

Players at Derbyshire County Cricket Club formed Derby FC in 1884. Their first kit was a strange mix of amber, brown and blue.

They were invited to join the Football League for its first season and in 1892 the club's greatest ever striker, Steve Bloomer, joined Derby. Three years later they'd moved to the Baseball Ground.

In their early years, Derby's form in the FA Cup was incredible, though they lost three finals between 1898 and 1903, including a record 6-0 defeat against Bury at Crystal Palace.

FA Cup success came in 1946 against Charlton, but after almost 30 years in the top flight they were relegated in 1953 and 1955.

The legendary Brian Clough arrived in 1967 and turned Derby into a dominant side, winning the title in 1972. Even when Clough left for Leeds, it didn't stop Derby, who won the title again in 1975.

After that league success, Arthur Cox took Derby to a fifth place finish in Division One in 1989. Since then the club has never returned to those heights, and they were relegated from the top flight after picking up just one win all season in 2007-08!

Pride Park

CLUB STATS!

Stadium: Pride Park

Capacity: 33,540

Formed: 1884

Nickname: The Rams

Manager: Nigel Clough

Captain: Paul Connolly

Record signing: Rob Earnshaw from Norwich, £3.5 million

Biggest win: 12-0 v Finn Harps, 1976

Biggest defeat: 11-2 v Everton, 1890

Highest attendance: 41,826 v Tottenham, 1969 (at the Baseball Ground)

Home kit: White shirts and socks, black shorts

Away kit: Black shirts and socks, silver shorts

Honours:
English League title (2), Championship (4), Division Three North (1), FA Cup (1), Texaco Cup (1)

FA Cup winners, 1946

⚽ Derby boss Nigel Clough is following in his dad's footsteps after joining from Burton in 2009. Brian Clough was manager of Derby from 1967-73, leading The Rams to the league title in 1972!

⚽ Derby have a massive rivalry with East Midlands neighbours Nottingham Forest. The clubs met four times in the 2008-09 season, with The Rams winning two and drawing two games!

⚽ The Rams had a goal-fest in their first ever league match in 1888-89. Derby battled back from 3-0 down to beat Bolton 6-3, but they eventually finished the season in tenth place!

Paul Connolly

FAB FACT!
A 500-seater mini stadium that sits next to The Keepmoat is used by Doncaster's reserve and women's teams!

Doncaster celebrate Gareth Roberts' strike at Portman Road

Rovers celebrate their win over Leeds in the 2008 League 1 Play-off Final

CLUB HISTORY!

Albert Jenkins formed the club in 1879 after a match was played against the Yorkshire Institution for the Deaf and Dumb. They achieved a place in the Football League in 1901, replacing New Brighton Tower, but were relegated after two seasons.

After World War One, non-League Doncaster were homeless and in 1922, 10,000 fans watched the club's first match at their new stadium – Belle Vue. A year later Rovers were back in the league.

The 1932 season saw Doncaster wear their famous red and white hoops for the first time, and within three years they had stormed back to the Championship.

Doncaster won Division Three North in 1947 and 1950, but relegations in the 1950s sent them back to the bottom division. They remained in League 2, apart from spells in League 1 in the 1980s, until 1998 when they dropped to the Blue Square Premier.

Dave Penney won successive promotions in 2003 and 2004 as Rovers fought their way back up the leagues. Sean O'Driscoll continued the job as Rovers reached the Championship in 2008!

Keepmoat Stadium

CLUB STATS!

Stadium: Keepmoat Stadium
Capacity: 15,269
Formed: 1879
Nickname: Rovers
Manager: Sean O'Driscoll
Captain: Brian Stock
Record signing: James Hayter from Bournemouth, £200,000
Biggest win: 10-0 v Darlington, 1964
Biggest defeat: 12-0 v Small Heath, 1903
Highest attendance: 37,149 v Hull, 1948
Home kit: Red and white hooped shirts, black shorts and socks
Away kit: Black shirts, red shorts and socks
Honours:
League 1 (1), Division Three North (3), League 2 (2), Blue Square Premier (1), Johnstone's Paint Trophy (1)

Captain Stuart Robertson shows off Doncaster's silverware in 1969

⚽ Doncaster's 1-0 victory against Yorkshire rivals Leeds in the 2008 League 1 Play-off Final saw the club return to the Championship for the first time in 50 years!

⚽ Rovers were 2-0 up after five minutes in the 2007 Johnstone's Paint Trophy Final, but a big Bristol Rovers fightback forced extra-time. Doncaster captain Graeme Lee sealed the famous win!

⚽ Doncaster were the first club to bag promotion to League 2 via the Blue Square Premier play-offs. Francis Tierney's golden goal extra-time winner gave Donny a 3-2 win in 2003!

Brian Stock

CLUB LEGENDS!

MATCH checks out the club's greatest players!

PAUL GREEN

The ace midfielder began his career at Rovers and won promotions in 2003, 2004 and 2008, before signing for Derby in May 2008!

IAN SNODIN

Snodin played 188 league matches in midfield for Rovers in the 1980s, before moving on to Leeds and Everton. He returned as Donny player-boss in 1998!

JAMES COPPINGER

The attacking midfielder scored a hat-trick against Southend in the 2008 League 1 play-off semi-finals as Doncaster stormed to promotion!

EVERTON

FAB FACT!
The tower on Everton's club crest is a copy of *Prince Rupert's Tower*, an old prison that was used to lock up criminals in the 1700s!

Tim Cahill and Leon Osman

Louis Saha strikes in the 2009 FA Cup Final

CLUB HISTORY!

Everton were the first club in Liverpool after being formed in 1878 by St. Domingo's Methodist Church. Playing their early seasons at Priory Road and Anfield, the club moved across Stanley Park to Goodison in 1892, a season after they won their first title.

In the early 20th Century, Everton won the FA Cup (1906) and another title (1915). Then ten years later they signed Dixie Dean and won their third title in 1928, and by World War Two another two titles were in the bag. Everton were relegated in 1951, but bounced back in 1954 and have been in the top flight ever since.

After lifting the title in 1970, Everton failed to bag any silverware until Howard Kendall took over in 1981. They then became a force in English football, winning two titles, reaching three FA Cup finals in a row and lifting the Cup Winners' Cup, their only European trophy.

A 1-0 win against Man. United in the 1995 Cup Final ended a trophy drought, but it wasn't until David Moyes arrived from Preston that Everton became a serious threat again in the Premier League, having always finished sixth or higher since 2006-07!

Captain Brian Labone shows off the FA Cup trophy in 1966

⚽ Everton staged a great comeback in the 1966 FA Cup Final. Facing defeat at 2-0 down in the second half, The Toffees scored three goals against Sheffield Wednesday to lift the trophy!

⚽ In the 2008-09 FA Cup fourth-round replay against Liverpool, Dan Gosling scored an extra-time winner for The Toffees, but TV viewers missed the goal because adverts were being shown!

⚽ Toffees striker Louis Saha rifled home the quickest goal in FA Cup final history against Chelsea in 2009. Everton's No.9 smashed the ball past Petr Cech after just 25 seconds!

Goodison Park

CLUB STATS!

Stadium: Goodison Park

Capacity: 40,157

Formed: 1878

Nickname: The Toffees

Manager: David Moyes

Captain: Phil Neville

Record signing: Marouane Fellaini from Standard Liege, £15 million

Biggest win: 11-2 v Derby, 1890

Biggest defeat: 10-4 v Tottenham, 1958

Highest attendance: 78,299 v Liverpool, 1948

Home kit: Blue shirts, white shorts and socks

Away kit: Black shirts with pink pin hoops, black shorts and socks

Honours: English League title (9), Championship (1), FA Cup (5), European Cup Winners' Cup (1), Community Shield (9, 1 shared)

Marouane Fellaini

CLUB LEGENDS!

MATCH checks out the club's greatest players!

DIXIE DEAN

William 'Dixie' Dean is one of the greatest strikers of all time. Dean blasted 60 goals in just 39 matches in 1928-29, an English record for one season!

NEVILLE SOUTHALL

The legendary Wales keeper played a record 750 games for Everton after joining from Bury in 1981. He's the only Toffees star to win two FA Cups!

GARY STEVENS

Everton and England's flying full-back won two league titles, reached three FA Cup finals and bagged the European Cup Winners' Cup in the 1980s!

FULHAM

FAB FACT!
Fulham's *Craven Cottage* stadium used to be a hunting lodge for the Royal Family. They also played croquet and lawn bowls there!

Clint Dempsey

Andy Johnson strikes against Tottenham

CLUB HISTORY!

Fulham are the oldest of London's top-flight clubs, after forming under the enormous name Fulham St. Andrew's Church Sunday School FC way back in 1879. Luckily for today's commentators, they became known as Fulham FC in 1888.

Fulham stayed in the Championship for 21 years after they were promoted to the Football League in 1907. It wasn't until 1948-49 that they reached the old Division One, pipping West Brom to the Championship title by just one point. Boxing Day 1952 goes down in club history as the day legend Johnny Haynes made his debut.

Fulham made their only appearance in an FA Cup final in 1975, but lost 2-0 to West Ham, and a year later former Man. United hero George Best moved to Craven Cottage.

By the mid-1980s top-flight football seemed a long way off as Fulham battled it out in League 1, but thanks to Louis Saha's goals The Cottagers clawed their way to the Premier League in 2001.

Chris Coleman kept Fulham up before Roy Hodgson secured a great escape with victory on the last day of the 2007-08 season!

Fulham's 1975 FA Cup Final squad

⚽ Fulham had one of their best ever top-flight seasons in 2008-09. The Cottagers qualified for the Europa League for the second time in their history after finishing in seventh place!

⚽ Wicked gaffer Roy Hodgson has coached 15 different teams since becoming a manager in 1976. The 62-year-old has been the boss of Blackburn, Inter Milan, Switzerland and Finland!

⚽ Craven Cottage's Riverside Stand marks part of the famous Oxford-Cambridge Boat Race course, which takes place between the two universities on the River Thames every year!

Craven Cottage

CLUB STATS!

Stadium:	Craven Cottage
Capacity:	25,478
Formed:	1879
Nickname:	The Cottagers
Manager:	Roy Hodgson
Captain:	Danny Murphy
Record signing:	Steve Marlet from Lyon, £11.5 million
Biggest win:	10-1 v Ipswich, 1963
Biggest defeat:	10-0 v Liverpool, 1986
Highest attendance:	49,335 v Millwall, 1938
Home kit:	White and black shirts, black shorts, white socks
Away kit:	Red and black shirts, black shorts and socks
Honours:	Championship (2), League 1 (1), Division Three South (1), Intertoto Cup (1)

Danny Murphy scores against Man. United

CLUB LEGENDS!

MATCH checks out the club's greatest players!

JOHNNY HAYNES

Fulham's legendary striker played 657 games between 1952 and 1970, and scored 157 goals. Haynes was the first British player to earn £100-a-week!

CHRIS COLEMAN

The influential club captain won promotion under Kevin Keegan in 1999. His career was cut short after a car crash in 2001, but he became boss in 2003!

LOUIS SAHA

After an unsuccessful loan spell at Newcastle, Saha joined from Metz in 2000 and scored 27 goals in his debut season to fire Fulham into the Premier League!

EXETER CITY
★ COCA-COLA LEAGUE 1 ★

FAB FACT!
No-one knows the origin of the club's nickname, The Grecians, but it's thought it was first given to people who lived outside the city walls!

CLUB STATS!

Stadium: St. James Park
Capacity: 9,036
Formed: 1904
Nickname: The Grecians
Manager: Paul Tisdale
Captain: Matt Taylor
Record signing: Tony Kellow from Blackpool, £65,000
Biggest win: 14-0 v Weymouth, 1908
Biggest defeat: 9-0 v Notts County (1948) and Northampton (1958)
Highest attendance: 20,984 v Sunderland, 1931
Home kit: Red and white striped shirts, white shorts and socks
Away kit: Black shirts, white shorts and socks
Honours: League 2 (1990)

Exeter host a 'Brazil Masters' team in 2004

CLUB HISTORY!

Exeter City played their first ever match in green and white kits against the 110th Battery of the Royal Artillery in 1904. Changing to their now red and white stripes, Exeter joined the old Division Three in 1920, beating Brentford 3-0 in their first match. The club's best run in the FA Cup came in 1931, when a record crowd saw The Grecians lose 4-2 to Sunderland in the sixth round. After World War Two, Exeter played in the lower leagues and slipped into the Blue Square Premier in 2003. They won back-to-back promotions in 2008 and 2009!

⚽ Exeter toured South America in 1914. Their friendly against Brazil is believed to be The Samba Boys' first ever match, played in Fluminense's Laranjeiras stadium!

⚽ St. James Park used to be a field for fattening pigs. In 1904 it was given to the club after it was agreed that no shows or circuses would be allowed on the pitch!

⚽ Arsenal legend Cliff Bastin played one season for Exeter in 1928-29. The forward went on to score 178 goals for The Gunners, a record that stood until 1997!

Exeter's 1990 promotion party

GILLINGHAM

★ COCA-COLA LEAGUE 1 ★

PLAY OFF WINNERS 2009

Coca-Cola

COCA-COLA LEAGUE 2 PLAY OFF WINNERS
GILLINGHAM F.C.

FAB FACT!
Gillingham are the only league club from Kent! Maidstone United spent three years in League 2, but they were forced to resign in 1992!

CLUB STATS!

Stadium: Priestfield Stadium

Capacity: 11,440

Formed: 1893

Nickname: The Gills

Manager: Mark Stimson

Captain: Barry Fuller

Record signing: Carl Asaba from Reading, £600,000

Biggest win: 10-0 v Chesterfield, 1987

Biggest defeat: 9-2 v Nott'm Forest, 1950

Highest attendance: 23,002 v QPR, 1948

Home kit: Blue and white shirts, blue shorts and socks

Away kit: Yellow and blue shirts, yellow shorts and socks

Honours: League 2 (1964), Southern League (1947 & 1949), Southern League Division Two (1895), Southern League Cup (1947)

Simeon Jackson heads The Gills into League 1

CLUB HISTORY!

Gillingham have played at Priestfield since they were formed as Brompton in 1893. A name change in 1913 and election to the old Division Three in 1920 was the club's highlight before World War Two, as The Gills battled it out in non-league footy until 1950. The club finally won the League 2 title in 1964, then bounced between the bottom two divisions until two promotions in the late 1990s, and an FA Cup quarter-final appearance against Chelsea in 2000. After relegation in 2008, The Gills battled straight back to League 1 in 2008-09!

⚽ Goal machine Simeon Jackson became a legend at Priestfield when his header won the 2008-09 League 2 Play-off Final against Shrewsbury at Wembley!

⚽ Sunderland gaffer Steve Bruce used to play for Gillingham. Before moving to Norwich and then joining Man. United, Bruce played over 200 games for The Gills!

⚽ Gills megastar Ron Hillyard holds the record for the most league and cup games for the club. The keeper played 657 matches in a 17-year spell at Priestfield!

The 2000 play-off run

GRIMSBY TOWN
★ COCA-COLA LEAGUE 2 ★

11

CLUB STATS!

Stadium: Blundell Park
Capacity: 10,033
Formed: 1878
Nickname: The Mariners
Manager: Mike Newell
Captain: Ryan Bennett
Record signing: Lee Ashcroft from Preston, £500,000
Biggest win: 9-2 v Darwen, 1899
Biggest defeat: 9-1 v Arsenal, 1931
Highest attendance: 31,657 v Wolves, 1937
Home kit: Black and white striped shirts, black shorts and white socks
Away kit: Blue shirts, shorts and socks
Honours:
Championship (1901 & 1934),
League 1 (1980),
League 2 (1972),
Division Three North (1926 & 1956),
Johnstone's Paint Trophy (1998)

Mike Newell

⚽ Legendary Liverpool manager Bill Shankly used to be Grimsby's gaffer. Before having mega success at Anfield, Shankly was Mariners boss between 1951 and 1954!

⚽ Current Grimsby gaffer Mike Newell scored the Premier League's 1,000th goal and the quickest ever Champions League hat-trick when he played for Blackburn!

⚽ Former England manager Graham Taylor used to play for Grimsby. The BBC Radio 5 Live commentator made nearly 200 appearances for The Mariners as a defender!

CLUB HISTORY!

Grimsby were formed at a meeting in the Wellington Arms pub on the town's Freeman Street. Some at the meeting were cricketers who wanted a sport to play in the winter and called the team Grimsby Pelham, after the family name of the local Earl of Yarborough. Between the World Wars, The Mariners were a regular top-flight side and reached the FA Cup semis in 1939, but lost 5-0 to Wolves. By the late 20th Century, Grimsby returned to the Championship, and even knocked Liverpool out of the League Cup in 2001, but only just survived in League 2 in 2008-09!

Wembley glory in 1998

HARTLEPOOL UNITED
★ COCA-COLA LEAGUE 1 ★

FAB FACT!
Nottingham Forest legend Brian Clough became the Football League's youngest gaffer when he took over at Hartlepool in 1965 aged 30!

CLUB STATS!

Stadium: Victoria Park
Capacity: 7,787
Formed: 1908
Nickname: The Pool
Manager: Chris Turner
Captain: Ritchie Humphreys
Record signing: Darrell Clarke from Mansfield, Gary Jones from Notts County and Chris Freestone from Northampton, £75,000
Biggest win: 10-1 v Barrow, 1959
Biggest defeat: 10-1 v Wrexham, 1962
Highest attendance: 17,426 v Man. United, 1957
Home kit: White shirts, blue shorts and white socks
Away kit: Black and red striped shirts, black shorts and socks
Honours: None

Hartlepool gets bombed in 1914

CLUB HISTORY!

After the town's rugby club went bust in 1908, Hartlepools United Football Athletic Company moved into Victoria Park and joined the Football League in 1921.
In 1957, Hartlepool lost 4-3 to Man. United in the FA Cup, with Sir Matt Busby calling it the most exciting match he'd ever watched. A year after Brian Clough left for Derby, the club won their first ever promotion in 1968, but were relegated back to League 2 in 1969 and failed to return for over 20 years. The Pool survived in League 1 by a point at the end of 2008-09, a year after turning 100!

⚽ Hartlepool's biggest North-East rivals are Darlington. In 134 league meetings, The Pool have won 56 games and drawn 26, one of which was a 5-5 thriller in 1936!

⚽ During World War One, parts of Hartlepool's ground were destroyed by a German Zeppelin airship and a naval bombardment off the coast of the town!

⚽ Hartlepool fans are known as the Monkey Hangers, after a monkey that was hanged in the town during the 1800s because the locals thought it was a French spy!

Hartlepool, 1971-72

HEREFORD UNITED

★ COCA-COLA LEAGUE 2 ★

FAB FACT! The Bulls wore shorts made out of blackout curtains during World War Two, because there was a shortage of white material!

CLUB STATS!

Stadium: Edgar Street

Capacity: 7,149

Formed: 1924

Nickname: The Bulls

Manager: John Trewick

Captain: Kenny Lunt

Record signing: Dean Smith from Walsall, £80,000

Biggest win: 6-0 v Burnley, 1987

Biggest defeat: 7-0 v Middlesbrough, 1996

Highest attendance: 18,114 v Sheffield Wednesday, 1958

Home kit: White shirts with black trim, black shorts and white socks

Away kit: Blue and yellow shirts, blue shorts and socks

Honours: League 1 (1976), Welsh Cup (1990)

Edgar Street

CLUB HISTORY!

Hereford started playing non-league footy in 1924 after local clubs RAOC and St. Martins teamed up, and then won promotion to the Southern League just before World War Two. The 1970s saw Hereford knock top-flight Newcastle out of the FA Cup and bag promotion to the Championship, but by 1979 they were back in the bottom division, where they stayed for 19 years. Following Blue Square Premier League footy from 1997 to 2006, Hereford charged up the leagues, but are now in League 2 after finishing bottom of League 1 in 2008-09!

⚽ Former manager John Sillett led Hereford to their highest finish, 22nd in the Championship, in 1976-77. Sillett also won the FA Cup with Coventry City in 1987!

⚽ After twice going behind in the 2006 Blue Square Premier Play-off Final, Ryan Green hit the winner as The Bulls won 3-2 to return to the league after nine years!

⚽ Back when Hereford were a non-league side, the teams had to get changed at the nearby Wellington Hotel and walk to Edgar Street in time for kick-off!

Hereford 2-1 Newcastle, 1972

HUDDERSFIELD TOWN

★ COCA-COLA LEAGUE 1 ★

FAB FACT!
Huddersfield's first ground, Leeds Road, had no changing rooms! Players got ready for matches in a tram, a tent or a nearby pub!

CLUB STATS!

Stadium: *Galpharm Stadium*
Capacity: *24,500*
Formed: *1908*
Nickname: *The Terriers*
Manager: *Lee Clark*
Captain: *Peter Clarke*
Record signing: *Marcus Stewart from Bristol Rovers, £1.2 million*
Biggest win: *10-1 v Blackpool, 1930*
Biggest defeat: *10-1 v Man. City, 1987*
Highest attendance: *67,037 v Arsenal, 1932 (at Leeds Road)*
Home kit: *Blue and white striped shirts, white shorts, blue and white socks*
Away kit: *Black, red and white shirts, black shorts and socks*
Honours:
English League title (1924, 1925 & 1926), Championship (1970), League 2 (1980), FA Cup (1922), Community Shield (1922)

Marcus Stewart goes for goal against Wimbledon in 1998

⚽ The Galpharm Stadium was designed by the same architects who created the awesome new Wembley stadium and Wimbledon's Centre Court!

⚽ Manager Lee Clark played in midfield for loads of top clubs including Fulham, Sunderland and Newcastle twice. He scored 66 goals between 1989 and 2007!

⚽ The club's record signing is striker Marcus Stewart, who they bought for £1.2 million in 1996. They sold the goal machine for £2.75 million three-and-a-half years later!

CLUB HISTORY!

Due to the popularity of rugby, football only started in Huddersfield in 1908 after the club decided to buy the Leeds Road playing fields for a bargain £500.
The club nearly closed with massive debts in 1919 and lost the 1920 FA Cup Final, but two years later they beat Preston in the final and won three straight top-flight titles between 1924 and 1926.
After 1,554 matches at Leeds Road, The Terriers switched to the Galpharm in 1994. Play-off success then followed for the West Yorkshire club in 1995 and 2004!

The 1922 FA Cup winners

FAB FACT! Tough-tackling defender *Michael Turner* was named The Tigers' Player Of The Year in 2008 and 2009!

Ian Ashbee and Michael Turner

Hull celebrate Kamil Zayatte's goal against West Brom in 2008

CLUB HISTORY!

After forming way back in 1904, it took Hull City a massive 104 years to finally reach the top flight of English football.

The Tigers almost stormed into the top division in 1909-10, but just missed out on goal difference after losing 3-0 to Oldham on the last day of the season. In 1930, Hull reached the semi-finals of the FA Cup, only to lose 1-0 to Arsenal in a replay after the first match had finished 2-2.

After World War Two, Championship and League 1 action was played at Boothferry Park. The old ground even saw a club-record crowd for a sixth-round FA Cup clash against Man. United.

Under Brian Horton, The Tigers surprised the pundits with a five-year stay in the Championship between 1986 and 1991, but they were struggling in League 2 by 2003. The arrival of Peter Taylor saw back-to-back promotions in 2004 and 2005, before Phil Brown took over at the KC Stadium in 2007.

After finishing third in 2007-08, they won promotion to the Premier League after a 1-0 play-off final victory over Bristol City.

The KC Stadium

CLUB STATS!

Stadium: KC Stadium
Capacity: 25,417
Formed: 1904
Nickname: The Tigers
Manager: Phil Brown
Captain: Ian Ashbee
Record signing: Jimmy Bullard from Fulham, £5 million
Biggest win: 11-1 v Carlisle, 1939
Biggest defeat: 8-0 v Wolves, 1911
Highest attendance: 55,019 v Man. United, 1949 (at Boothferry Park)
Home kit: Amber and black striped shirts, black shorts and socks
Away kit: Grey shirts, shorts and socks
Honours: League 1 (1), Division Three North (2)

Phil Brown

The Tigers go crazy on the final day of the 2008-09 season

⚽ Hull defender Steven Mouyokolo helped his former club Boulogne win promotion to the French top flight for the first time in their history in 2008-09!

⚽ The KC Stadium's biggest ever crowd was on the final day of the 2008-09 season when a whopping 24,945 fans watched Hull lose 1-0 to Premier League champions Man. United!

⚽ Hull skipper Ian Ashbee is a footy legend. The midfielder, who has been with The Tigers since July 2002, is the only player to have captained the same club in all four league divisions!

CLUB LEGENDS!

MATCH checks out the club's greatest players!

DEAN WINDASS

Deano had three spells with his hometown club. At 39 years old, he even scored an unbelievable volley against Bristol City to send Hull into the Prem!

KEN WAGSTAFF

'Waggy' scored on his Tigers debut in 1964-65 and went on to net 23 goals that season. The deadly striker eventually bagged 173 league goals in 374 games!

IAN ASHBEE

Despite being sent off on his debut against Southend, the midfielder has since scored in all four leagues and played over 200 games for The Tigers!

FAB FACT!
Ipswich beat Man. United 6-0 back in 1980. It would have been even more, but United goalkeeper Gary Bailey saved three penalties!

Jon Stead

Bobby Robson's Ipswich side win the FA Cup in 1978

CLUB HISTORY!

Ipswich Town Hall was the venue for the creation of the original Ipswich amateur side in 1878, but it wasn't until 1936 that the club turned professional. They were elected to the Football League in 1938 after winning the Southern League.

In August 1955, Alf Ramsey was named Ipswich boss and led the club to their only league title seven years later. They qualified for the European Cup, but lost to AC Milan in the second round.

Bobby Robson took over at Portman Road in January 1969, and won the FA Cup a century after the club was formed when a Roger Osbourne goal beat Arsenal 1-0 at Wembley.

Robson's success didn't end there, as Ipswich lifted the UEFA Cup in 1981 after a 5-4 aggregate win over AZ Alkmaar. Robson then followed in Ramsey's footsteps and became England boss in 1982.

The formation of the Prem saw Ipswich reach the top flight, but they were relegated under George Burley. They bounced back in 2000, finishing fifth in the Prem a season later. They went down again in 2002 and have been in the Championship ever since!

Portman Road

Alf Ramsey chats to his players in 1961

⚽ Two legendary England bosses were also Ipswich gaffers. Sir Alf Ramsey managed Ipswich from 1955 to 1963 and Sir Bobby Robson was at Portman Road from 1969 to 1982!

⚽ Ipswich have a massive rivalry with East Anglian neighbours Norwich. The Tractor Boys have won 38 league matches to Norwich's 28 since they first played each other in 1946!

⚽ Loads of Ipswich players stood in for Hollywood greats during the making of footy film Escape To Victory. Paul Cooper played Sly Stallone and Kevin Beattie was Michael Caine!

CLUB STATS!

Stadium: Portman Road
Capacity: 30,311
Formed: 1878
Nickname: Tractor Boys
Manager: Roy Keane
Captain: Gareth McAuley
Record signing: Matteo Sereni from Sampdoria, £5 million
Biggest win: 10-0 v Floriana, 1962
Biggest defeat: 10-1 v Fulham, 1963
Highest attendance: 38,010 v Leeds, 1975
Home kit: Blue and white shirts, white shorts, blue socks
Away kit: Red and black shirts, red shorts and socks
Honours: English League title (1), Championship (3), Division Three South (2), UEFA Cup (1), FA Cup (1)

Gareth McAuley

CLUB LEGENDS!

MATCH checks out the club's greatest players!

TOM GARNEYS

The legendary centre-forward once smashed home four goals in a 5-1 win over Doncaster, and netted 143 times in 274 games for The Tractor Boys!

JOHN WARK

For a midfielder, Wark had an incredible goalscoring record. In three spells at the club, the Scotland international fired home an amazing 181 goals!

PAUL MARINER

Now working in the MLS, the former England striker will always be remembered by Ipswich fans for scoring in the 1981 UEFA Cup Final!

LEEDS UNITED
★ COCA-COLA LEAGUE 1 ★

FAB FACT!
Jermaine Beckford scored more goals than Prem Golden Boot winner Nicolas Anelka in 2008-09. The deadly striker smashed home 34 goals!

Jermaine Beckford

Leeds captain Billy Bremner lifts the Fairs Cup in 1971

CLUB LEGENDS!

MATCH checks out the club's greatest players!

BILLY BREMNER

The fiery midfielder played 772 games for Leeds and captained the club during the Don Revie years. Bremner is honoured with a statue outside Elland Road!

NORMAN HUNTER

Nicknamed 'Bite Yer Legs' because of his ferocious tackling, the fearsome centre-back spent 14 successful years at the club in the 1960s and 1970s!

NIGEL MARTYN

Leeds' first-choice keeper for six seasons, Martyn was in electric form between the sticks when they reached the semi-finals of the Champions League in 2001!

CLUB HISTORY!

After making illegal payments to players, The FA forced Leeds City to close in October 1919. A meeting held by Alf Masser saw the new Leeds form, and they played their first match a month later.

During the 1920s and 1930s Leeds were promoted and relegated on a regular basis, and it was only after World War Two, and the appointment of Don Revie in 1961, that they started going places.

By 1974, Revie and Leeds legends Billy Bremner and Norman 'Bite Yer Legs' Hunter had won eight trophies, including two top-flight titles, an FA Cup and two European successes.

Leeds' stay in the top flight was over by 1982. They returned under Howard Wilkinson, winning promotion in 1990 and then the league title in 1992, the last season before the Premier League.

David O'Leary took over the manager's hotseat in 1998 and led Leeds to third spot in the Prem, and semi-finals in the UEFA Cup and the Champions League. Leeds then started to falter under a succession of managers, including Kevin Blackwell and Dennis Wise. The West Yorkshire club slipped down into League 1 in 2007.

Elland Road

CLUB STATS!

Stadium: Elland Road
Capacity: 39,450
Formed: 1919
Nickname: The Whites
Manager: Simon Grayson
Captain: Richard Naylor
Record signing: Rio Ferdinand from West Ham, £18 million
Biggest win: 10-0 v Lyn Oslo, 1969
Biggest defeat: 8-1 v Stoke, 1934
Highest attendance: 57,892 v Sunderland, 1967
Home kit: White shirts, shorts and socks
Away kit: Yellow and blue shirts and shorts, yellow socks
Honours: English League title (3), Championship (3), FA Cup (1), League Cup (1), Community Shield (2), Inter-Cities Fairs Cup (2)

Rio Ferdinand joins Leeds for £18 million

Richard Naylor

⚽ Leeds United fought back from a minus 15-point start to the 2007-08 season to bag a League 1 play-off place. They reached the final, but lost 1-0 to Doncaster at Wembley!

⚽ England centre-back Rio Ferdinand set two club transfer records at Elland Road in 2000 and 2002. Leeds bought Rio for £18 million, then sold him for a massive £30 million!

⚽ Leeds had an incredible Champions League run in 2001. David O'Leary's young side stormed to the semi-finals, before losing 3-0 on aggregate to Spanish giants Valencia!

Steve Howard

FAB FACT!
Striker *Ashley Chambers* became the club's youngest player when he came off the bench against Blackpool in 2005. He was just 15 years old!

The Foxes storm to the League 1 title in 2009

CLUB HISTORY!

Originally called Leicester Fosse after they were formed at a house on the Roman Fosse Way in 1884, The Foxes became Leicester City in 1919 after a brief spell in Division One in 1908-09.

Leicester finished second in the top flight in 1928-29, just one point behind champions Sheffield Wednesday, but by 1939 they were back in the Championship.

An FA Cup final appearance in 1949 ended in disappointment as they were beaten 3-1 by Wolves, an achievement that was repeated in 1961, 1963 and 1969. Silverware did arrive at Filbert Street in 1964, though, in the form of the League Cup.

The 1970s saw a long spell in Division One, and a young striker called Gary Lineker made his first appearance by the end of the decade. By the late 1980s, Leicester were back in the second tier.

After play-off final defeats in 1992 and 1993, they won promotion at the third attempt and, under Martin O'Neill, lifted two League Cups and played in the UEFA Cup. The Foxes are now hoping for a return to those days after winning League 1 in 2009!

Leicester Fosse, 1895

⚽ Leicester only spent one season in League 1 after getting relegated in 2007-08. Under Nigel Pearson, The Foxes destroyed the division as they won the title with 96 points!

⚽ The Foxes reached Wembley three times in four seasons under Martin O'Neill. Leicester reached the League Cup final in 1997, 1999 and 2000, lifting the trophy twice!

⚽ The quickest goal scored by a Leicester player was in the Championship in 2006, when deadly striker Matty Fryatt netted against Preston after just nine seconds!

The Walkers Stadium

CLUB STATS!

Stadium: The Walkers Stadium

Capacity: 32,312

Formed: 1884

Nickname: The Foxes

Manager: Nigel Pearson

Captain: Stephen Clemence

Record signing: Ade Akinbiyi from Wolves, £5 million

Biggest win: 13-0 v Notts. Olympic, 1894

Biggest defeat: 12-0 v Nottingham Forest, 1909

Highest attendance: 47,298 v Tottenham, 1928 (at Filbert Street)

Home kit: Blue and white shirts, white shorts, blue socks

Away kit: Black shirts, shorts and socks

Honours: Championship (6), League 1 (1), League Cup (3), Community Shield (1)

Stephen Clemence

CLUB LEGENDS!

MATCH checks out the club's greatest players!

ARTHUR CHANDLER

Leicester's record scorer with 273 goals, Chandler is best remembered for the six he scored in one match against Portsmouth in 1928!

GORDON BANKS

England's 1966 World Cup-winning goalkeeper played 293 league games for Leicester from 1959 to 1967, and helped them win their first League Cup!

GARY LINEKER

Before playing for Everton, Barcelona and Spurs, Lineker hit 95 goals for his hometown club. He was top scorer in 1985-86 with 24 goals!

LEYTON ORIENT
★ COCA-COLA LEAGUE 1 ★

FAB FACT!
The strange creatures on Orient's badge are known as Wyverns, which are half dragon and half serpent reptiles!

CLUB STATS!

Stadium: Brisbane Road

Capacity: 9,271

Formed: 1881

Nickname: The O's

Manager: Geraint Williams

Captain: Stephen Purches

Record signing: Paul Beesley from Wigan, £175,000

Biggest win: 8-0 v Crystal Palace (1955), Rochdale (1987), Colchester (1988) and Doncaster (1997)

Biggest defeat: 8-0 v Aston Villa, 1929

Highest attendance: 34,345 v West Ham, 1964

Home kit: Red shirts, shorts and socks

Away kit: Black shirts, shorts and socks

Honours:
League 1 (1970),
Division Three South (1956)

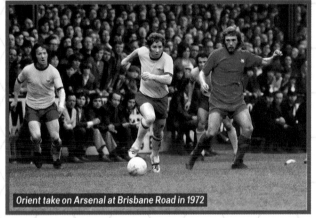
Orient take on Arsenal at Brisbane Road in 1972

CLUB HISTORY!

Like Sheffield Wednesday, the club was formed by a cricket team, and didn't become known as Leyton Orient until 1946. The 'Orient' part of the team's name came about because one player worked for the Orient Shipping Line, which took passengers from Britain to Australia. The club was then known as Orient between 1966 and 1987. The O's spent one season in the top flight in 1962-63, but finished bottom. An 11-year spell in League 2 ended in 2006 when a last-gasp winner saw them reach League 1, where they finished 14th in 2008 and 2009!

⚽ Legendary keeper Peter Shilton played his 1,000th league match for Leyton Orient in December 1996. Shilts kept a clean sheet in a 2-0 win against Brighton!

⚽ Leyton Orient reached the semi-finals of the FA Cup in 1978, but lost 3-0 to London rivals Arsenal at Stamford Bridge. The Gunners were beaten 1-0 by Ipswich in the final!

⚽ West End star Sir Andrew Lloyd Webber is said to be an Orient fan. The world-famous musician is famous for composing music for Cats, Joseph and The Sound Of Music!

Orient take on Man. United in 1962

LINCOLN CITY
★ COCA-COLA LEAGUE 2 ★

CLUB STATS!

Stadium: Sincil Bank Stadium

Capacity: 10,120

Formed: 1884

Nickname: The Red Imps

Manager: Peter Jackson

Captain: Scott Kerr

Record signing: Dean Walling from Carlisle and Tony Battersby from Bury, £75,000

Biggest win: 11-1 v Crewe, 1951

Biggest defeat: 11-3 v Man. City, 1895

Highest attendance: 23,196 v Derby, 1967

Home kit: Red and white striped shirts, black shorts and red socks

Away kit: Silver and blue shirts, blue shorts and socks

Honours:
League 2 (1976),
Division Three North (1932, 1948 & 1952),
Blue Square Premier (1988)

Keith Alexander gives his orders from the dugout

CLUB HISTORY!

Formed as an amateur side, Lincoln turned professional ahead of the 1891-92 season, moving to Sincil Bank four years later. The club's highest ever finish was in 1902 when they ended the season in fifth place in the Championship. They also reached the last 16 of the FA Cup, but lost to Derby. The Red Imps spent 14 years in League 2 after relegation in 1961-62, and one season in the Blue Square Premier in 1987-88. Since their fifth play-off disaster in a row in 2007, Lincoln have only reached mid-table in League 2 under gaffer Peter Jackson!

⚽ Under ex-boss Keith Alexander, Lincoln set an incredible record. Between 2003 and 2006 they reached the play-offs each season, but never got promoted!

⚽ Former Newcastle goal machine Alan Shearer made his debut against Lincoln after joining the North-East club for a world record £15 million fee in July 1996!

⚽ At the end of the 1986-87 season, Lincoln became the first team to be automatically relegated from the Football League, and were replaced by Scarborough!

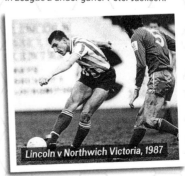

Lincoln v Northwich Victoria, 1987

NEVILLE
18

FAB FACT!
Liverpool's youngest ever goalscorer is former striker *Michael Owen,* who was just 17 when he netted against Wimbledon in 1997!

Fernando Torres

Liverpool celebrate their comeback against AC Milan in the 2005 Champions League Final

CLUB HISTORY!

Everton were forced to move out of Anfield in 1892 after a row with owner John Houlding, which led to the formation of Liverpool FC. Before World War One, The Reds won the title twice and finished runners-up in the 1914 FA Cup Final. More league titles arrived in 1922, 1923 and 1947, but by 1954 they were in the Championship.

The appointment of Bill Shankly in 1959 was a masterstroke as the great Scot transformed Liverpool, winning seven trophies during his 15-year reign. Bob Paisley replaced him and was even more successful, as he picked up 19 trophies in nine seasons.

After the Heysel Stadium disaster in 1985, striker Kenny Dalglish became player-manager and won the double in his first season. The club's FA Cup victory in 1989 was overshadowed by the Hillsborough disaster, when 96 Liverpool fans lost their lives.

Graeme Souness and Roy Evans picked up one trophy each in the 1990s, then Gerard Houllier led The Reds to an amazing treble in 2001. Spanish boss Rafa Benitez took over at Anfield in 2004, and has since won the Champions League and FA Cup!

Anfield

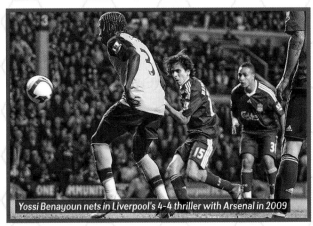

Yossi Benayoun nets in Liverpool's 4-4 thriller with Arsenal in 2009

⚽ Liverpool skipper Steven Gerrard loves playing in major finals. The midfield superstar has scored in the Champions League, UEFA Cup, FA Cup and League Cup finals for The Reds!

⚽ Spain striker Fernando Torres bagged the Anfield club's 1,000th Premier League goal during their 3-2 win against Man. City at Eastlands in October 2008!

⚽ Incredibly, Liverpool drew 4-4 twice in a week in 2008-09. After battling it out in the Champions League quarter-finals against Chelsea, The Reds were held by Arsenal at Anfield!

CLUB STATS!

Stadium: Anfield
Capacity: 45,362
Formed: 1892
Nickname: The Reds
Manager: Rafael Benitez
Captain: Steven Gerrard
Record signing: Fernando Torres from Atletico Madrid, £26.5 million
Biggest win: 11-0 v Stromsgodset Drammen, 1974
Biggest defeat: 9-1 v Birmingham, 1954
Highest attendance: 61,905 v Wolves, 1952
Home kit: Red shirts, shorts and socks
Away kit: Black shirts, shorts and socks
Honours: English League title (18), Championship (4), FA Cup (7), League Cup (7), Champions League (5), UEFA Cup (3), European Super Cup (3)

Glen Johnson joins Liverpool

CLUB LEGENDS!

MATCH checks out the club's greatest players!

KENNY DALGLISH

'King Kenny' netted 172 goals for Liverpool, including the winner in the 1978 European Cup Final and a title-winning strike at Stamford Bridge in 1986!

IAN RUSH

Rushy bagged 346 goals for Liverpool, won the European Golden Boot in 1984 and bagged ten goals for The Reds in major cup finals. What a striker!

STEVEN GERRARD

One of the world's best box-to-box midfielders, The Reds captain scored his 100th Liverpool goal against PSV in the 2008-09 Champions League!

FAB FACT!
The 2007-08 season saw City do the league double over local rivals Man. United, winning 1-0 at Eastlands then 2-1 at Old Trafford!

Stephen Ireland

Samba star Robinho nets against Tottenham at Eastlands

MATCH checks out the club's greatest players!

FRANK SWIFT

City's 1937 title-winning keeper played nearly 400 matches before becoming a journalist. Swift died in the Munich air disaster in February 1958!

BERT TRAUTMANN

Legendary German goalkeeper Trautmann played 545 games for City and famously carried on after breaking his neck in the 1956 FA Cup Final!

RICHARD DUNNE

Dunne may hold the Prem red card record, but his City career has been incredible. The Ireland defender was the club's Player Of The Year from 2005 to 2008!

CLUB HISTORY!

The roots of Man. City can be traced back to 1880, when St. Mark's Church formed a football team. They moved to Hyde Road in 1887 and changed their name to Ardwick, who later became Man. City.

The club picked up their first major honour in 1904 with a 1-0 win against Bolton in the FA Cup final, then moved to Maine Road in 1923 after their Hyde Road ground was destroyed by fire.

The 1930s saw another FA Cup added to City's trophy cabinet, as well as the league title in 1937. Their appearances at Wembley continued in the 1950s, as they reached two cup finals on the spin.

Under Joe Mercer and Malcolm Allison, City won the title again in 1968, the FA Cup a season later and the European Cup Winners' Cup in 1970. But the 1980s saw two relegations from the top flight, and by 1998-99 they were down in League 1.

Kevin Keegan's reign brought a return to the top flight in 2002, but Stuart Pearce and Sven-Goran Eriksson couldn't bring any trophies to Eastlands. Now with his billionaire bosses, the Abu Dhabi United Group, Mark Hughes will be hoping to change that!

The City Of Manchester Stadium

CLUB STATS!

Stadium: The City of Manchester Stadium

Capacity: 47,715

Formed: 1887

Nickname: The Citizens

Manager: Mark Hughes

Captain: Richard Dunne

Record signing: Robinho from Real Madrid, £32.5 million

Biggest win: 10-1 v Swindon (1930) and Huddersfield (1987)

Biggest defeat: 9-1 v Everton, 1906

Highest attendance: 85,569 v Stoke, 1934 (at Maine Road)

Home kit: Sky blue shirts, white shorts and socks

Away kit: Black shirts, shorts and socks

Honours: English League title (2), Championship (7), European Cup Winners' Cup (1), FA Cup (4), League Cup (2)

The great Man. City team of the late 1960s

Carlos Tevez swaps Man. United for Man. City

⚽ City broke the British transfer record in 2008 when they splashed out on Real Madrid forward Robinho. The Brazilian skill machine joined on transfer deadline day for £32.5 million!

⚽ Man. City star Micah Richards set an England record on his debut against Holland in November 2006. Aged just 18 years and five months, he became England's youngest ever defender!

⚽ Man. City's £25 million summer signing from Arsenal, Togo international Emmanuel Adebayor, was named African Footballer Of The Year back in 2008!

MANCHESTER UNITED

★ BARCLAYS PREMIER LEAGUE ★

FAB FACT!
Wayne Rooney's United career got off to a top start in 2004 when he bagged a hat-trick on his debut against Fenerbahçe!

Wayne Rooney

United beat Benfica to lift the European Cup at Wembley in 1968

CLUB HISTORY!

The club was founded as Newton Heath in 1878, but they were almost forced into bankruptcy in 1902. Man. United were formed as a result and immediately switched to their famous red shirts.

United's first league title was won in 1908 and they only had to wait another season before lifting the FA Cup. Old Trafford opened its gates for the first time in 1910, but the club began to slump and by the early 1930s were back in the Championship.

Sir Matt Busby was appointed as manager in 1945 and won three league titles with his 'Busby Babes', before the Munich air disaster killed eight players in 1958. Busby rebuilt his team, and with the likes of Bobby Charlton, Denis Law and George Best, The Red Devils won the European Cup at Wembley in 1968.

A period of decline set in after Busby resigned and it wasn't until Sir Alex Ferguson arrived in 1986 that the club became serious contenders for the title. Fergie has since won more trophies in English football than any other manager, winning the Treble in 1999 and being knighted for his achievement!

Old Trafford

CLUB STATS!

Stadium: Old Trafford

Capacity: 76,212

Formed: 1878

Nickname: The Red Devils

Manager: Sir Alex Ferguson

Captain: Gary Neville

Record signing: Dimitar Berbatov from Tottenham, £30.75 million

Biggest win: 10-0 v Anderlecht, 1956

Biggest defeat: 7-0 v Blackburn, 1926

Highest attendance: 76,962 v Wolves, 1939

Home kit: Red shirts, white shorts, black socks

Away kit: Black shirts, shorts and socks

Honours: English League title (18), Championship (2), Champions League (3), European Cup Winners' Cup (1), European Super Cup (1), FIFA Club World Cup (1), FA Cup (11), League Cup (3)

Man. United claim their 18th league title in 2009

⚽ Man. United achieved an awesome title-winning record after topping the Prem in 2009. It was the second time they'd won three in a row, with the first treble coming between 1999 and 2001!

⚽ Former Man. United superstar Cristiano Ronaldo set a world record when he moved to Real Madrid last summer. The Portugal wing wizard cost the La Liga giants £80 million!

⚽ Sir Alex Ferguson seems to have been the Man. United manager forever. The former Aberdeen boss arrived at the Theatre Of Dreams way back in November 1986!

Sir Alex Ferguson's 2009 summer signings

CLUB LEGENDS!

MATCH checks out the club's greatest players!

SIR BOBBY CHARLTON

England's all-time leading goalscorer was a Man. United hero, making 758 appearances and being named European Player Of The Year in 1966!

BRYAN ROBSON

'Captain Marvel' broke the British transfer record when he joined United for £1.5 million in 1981, and went on to win eight major trophies at Old Trafford!

CRISTIANO RONALDO

The Portugal midfielder won the European Golden Shoe, the FIFA World Player Of The Year award and the Ballon d'Or after netting 42 goals in 2007-08!

FAB FACT!
Former Middlesbrough keeper *Mark Schwarzer* has helped write a footy book series. The first was called 'Megs and the Vootball Kids'!

Tuncay

Chris Riggott scores against Steaua Bucharest in the 2006 UEFA Cup semi-final

CLUB HISTORY!

The gym at the Albert Park Hotel was the venue for the club's formation by members of the town's cricket club in 1876. In 1903 Boro moved into Ayresome Park, their home for the next 92 years.

Boro were the first club to spend £1,000 on a player when Alf Common was signed from Sunderland in 1905. They finished third in Division One in 1914, but were soon moving between the leagues on a regular basis, winning the Championship in 1927 and 1929.

The 1970s saw an upturn in Boro's fortunes as Jack Charlton led them to Championship glory in 1974, then the semi-finals of the League Cup in 1976. After he was sacked, they soon dropped into League 1, but Bruce Rioch had them back in the top flight by 1988.

Under Bryan Robson in the 1990s, the North-East club reached three major cup finals in two seasons, but silverware didn't arrive until Steve McClaren won the Carling Cup in 2004.

Boro beat all the odds to reach the 2006 UEFA Cup Final, but lost 4-0 to Sevilla. Gareth Southgate took over after McClaren became England boss, but couldn't stop Boro sliding out the Prem in 2009!

The 1894-95 Middlesbrough squad

⚽ Boro twice came back from 3-0 down on aggregate on their run to the 2006 UEFA Cup Final. They knocked out Basle in the quarter-final and Steaua Bucharest in the semi-final!

⚽ Middlesbrough captain Emanuel Pogatetz also wears the armband for his country. The Austria defender has been the skipper of his national team since March 2009!

⚽ Gareth Southgate was the first Boro player to lift a domestic cup when they beat Bolton in the 2004 Carling Cup Final. The ace defender made 160 league appearances for the club!

The Riverside Stadium

CLUB STATS!

Stadium: Riverside Stadium
Capacity: 35,041
Formed: 1876
Nickname: Boro
Manager: Gareth Southgate
Captain: Emanuel Pogatetz
Record signing: Afonso Alves from Heerenveen, £12 million
Biggest win: 9-0 v Brighton, 1958
Biggest defeat: 9-0 v Blackburn, 1954
Highest attendance: 53,536 v Newcastle, 1949 (at Ayresome Park)
Home kit: Red and white shirts, white shorts and socks
Away kit: Light blue shirts, shorts and socks
Honours: Championship (4), League Cup (1)

Emanuel Pogatetz

CLUB LEGENDS!

MATCH checks out the club's greatest players!

BRIAN CLOUGH

Before making his name as a manager, Cloughie was a deadly marksman for Boro. He hit 204 goals in 222 appearances before moving to rivals Sunderland!

GARY PALLISTER

After arriving from Billingham in exchange for kits, Gary became a Boro legend in two spells and made his England debut while still a Championship player!

MARK SCHWARZER

Boro's Australian international keeper was class for 11 seasons. His vital shoot-out saves against Everton and Spurs took them to the 2004 Carling Cup Final!

MACCLESFIELD
★ COCA-COLA LEAGUE 2 ★

FAB FACT!
Macclesfield's training regime before the 1890 Cheshire Senior Cup Final was dieting, no smoking, country walks and Turkish baths!

CLUB STATS!

Stadium: *Moss Rose*

Capacity: *6,335*

Formed: *1874*

Nickname: *The Silkmen*

Manager: *Keith Alexander*

Captain: *Sean Hessey*

Record signing: *Danny Swailes from Bury, £40,000*

Biggest win: *15-0 v Chester St. Marys, 1886*

Biggest defeat: *8-1 v Davenham, 1885*

Highest attendance: *9,008 v Winsford United, 1948*

Home kit: *Blue and white shirts, white shorts, blue socks*

Away kit: *Black and yellow shirts, black shorts, yellow socks*

Honours: *Blue Square Premier (1995 & 1997), Unibond Premier Division (1969, 1970 & 1987), The FA Trophy (1970 & 1996)*

Paul Ince at Moss Rose

CLUB HISTORY!

Macclesfield started out as a rugby union team, only adopting footy rules in 1874. The Silkmen were a non-league side until they were crowned Blue Square Premier champions under Sammy McIlroy in 1997. McIlroy's success didn't stop there, though, as The Silkmen won promotion to League 1 a season later after finishing in third place. But after McIlroy's departure to become Northern Ireland boss in 2000, the club slipped back down to League 2, and a play-off place in 2005 is the closest they've come to promotion since!

⚽ Under Paul Ince, Macclesfield survived the drop from League 2 in 2006-07. Seven points off their closest rivals when he joined, they beat relegation by one point!

⚽ The brother of Man. United striker Wayne Rooney plays for Macclesfield. John Rooney, who plays up front like his brother, scored two goals in 14 appearances last season!

⚽ Macclesfield won the Blue Square Premier in 1994-95, but were denied promotion to the Football League because their Moss Rose stadium wasn't good enough!

Umbro Trophy winners, 1996

MILLWALL
★ COCA-COLA LEAGUE 1 ★

FAB FACT!
Dragons' Den star Theo Paphitis used to be Millwall chairman, and was in charge when they reached the FA Cup Final in 2004!

CLUB STATS!

Stadium: The Den
Capacity: 20,146
Formed: 1885
Nickname: The Lions
Manager: Kenny Jackett
Captain: Paul Robinson
Record signing: Paul Goddard from Derby, £800,000
Biggest win: 9-1 v Torquay, 1927
Biggest defeat: 9-1 v Aston Villa, 1946
Highest attendance: 20,093 v Arsenal, 1994
Home kit: Blue shirts, shorts and socks
Away kit: White shirts, black shorts and socks
Honours:
Championship (1988),
League 1 (2001),
Division Three South (1928 & 1938),
League 2 (1962),
Football League Group Cup (1983)

The Lions take on Man. United in the 2004 FA Cup Final

CLUB HISTORY!

Workers at the Morton's Jam Factory set up Millwall Rovers in 1885, and decided to wear a blue and white kit as many of them were Scottish. They were a non-league side until 1920, but became the first team from the old Division Three to reach the FA Cup semis. Promotion and relegation followed in the decades after World War Two, but in 1988 they reached the top flight where Teddy Sheringham's goals ensured tenth spot. Since 1997, fans have seen Tim Cahill wear the Lions' kit, UEFA Cup action and a trip to Wembley in a memorable 2008-09 season!

⚽ Millwall just missed out on promotion from League 1 in 2008-09. With 20 minutes to go in the play-off final against Scunthorpe, they let a 2-1 lead slip and lost 3-2.

⚽ The Lions became only the second team from outside the top flight to reach the FA Cup final since 1982 when they lost 3-0 to Man. United in 2004!

⚽ Millwall gaffer Kenny Jackett played in midfield for Watford in the 1984 FA Cup Final. The Hornets lost 2-0 to Everton in their only final appearance!

Southern League champions, 1895

MK DONS
★ COCA-COLA LEAGUE 1 ★

Coca-Cola LEAGUE 2
CHAMPIONS 2008
MILTON KEYNES DONS F.C.

FAB FACT! MK Dons' stadium could be expanded to a massive 40,000 capacity if it's chosen as a venue for the 2018 World Cup!

CLUB STATS!

Stadium: Stadiummk
Capacity: 22,000
Formed: 2004
Nickname: The Dons
Manager: Paul Ince
Captain: Dean Lewington
Record signing: Stephen Gleeson from Wolves, Undisclosed
Biggest win: 5-0 v Accrington Stanley, 2007
Biggest defeat: 5-0 v Hartlepool, 2005
Highest attendance: 17,717 v Leicester, 2009
Home kit: White and black shirts, white shorts and socks
Away kit: Red shirts, shorts and socks
Honours: League 2 (2008), Johnstone's Paint Trophy (2008)

Paul Ince and chairman Pete Winkelman

CLUB HISTORY!

The MK Dons started life at the National Hockey Stadium following Wimbledon's relocation to Milton Keynes in 2004. After escaping relegation from League 1 on the last day of the 2004-05 season, The Dons slipped into League 2 in 2006. Paul Ince replaced Martin Allen as manager in 2007 and picked up the club's first silverware in his first season in charge. After Ince moved to Blackburn, Roberto di Matteo took charge of The Dons in his first manager's post, but saw his side lose to Scunthorpe in last season's play-offs!

⚽ MK Dons used to be known as Wimbledon, before the South London club relocated to Milton Keynes in July 2004. Wimbledon had won the FA Cup in 1988!

⚽ Paul Ince won a league and cup double in his first season, beating Grimsby 2-0 in the Johnstone's Paint Trophy final and taking the League 2 title by five points!

⚽ Former MK Dons boss Roberto di Matteo scored one of the quickest FA Cup final goals ever when he netted after 43 seconds for Chelsea back in 1997!

Glory at Wembley in 2008

MORECAMBE
★ COCA-COLA LEAGUE 2 ★

CLUB STATS!

Stadium: Christie Park
Capacity: 6,030
Formed: 1920
Nickname: The Shrimps
Manager: Sammy McIlroy
Captain: Jim Bentley
Record signing: Carl Baker from Southport, Undisclosed
Biggest win: 16-0 v Rossendale United, 1967
Biggest defeat: 11-0 v Crewe Alexandra 'A', 1989
Highest attendance: 9,383 v Weymouth, 1962
Home kit: Red and white shirts, white shorts, red socks
Away kit: Blue shirts, shorts and socks
Honours: FA Trophy (1974), Northern Premier League Presidents Cup (1992)

Morecambe stun Preston at Deepdale

⚽ England Under-21 keeper Joe Lewis played 19 league matches for Morecambe while on loan from Peterborough during the 2007-08 season!

⚽ Morecambe's first competitive win over local rivals Preston was in the Carling Cup in 2007. The Shrimps' 2-1 victory came during their first ever League Cup tie!

⚽ Morecambe will move to a wicked new stadium at the start of the 2010-11 season. The new ground will be able to hold 6,800 fans and has a hotel next to it!

CLUB HISTORY!

Morecambe FC was formed in 1920 at the West View Hotel. They played their early games at a ground they shared with a local cricket club before moving to Roseberry Park, which was later named after Joseph Christie. The Shrimps were finally promoted to the Football League in May 2007 after beating Exeter 2-1 in the Blue Square Premier play-off final, just a year after Sammy McIlroy's side had lost in the semi-finals. The club's only previous national success had come in the 1974 FA Trophy Final, when they beat Dartford 2-1!

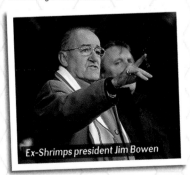
Ex-Shrimps president Jim Bowen

NEWCASTLE UNITED

★ COCA-COLA CHAMPIONSHIP ★

FAB FACT!

Newcastle haven't always played in black and white striped shirts. The Magpies used to wear red and white stripes, just like rivals Sunderland!

Steven Taylor

Kevin Keegan's Newcastle side celebrate their promotion charge in 1993

FAB FACT! Famous Newcastle fans include TV presenters Ant 'n' Dec and Former Prime Minister Tony Blair!

CLUB HISTORY!

Newcastle United were officially formed in December 1892 after a merger between the city's East End and West End clubs.

United won three titles and reached five FA Cup finals in seven seasons in the early 1900s, lifting the cup just once in 1910. They won the FA Cup again in 1924, before their last title arrived in 1927.

The Toon Army enjoyed more trips to Wembley after World War Two, as they won the FA Cup three times in five seasons (1951, 1952 and 1955). Joe Harvey's side then won the Fairs Cup in 1969.

Newcastle were down in the Championship by the 1980s, but with Kevin Keegan's goals they battled back to the top flight. The club remained there until 1989, then almost slipped into League 1 before fans' favourite Keegan returned as boss in 1992.

Within four seasons Newcastle were playing some of the Prem's most entertaining football, nearly winning the title in 1996 and finishing third under Sir Bobby Robson in 2003. Keegan's 2008 return lasted only 232 days, and sadly for Newcastle fans they were relegated in 2008-09 despite appointing Shearer as boss!

Newcastle's 1905 title-winning team

⚽ St. James' Park is the third biggest league ground in England after Old Trafford and The Emirates. The giant stadium's Gallowgate End is named after the city's old gallows!

⚽ Alan Shearer broke the world transfer record when he joined Newcastle in 1996 for £15 million. It was broken a year later when Ronaldo moved from Barça to Inter Milan for £19.5 million!

⚽ Back in 1923-24, Newcastle and Derby scored a massive 20 goals in one FA Cup tie. After three 2-2 draws, the fourth match saw The Magpies win 5-3 to reach the third round!

St. James' Park

CLUB STATS!

Stadium: St. James' Park

Capacity: 52,387

Formed: 1892

Nickname: The Magpies

Manager: Chris Hughton

Captain: Nicky Butt

Record signing: Michael Owen from Real Madrid, £17 million

Biggest win: 13-0 v Newport, 1946

Biggest defeat: 9-0 v Burton, 1885

Highest attendance: 68,386 v Chelsea, 1930

Home kit: Black and white striped shirts, black shorts, black and white socks

Away kit: Yellow and white striped shirts, yellow shorts, yellow and white socks

Honours: English League title (4), Championship (2), Inter-Cities Fairs Cup (1), FA Cup (6)

Toon legend Alan Shearer

CLUB LEGENDS!

MATCH checks out the club's greatest players!

JACKIE MILBURN

Known as 'Wor Jackie' to thousands of Newcastle fans, the lightning-fast striker smashed home 239 goals in 494 appearances for The Magpies!

PAUL GASCOIGNE

Jackie Milburn described Gazza as 'the best in the world' after the local lad led Newcastle to Youth Cup glory in 1985. He went on to play 107 games for the club!

LES FERDINAND

'Sir Les' became a Gallowgate legend after netting 50 goals during a two-year spell on Tyneside. His strike partnership with Alan Shearer was lethal!

NORTHAMPTON TOWN

★ COCA-COLA LEAGUE 2 ★

FAB FACT! Northampton are called The Cobblers because the East Midlands town used to be famous for its leather and shoe-making industries!

CLUB STATS!

Stadium: Sixfields Stadium

Capacity: 7,653

Formed: 1897

Nickname: The Cobblers

Manager: Stuart Gray

Captain: Craig Hinton

Record signing: Josh Low from Oldham, £165,000

Biggest win: 10-0 v Sutton (1907) and Walsall (1927)

Biggest defeat: 11-0 v Southampton, 1901

Highest attendance: 24,523 v Fulham, 1966 (at the County Ground)

Home kit: Claret shirts, white shorts and claret socks

Away kit: Sky blue shirts, shorts and socks

Honours:
League 1 (1963),
League 2 (1987)

Peterborough v Northampton, 2001

CLUB HISTORY!

A group of teachers and a solicitor called A.J. Darnell formed the club in 1897 and moved into the County Ground, where they stayed for the next 97 years. The 1960s saw the club reach the top flight before plummeting back to the old Division Four within just three seasons. Man. United legend George Best even scored six goals against The Cobblers in an 8-2 FA Cup fifth-round tie in 1970. They've been in Leagues 1 and 2 ever since, and only just escaped relegation to the Blue Square Premier in 1994!

⚽ Northampton's biggest rivals are Championship side Peterborough. In 50 league matches between the clubs, The Cobblers have won 14, with 13 draws!

⚽ The road that leads to Sixfields is called Walter Tull Way. Northampton signed Tull, who was the league's first black outfield player, from Spurs in 1911!

⚽ Northampton spent their only season in the top flight in 1965-66. The Cobblers finished second from bottom and were relegated after just ten wins!

George Best destroys The Cobblers

NORWICH CITY
★ COCA-COLA LEAGUE 1 ★

FAB FACT!
Norwich's big rivals are East Anglian neighbours Ipswich! In 80 League meetings, The Canaries have won 28 games and drawn 14!

CLUB STATS!

Stadium: Carrow Road
Capacity: 26,034
Formed: 1902
Nickname: The Canaries
Manager: Bryan Gunn
Captain: Gary Doherty
Record signing: Dean Ashton from Crewe, £3.4 million
Biggest win: 10-2 v Coventry, 1930
Biggest defeat: 10-2 v Swindon, 1908
Highest attendance: 43,984 v Leicester, 1963
Home kit: Yellow and green shirts, green shorts, yellow socks
Away kit: White shirts, shorts and socks
Honours:
Championship (1972, 1986 & 2004),
Division Three South (1934),
League Cup (1962 & 1985)

Jeremy Goss nets against Bayern Munich at Carrow Road in 1993

⚽ Norwich thrashed Barnsley 4-0 in Bryan Gunn's first match as boss last season, but three defeats in their last three matches saw City relegated to League 1!

⚽ In the first Premier League season in 1992-93, Norwich topped the table for most of the campaign, but finished third behind champions Man. United and Aston Villa!

⚽ Norwich became the first British team to beat Bayern Munich in their old Olympic Stadium. The Canaries won 2-1 in a UEFA Cup second-round clash in October 1993!

CLUB HISTORY!

Life for the League 1 club began 107 years ago in 1902 after a meeting between a group of footballers in the city's Criterion Café. Before World War Two, Norwich played in a disused chalk pit called The Nest, until they moved to their Carrow Road home in 1935. The club's iconic yellow and green home kit was first worn in 1907. Norwich lost the League Cup final twice in the 1970s before beating Sunderland 1-0 in 1985. Seven years later they were in the Prem, but only lasted three seasons before being relegated to the Championship!

Dave Watson lifts the League Cup

NOTTINGHAM FOREST
★ COCA-COLA CHAMPIONSHIP ★

FAB FACT!
Nottingham Forest's biggest League victory was a huge 12-0 win against Leicester Fosse in 1909. Three players bagged hat-tricks!

Robert Earnshaw

Brian Clough shows off his second European Cup in 1980

CLUB HISTORY!

The second oldest existing league club in England started life in 1865, just months after neighbours Notts County. A group of 'shinney' players formed the club, a sport that's similar to hockey. Forest played well in early FA Cup competitions and reached the semi-finals in 1879, before lifting the trophy in 1898 after a 3-1 win against mega rivals Derby at Crystal Palace. It wasn't until after World War Two that Forest started to improve in the League.

Under Brian Clough and his assistant Peter Taylor, who joined in 1975, Forest had their most successful period. Back-to-back European Cups in 1979 and 1980 followed a top-flight title in 1978. Clough remained in charge until Forest were relegated in 1993.

Managed by Frank Clark, and with Stan Collymore's goals, Forest returned to the Premier League the following season, finished third and reached the UEFA Cup quarter-finals in 1996.

Following on from David Platt and Joe Kinnear, Colin Calderwood became the club's 12th boss in 13 years in 2006. He took Forest up to the Championship, but was replaced by Billy Davies in 2009!

The City Ground

CLUB STATS!

Stadium: City Ground
Capacity: 30,576
Formed: 1865
Nickname: Reds
Manager: Billy Davies
Captain: James Perch
Record signing: Pierre van Hooijdonk from Celtic, £3.5 million
Biggest win: 14-0 v Clapton, 1891
Biggest defeat: 9-1 v Blackburn, 1937
Highest attendance: 49,946 v Man. United, 1967
Home kit: Red and white shirts, white shorts, red socks
Away kit: White shirts and socks, red shorts
Honours: English League title (1), Championship (2), Division Three South (1), FA Cup (2), League Cup (4), Full Members Cup (2), Champions League (2), UEFA Cup (1)

Roy Dwight strikes at Wembley in 1959

⚽ The uncle of music legend Elton John scored the first goal for Nottingham Forest in the 1959 FA Cup Final. Roy Dwight then broke his leg, but The Reds went on to win the game 2-1!

⚽ Nottingham Forest are the reason Premier League giants Arsenal wear red home shirts. The City Ground outfit donated red kits to the North London club in 1886!

⚽ England Under-21 boss Stuart Pearce is the most-capped player in Nottingham Forest history. The rock-solid left-back won 78 caps for England between 1985 and 1997!

Billy Davies

CLUB LEGENDS!

MATCH checks out the club's greatest players!

PETER SHILTON

Forest splashed out £250,000 on Stoke's No.1 in 1977. Shilts was named PFA Player Of The Year in 1978 and won the European Cup twice under Brian Clough!

STUART PEARCE

Before taking over as caretaker manager in 1996, 'Psycho' was club captain, played 401 league games and scored a free-kick in the 1991 League Cup Final!

DES WALKER

After being handed his debut at the age of 18 by Brian Clough, the speedy England centre-back went on to play a massive 321 games for Forest!

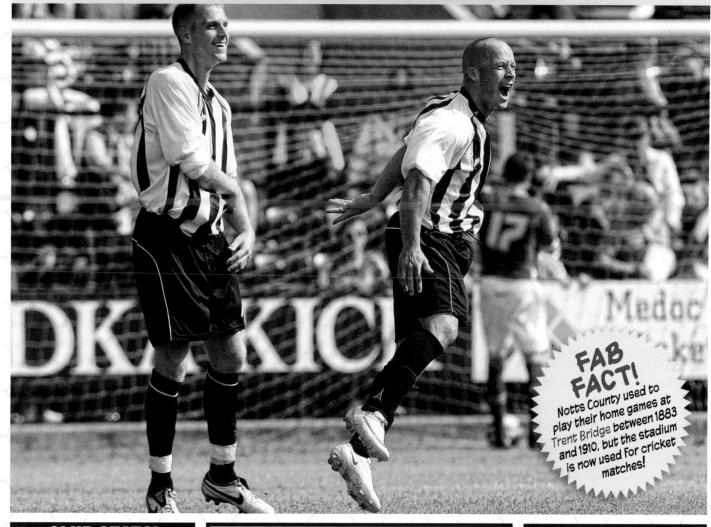

FAB FACT! Notts County used to play their home games at Trent Bridge between 1883 and 1910, but the stadium is now used for cricket matches!

CLUB STATS!

Stadium: Meadow Lane

Capacity: 20,300

Formed: 1864

Nickname: Magpies

Manager: Ian McParland

Captain: John Thompson

Record signing: Tony Agana from Sheffield United, £650,000

Biggest win: 15-0 v Rotherham, 1885

Biggest defeat: 9-1 v Aston Villa (1888), Blackburn (1889) and Portsmouth (1927)

Highest attendance: 47,310 v York, 1955

Home kit: Black and white striped shirts, black shorts and socks

Away kit: Claret and sky blue halved shirts, claret shorts and sky blue socks

Honours:
Championship (1897, 1914 & 1923)
Division Three South (1931 & 1950),
League 2 (1998 & 1971),
FA Cup (1894),
Anglo-Italian Cup (1995)

NOTTS COUNTY FC

THE WORLD'S OLDEST FOOTBALL LEAGUE CLUB

Sven-Goran Eriksson arrives at Meadow Lane

⚽ Notts County is the oldest professional club in the world. There's evidence that a team existed in 1862, but they were officially formed on December 7, 1864!

⚽ Former England and Man. City boss Sven-Goran Eriksson shocked the footy world when he took over as Notts County's director of football in July 2009!

⚽ Meadow Lane and Nottingham Forest's City Ground are the closest footy stadiums in England. They're just 300 metres apart, separated by the River Trent!

CLUB HISTORY!

With the Football League only existing from 1888, Notts County were forced to play friendlies after their formation in 1864. They reached the FA Cup final in 1891, losing 3-1 to Blackburn, but three years later they crushed Bolton 4-1 at Everton's Goodison Park stadium to lift the trophy. Relegation to Division Two followed in 1926, and County had to wait for 55 years to return to the top flight, where they stayed between 1982 and 1984 and again from 1991 to 1992. The ancient club could now be transformed after a takeover by Middle East millionaires!

The 1894 FA Cup winners

OLDHAM ATHLETIC
★ COCA-COLA LEAGUE 1 ★

FAB FACT!
At 509 feet above sea level, Boundary Park is the third-highest football ground in England behind West Brom and Port Vale!

CLUB STATS!

Stadium: Boundary Park

Capacity: 10,850

Formed: 1895

Nickname: The Latics

Manager: Dave Penney

Captain: Neal Eardley

Record signing: Ian Olney from Aston Villa, £750,000

Biggest win: 11-0 v Southport, 1962

Biggest defeat: 13-4 v Tranmere, 1935

Highest attendance: 46,471 v Sheffield Wednesday, 1930

Home kit: Blue and white shirts, blue shorts and white socks

Away kit: Blue and orange shirts and socks, blue shorts with orange trim

Honours: Championship (1991), League 1 (1974), Division Three North (1953)

Andy Ritchie strikes against Man. United in 1990

CLUB HISTORY!

For the first four years of their existence, Oldham were known as Pine Villa. They changed their name in 1899 and within 11 years were playing Division One footy. Relegation followed in 1923 and it would take another 68 years before they returned to the top flight in 1991. Oldham spent two seasons in the Prem, before slipping back into the second tier. High-profile managers including Iain Dowie, Neil Warnock and the return of Joe Royle couldn't get Oldham promoted, paving the way for Dave Penney to take over in 2009!

Joe Royle

⚽ Oldham reached the FA Cup semi-finals in 1990 and 1994, but were beaten by local rivals Man. United after replays on both occasions!

⚽ Oldham did reach Wembley in 1990 when they played Nottingham Forest in the League Cup final, but lost the match 1-0 thanks to a Nigel Jemson strike!

⚽ Joe Royle has been manager of Oldham twice. In his first spell at Boundary Park, he guided the club to the Premier League before resigning after 12 years in charge!

FAB FACT!
Peterborough manager Darren Ferguson is the son of Man. United boss Sir Alex! Fergie Junior played 30 games for United in the early 1990s!

Craig Mackail-Smith

POSH ARE GOING UP!
www.theposh.com

Peterborough celebrate promotion from League 1 in 2009

CLUB HISTORY!

The original Peterborough & Fletton club was suspended by The FA in 1932-33, and two years later United were formed after a meeting at the now-demolished Angel Hotel.

After World War Two, Posh won six Midland League titles, including five on the bounce from 1956 to 1960, then lifted the Division Four title in their first Football League season in 1961.

After missing out on promotion to the Championship in the last match of the 1978 season, Peterborough were relegated and spent 12 seasons back in League 2. By 1991, they returned to League 1.

The 1991-92 season is remembered for knocking Newcastle and Liverpool out the League Cup, and a play-off final victory against Stockport at Wembley. The following season the club were tenth in the Championship, their highest ever finish.

Posh slowly slipped down the leagues, but under boss Barry Fry they beat Darlington 1-0 in the 2000 League 2 play-off final. After a five-season stay in League 1, relegation followed, but Darren Ferguson has since led them back to the Championship!

Terry Bly in action against Portsmouth in 1961

⚽ In Peterborough's first season in the Football League in 1960-61, super striker Terry Bly scored an incredible 52 goals as Posh were crowned League 2 champions!

⚽ Peterborough's Argentina-inspired away kit for the 2009-10 season was first used as the club's home strip in 1978 and 1979, when Posh were stuck in League 1!

⚽ After taking over as Posh boss in 2007, Darren Ferguson won two promotions in a row as the London Road side climbed back to the Championship for the first time since 1994!

Welcome to Peterborough United
London Road

CLUB STATS!

Stadium: London Road
Capacity: 15,000
Formed: 1934
Nickname: The Posh
Manager: Darren Ferguson
Captain: Russell Martin
Record signing: Joe Lewis from Norwich, £400,000
Biggest win: 9-1 v Barnet, 1998
Biggest defeat: 8-1 v Northampton, 1946
Highest attendance: 30,096 v Swansea, 1965
Home kit: Blue and white shirts, white shorts and socks
Away kit: Sky blue and white striped shirts, black shorts, sky blue socks
Honours: League 2 (2)

Darren Ferguson (second from the right)

TOMMY ROBSON

The rapid left winger joined Peterborough from Newcastle in 1968 and stayed for 13 seasons, netting 111 goals before joining Nuneaton Borough in 1981!

KEN CHARLERY

'King Kenny' became a Posh legend after scoring twice in the 1992 League 1 Play-off Final against Stockport, including an 89th-minute winner!

SIMON DAVIES

The Wales midfielder was in top-class form at London Road in the late 1990s, which earned him a £700,000 move to Premier League side Tottenham!

PLYMOUTH ARGYLE
★ COCA-COLA CHAMPIONSHIP ★

FAB FACT!
The ship in the centre of Plymouth's badge is the *Mayflower*, which took the Pilgrims across the Atlantic to Plymouth, USA, in 1620!

Karl Duguid

The Pilgrims win promotion in 2004

CLUB HISTORY!

A coffee house called the Borough Arms was the meeting place for a group of students who formed Argyle Football Club in 1886. The Argyle name has been attributed to army regiment Argyll & Sutherland Highlanders, or a local street called Argyle Terrace.

The club became Plymouth Argyle after turning professional in 1903, and finished runners-up in Division Three South six seasons in a row between 1922 and 1927, but never got promoted.

In recent years, Plymouth almost reached Wembley with their incredible run to the FA Cup semi-finals in 1984. Then despite the appointment of goalkeeper Peter Shilton as player-manager in 1992, they were relegated to League 1 at the end of the season.

Paul Sturrock turned the club around, taking The Pilgrims from fourth-bottom of League 2 in 2000 to promotion in less than two years. The League 1 title then arrived in 2004.

Plymouth have since spent their last six campaigns in the Championship. After the return of Sturrock in November 2007, the club escaped relegation to League 1 by five points in 2008-09!

Home Park

CLUB STATS!

Stadium: Home Park

Capacity: 20,000

Formed: 1886

Nickname: The Pilgrims

Manager: Paul Sturrock

Captain: Karl Duguid

Record signing: Steve MacLean from Cardiff, £500,000

Biggest win: 8-1 v Millwall (1932) and Hartlepool (1994)

Biggest defeat: 9-0 v Stoke, 1960

Highest attendance: 43,596 v Aston Villa, 1936

Home kit: Green shirts and socks, white shorts

Away kit: White shirts and socks, green shorts

Honours: League 1 (2), Division Three South (2), League 2 (1)

Plymouth take on Watford at Villa Park in the 1984 FA Cup semi-final

⚽ Paul Sturrock is currently in his second spell in charge at Home Park. The Pilgrims won League 2 with a massive 102 points in 2001-02 during his first spell with the club!

⚽ Plymouth and Newcastle fans will have to travel for hours to watch their teams play each other in 2009-10. The clubs are 410 miles apart, the furthest distance between two league clubs!

⚽ The Pilgrims shocked the football world in 1984 when, as a struggling League 1 side, they reached the FA Cup semi-finals. They eventually lost 1-0 to runners-up Watford!

Paul Sturrock gives his orders

CLUB LEGENDS!

MATCH checks out the club's greatest players!

TOMMY TYNAN

Tynan moved to Plymouth after failing to break into the Liverpool first team in the 1970s. In 1985, the striker was top scorer in the Football League with 31 goals!

GRAHAM COUGHLAN

The defender's four-year spell at Home Park saw him crowned Player Of The Year in 2002. He played 177 league games for Plymouth and scored 25 goals!

SYLVAN EBANKS-BLAKE

Before his £1.5 million move to Wolves in 2008, the former Man. United trainee banged in 21 goals in 66 league games for The Pilgrims!

PORTSMOUTH
★ BARCLAYS PREMIER LEAGUE ★

FAB FACT!
Portsmouth were the First English club to play a match under Floodlights when they lost 2-0 to Newcastle at Fratton Park in February 1956!

Hermann Hreidarsson and Nadir Belhadj

2008 WINNERS

FAB FACT! Portsmouth held the FA Cup for seven years after beating Wolves in the 1939 Final! It wasn't played again until 1946 because of World War Two!

Pompey beat Cardiff at Wembley to win the 2008 FA Cup Final

CLUB HISTORY!

The club was founded on April 5, 1898 when a group of five sports and businessmen decided to buy a plot of land close to Goldsmith Avenue, which later became Portsmouth FC's home, Fratton Park.

By 1920, they were in Division Three South and won promotion in 1924. Two FA Cup final defeats followed in 1927 and 1934, but cup success finally arrived in 1939 with a 4-1 win over Wolves.

After World War Two, the league title arrived at Fratton Park in 1949 and 1950, but they had slumped to League 1 by the start of the 1961-62 season. Pompey bounced back a year later.

After crashing down to League 2 by the late 1970s, the fightback began as they clawed their way up to the top flight under Alan Ball. They also reached the FA Cup semi-finals under Jim Smith in 1992.

The 21st Century saw Harry Redknapp in charge for two spells. He guided Pompey to Prem survival in 2006 when they looked certain to be relegated, then FA Cup glory in 2008. Tony Adams was sacked shortly after taking over from Redknapp, so Paul Hart will be hoping for better luck in the 2009-10 season!

Fratton Park

John Portsmouth FC Westwood goes crazy at Portman Road

⚽ The club's most famous fan is called John Portsmouth FC Westwood. He officially changed his name by deed poll and has an incredible 60 tattoos plastered all over his body!

⚽ Pompey and England goalkeeper David James broke the Premier League appearance record in 2008-09 when he played his 536th match in a 2-0 win against Man. City!

⚽ Portsmouth have only ever taken part in one competitive penalty shoot-out. After a goalless draw in the 1992 FA Cup semi-final replay against Liverpool, they lost 3-1 on spot-kicks!

CLUB STATS!

Stadium: Fratton Park
Capacity: 20,338
Formed: 1898
Nickname: Pompey
Manager: Paul Hart
Captain: Sylvain Distin
Record signing: Peter Crouch from Liverpool, £11 million
Biggest win: 9-1 v Notts County, 1927
Biggest defeat: 10-0 v Leicester, 1928
Highest attendance: 51,385 v Derby, 1949
Home kit: Blue shirts, white shorts, red socks
Away kit: White shirts and socks, blue shorts
Honours: English League title (2), Championship (1), League 1 (3), FA Cup (2)

Sylvain Distin

CLUB LEGENDS!

MATCH checks out the club's greatest players!

JIMMY DICKINSON

Capped 48 times by England, 'Gentleman Jim' spent his whole career at Fratton Park, making 764 appearances and winning league titles in 1949 and 1950!

ALAN KNIGHT

The awesome goalkeeper is the only Pompey star to have played for the club in all four divisions. 'The Legend' was a Fratton Park hero from 1978 to 2000!

DAVID JAMES

Jamo took the England No.1 spot back from Paul Robinson after some ace displays for Pompey, and set a Premier League clean sheet record of 142 in 2007!

FAB FACT! Deepdale is home to the National Football Museum, which houses the ball that Sir Geoff Hurst hit a hat-trick with in the 1966 World Cup Final!

Neil Mellor and Sean St. Ledger

Preston captain Tom Smith shows off the FA Cup in 1938

CLUB HISTORY!

Preston's history can be traced back over 140 years to 1862, when North End Cricket and Rugby Club was formed. However, it wasn't until 1878 that the team began to take football seriously.

Preston signed goalkeeper Arthur Wharton in 1886, the first black player in English footy history, though he wasn't part of the team that won the double in 1889 or the league title a year later.

After moving between the top flight and the Championship, Preston lost the 1937 FA Cup Final before beating Huddersfield 1-0 to lift the trophy for the second time in 1938.

After World War Two, Preston suffered relegation to the Championship in 1961 and lost the 1964 FA Cup Final to West Ham. North End have never returned to the top flight since, even under big-name managers like Bobby Charlton and Alan Ball.

Promotion followed under David Moyes in 2000, and with Billy Davies in the hotseat they just missed out on promotion to the Prem after losing 1-0 to West Ham in the 2005 play-off final. Alan Irvine will be looking to go one better in 2009-10!

Preston's 1888-89 double-winning team

⚽ Preston almost reached the Championship play-off final in 2008-09 after ending the season in sixth place, but they lost 2-1 on aggregate to Sheffield United in the semi-finals!

⚽ The Lilywhites became the first ever winners of the double in 1888-89. Preston's greatest ever team were unbeaten throughout the entire season in both the league and the FA Cup!

⚽ Before taking over at Goodison Park, Everton manager David Moyes was in charge at Deepdale. Moyes led his North End side to the League 1 title in 2000!

Deepdale

CLUB STATS!

Stadium: Deepdale

Capacity: 24,000

Formed: 1881

Nickname: The Lilywhites

Manager: Alan Irvine

Captain: Callum Davidson

Record signing: David Healy from Man. United, £1.5 million

Biggest win: 26-0 v Hyde, 1887

Biggest defeat: 7-0 v Blackpool, 1948

Highest attendance: 42,684 v Arsenal, 1938

Home kit: White shirts and socks, blue shorts

Away kit: Red shirts, shorts and socks

Honours: English League title (2), Championship (3), League 1 (2), League 2 (1), FA Cup (2)

Callum Davidson

SIR TOM FINNEY

The Preston superstar only made his official debut at 24, but went on to spend his entire career with his hometown club and won 76 England caps!

BILL SHANKLY

Before becoming a legendary manager at Liverpool, Shankly played nearly 300 matches for North End and won the FA Cup in 1938 against Huddersfield!

YOUL MAWENE

Apart from missing 2006-07 with a cruciate ligament injury, Preston's awesome centre-back has been in great form since joining from Derby in 2004!

FAB FACT!
QPR haven't always played in blue and white hooped shirts. At the start of the 20th Century, Rangers wore green and white hoops!

Damion Stewart

Mike Keen lifts the League Cup at Wembley in 1967

CLUB LEGENDS!

MATCH checks out the club's greatest players!

RODNEY MARSH

After a spell at Fulham, Marsh moved to QPR and scored 44 goals in his first full season. He also netted the equaliser in the 1967 League Cup Final!

CLUB HISTORY!

Former students of Droop Street Board School formed the original club, St. Jude's, in 1882. They only became known as QPR after they merged with Christchurch Rangers in 1886.

The club played at 20 different grounds before finally settling at Loftus Road in 1917. Their first title arrived in 1948, when they were crowned Division Three South champions.

In March 1967, QPR became the first League 1 side to lift the League Cup, then spent a year in the top flight before a four-year stay in the Championship.

With legendary names such as Stan Bowles and Gerry Francis, they missed out on the top-flight title by a point in 1976. Terry Venables took over in 1980 and led them to the FA Cup final.

With Gerry Francis in the hotseat, QPR finished fifth in the first ever Premier League season. But after Francis left for Spurs, the West London club crumbled and by 2001 they were in League 1. After four managers in 2008-09, former Ipswich boss Jim Magilton was given the task of bringing the glory days back to Loftus Road!

Loftus Road

CLUB STATS!

Stadium:	Loftus Road
Capacity:	18,682
Formed:	1885
Nickname:	Rangers
Manager:	Jim Magilton
Captain:	Martin Rowlands
Record signing:	Alejandro Faurlin from Institute, £3.5 million
Biggest win:	9-2 v Tranmere, 1960
Biggest defeat:	8-1 v Mansfield (1965) and Man. United (1969)
Highest attendance:	35,353 v Leeds, 1974
Home kit:	Blue and white hooped shirts and socks, white shorts
Away kit:	Red and black hooped shirts and socks, red shorts
Honours:	Championship (1), League 1 (1), Division Three South (1), League Cup (1)

STAN BOWLES

Loftus Road's cult hero bagged Rodney Marsh's No.10 shirt in 1972, and went on to become one of Rangers' key players in their 1970s glory days!

QPR's famous plastic pitch

⚽ QPR became the first English league club to replace their grass pitch with an artificial surface in 1981-82. The Omniturf pitch was torn up after seven seasons!

⚽ The 1981-82 season marked the last time QPR reached a major cup final. Rangers lost 1-0 in the FA Cup final replay after drawing the first match 1-1 against Spurs!

⚽ QPR played in the UEFA Cup in 1976-77. After beating SK Brann 11-0 in the first round, they eventually lost on penalties to AEK Athens in the quarter-finals!

Mikele Leigertwood

LES FERDINAND

Before becoming a hero on Tyneside, 'Sir Les' was a QPR goal king. His £6 million move to Newcastle is still the most Rangers have got for a player!

READING
★ COCA-COLA CHAMPIONSHIP ★

FAB FACT!
Before joining Stoke in 2008, centre-back Ibrahima Sonko was nicknamed 'Superman' due to his powerful headers!

Shane Long

Steve Death denies the Arsenal forwards

CLUB HISTORY!

A meeting held at the Bridge Street Rooms in 1871 saw the formation of Reading, who took the nickname 'The Biscuitmen' after the Huntley & Palmers biscuit company in the town.

In 1896 the club moved to Elm Park, which was to remain their stadium for the next 102 years as they battled it out in the bottom two divisions of English football.

Reading were crowned champions of League 1 in 1986 and promotion to the Premier League nearly arrived in 1995, but The Royals threw away a 2-0 half-time lead in the play-off final and eventually lost 4-3 to Bolton after extra-time.

The club moved from Elm Park to the Madejski Stadium three years later and in March 2006 were promoted to the Premier League for the first time in their history, scoring 99 goals and losing just two matches in the entire Championship season.

Reading finished an impressive eighth in their first season in the top flight, but were relegated in 2008. Steve Coppell almost secured a return at the first attempt, but lost out in the play-offs!

Reading take the old Second Division title in 1992

⚽ Reading's Championship-winning side of 2005-06 set an unbelievable record. The Royals bagged an incredible 106 points as they ran away with the title!

⚽ Steve Coppell resigned as Reading boss after six seasons in charge in 2009. The Royals just missed out on bouncing back to the Premier League after losing to Burnley in the play-offs!

⚽ Reading fans have seen some legendary players wear the club's kit over the years, including Sir Matt Busby, George Best, Kerry Dixon, Steve Sidwell and Nicky Shorey!

The Madejski Stadium

CLUB STATS!

Stadium: Madejski Stadium

Capacity: 24,161

Formed: 1871

Nickname: The Royals

Manager: Brendan Rodgers

Captain: Ivar Ingimarsson

Record signing: Emerse Fae from Nantes, £2.5 million

Biggest win: 10-2 v Crystal Palace, 1946

Biggest defeat: 18-0 v Preston, 1894

Highest attendance: 33,042 v Brentford, 1927 (at Elm Park)

Home kit: Blue and white hooped shirts, blue shorts and socks

Away kit: White shirts and socks, green shorts

Honours: Championship (1), League 1 (2), Division Three South (1), League 2 (1), Full Members Cup (1)

Steve Coppell

ROBIN FRIDAY

Reading's Player Of The Millennium scored 46 goals in four seasons, including a volley from a corner which is regarded as the club's best ever strike!

STEVE SIDWELL

Aston Villa midfielder Sidwell was a key player in the club's 2006 title-winning side and scored 30 goals before moving to Chelsea on a free transfer!

KEVIN DOYLE

The Republic Of Ireland striker was Reading's Player Of The Season in 2006 and scored more headers than any other Premier League player in 2007!

PORT VALE
★ COCA-COLA LEAGUE 2 ★

FAB FACT! Darts legend Phil 'The Power' Taylor and pop superstar Robbie Williams are both massive Vale Fans!

CLUB STATS!

Stadium: Vale Park

Capacity: 18,982

Formed: 1876

Nickname: The Valiants

Manager: Micky Adams

Captain: Marc Richards

Record signing: Jon McCarthy from York and Gareth Ainsworth from Lincoln, £500,000

Biggest win: 9-1 v Chesterfield, 1932

Biggest defeat: 10-0 v Sheffield United (1892) and Notts County (1895)

Highest attendance: 49,768 v Aston Villa, 1960

Home kit: Black and white striped shirts, black and white shorts, black socks

Away kit: Black shirts with white pin stripes, white shorts, black socks

Honours:
Division Three North (1930 & 1954),
League 2 (1959),
Johnstone's Paint Trophy (1993 & 2001)

Port Vale celebrate cup glory in 2001

CLUB HISTORY!

Known as Burslem Port Vale after they were formed in 1876, The Valiants joined Division Two way back in 1892. Financial problems forced them to resign from the league in 1907, but they replaced Leeds City in 1919 and never looked back. A short stay in the Championship ended in 1957 and it took 32 years before Port Vale returned to the division via the play-offs. As the 21st Century arrived, the club slipped into massive debt and dropped down the league. Micky Adams will be aiming to get his new club out of League 2 in 2009-10!

⚽ Port Vale have a great record in the Johnstone's Paint Trophy. They've appeared in the final twice and won them both – against Stockport in 1993 and Brentford in 2001.

⚽ Ex-Port Vale midfielder Chris Birchall played for Trinidad & Tobago at World Cup 2006. He was the first white player to line up for the Soca Warriors at the Finals!

⚽ Due to its size and the plans the club had for its development, Vale Park was known as 'The Wembley Of The North' when the club first moved there in 1950!

Micky Adams

ROCHDALE
★ COCA-COLA LEAGUE 2 ★

FAB FACT!
Captain *Gary Jones* holds the record for the most appearances in a Rochdale shirt. The super skipper has played 347 times since 1998!

CLUB STATS!

Stadium: *Spotland Stadium*

Capacity: *10,208*

Formed: *1907*

Nickname: *The Dale*

Manager: *Keith Hill*

Captain: *Gary Jones*

Record signing: *Paul Connor from Stoke, £150,000*

Biggest win: *8-1 v Chesterfield, 1926*

Biggest defeat: *9-1 v Tranmere, 1931*

Highest attendance:
24,231 v Notts County, 1949

Home kit: *Black and blue striped shirts, white shorts, blue socks*

Away kit: *Purple shirts with white trim, purple shorts and socks*

Honours:
None

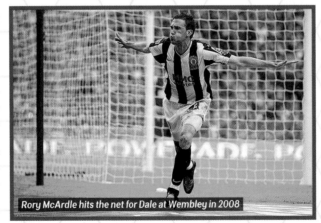
Rory McArdle hits the net for Dale at Wembley in 2008

CLUB HISTORY!

Since Rochdale were formed in 1907, Spotland has only seen one promotion (in 1969) and one relegation (in 1974) since they joined the league in 1921. Dale became the only club from the bottom division to reach an English cup final when they lost 4-0 to Norwich over two legs in the 1962 League Cup Final. Following relegation in 1974, they failed to finish in the top half of League 2 for another 14 years, but after coming close in the play-offs in recent years, a route out of the basement division can't be far away!

⚽ Rochdale reached the League 2 play-off semi-finals in 2002 and 2009, and were beaten 3-2 by Stockport in the 2008 final despite taking the lead at Wembley!

⚽ Rochdale fans must be sick of watching League 2 football. They've spent the last 35 years in the bottom division – longer than any other club!

⚽ The Spotland side used to play in black and white striped home shirts, but the club switched over to their blue kit at the start of the 1949-50 season!

Rochdale host Cambridge, 1974

ROTHERHAM UNITED
★ COCA-COLA LEAGUE 2 ★

CLUB STATS!

Stadium: Don Valley Stadium

Capacity: 25,000

Formed: 1870

Nickname: The Merry Millers

Manager: Mark Robins

Captain: Pablo Mills

Record signing: Tony Towner from Millwall, Lee Glover from Port Vale, Alan Lee from Burnley and Martin Butler from Reading, £150,000

Biggest win: 8-0 v Oldham, 1947

Biggest defeat: 11-1 v Bradford, 1928

Highest attendance: 25,170 v Sheffield United, 1952

Home kit: Red and white shirts, white shorts and red socks

Away kit: Sky blue and white shirts, shorts and socks

Honours:
League 1 (1981),
Division Three North (1951),
League 2 (1989),
Johnstone's Paint Trophy (1996)

Mark Robins (right) watches his players in action

⚽ Rotherham began the 2008-09 season on minus 17 points, but after 21 victories, Mark Robins' side steered clear of relegation by finishing in 14th spot!

⚽ Rotherham reached the first ever League Cup final in 1961, but after winning the first leg 2-0, The Merry Millers were beaten 3-0 by Aston Villa in the second leg!

⚽ Boss Mark Robins scored two goals for Norwich on the opening day of the first Premier League season in 1992-93 as The Canaries beat Arsenal 4-2 at Highbury!

CLUB HISTORY!

The club traces its roots back to 1870, but United were formed after Rotherham County and Rotherham Town teamed up in 1925. Their first kit was amber and black, but they changed to red and white in 1928. In 1954-55 Rotherham finished third in the Championship, but they were denied top-flight football on goal difference. The Millers then won the Johnstone's Paint Trophy in 1996 and secured promotions in 2000 and 2001. They dropped into League 2 in 2007, but will be aiming for big things at Don Valley in 2009-10!

Wembley joy in 1996

PLAY OFF WINNERS 2009

COCA-COLA LEAGUE 1 PLAY OFF WINNERS 2009
SCUNTHORPE UNITED F.C.

FAB FACT!
Scunthorpe's rivals include Doncaster, Grimsby and Lincoln, but their biggest derby is against Hull who play just across the Humber River!

CLUB STATS!

Stadium: Glanford Park

Capacity: 9,203

Formed: 1899

Nickname: The Iron

Manager: Nigel Adkins

Captain: Cliff Byrne

Record signing: Martin Paterson from Stoke, £425,000

Biggest win: 9-0 v Boston, 1953

Biggest defeat: 8-0 v Carlisle, 1952

Highest attendance: 23,935 v Portsmouth, 1954 (at the Old Showground)

Home kit: Claret and blue striped shirts, claret shorts, claret and blue socks

Away kit: Sky blue striped shirts, dark blue shorts, sky blue socks

Honours:
League 1 (2007),
Division Three North (1958)

Ian Botham gets his boots checked before a Scunthorpe reserve game

CLUB HISTORY!

Nigel Adkins is Scunthorpe's 25th boss since they teamed up with North Lindsey United to become Scunthorpe & Lindsey United, a name they kept until 1950 when they were elected to the Football League. Fourth place in the Championship in 1962 earned Scunthorpe's highest finish, but by 1968 they were back in the bottom league. The 1990s saw a move to Glanford Park and trips to Wembley in 1992 and 1999. Current manager Nigel Adkins then won League 1 in 2007, and bagged a return to the Championship via the play-offs in 2009!

⚽ Scunthorpe reached Wembley twice in 2008-09. The Iron beat Millwall 3-2 in the League 1 Play-off final, but lost to Luton 3-2 in the Johnstone's Paint Trophy final!

⚽ Cricket legend Sir Ian Botham, Liverpool greats Kevin Keegan and Ray Clemence, and Sheffield Wednesday boss Brian Laws all played for Scunthorpe!

⚽ Ex-Scunthorpe striker Billy Sharp was on fire in the 2006-07 season. On their way to the League 1 title, Sharp scored 32 goals before moving to Sheffield United!

League 1 champions, 2007

SHEFFIELD UNITED

★ COCA-COLA CHAMPIONSHIP ★

FAB FACT!
Before Bramall Lane started hosting Sheffield United's home games in 1899, the famous old ground was used for cricket matches!

Brian Howard

William 'Fatty' Foulke picks the ball out of the net against Tottenham in 1901

CLUB LEGENDS!

MATCH checks out the club's greatest players!

JIMMY HAGAN

Hagan earned just £7 a week and his United career was interrupted by World War Two, but the deadly forward still played nearly 400 games for the club!

KEITH EDWARDS

During two spells with the Yorkshire side in the 1970s and 1980s, Edwards' 171 goals in 293 starts saw The Blades climb out of lower league trouble!

CHRIS MORGAN

Sheffield United's captain has been sent off more times than any other Blades player, but he's still made over 200 league appearances since 2003!

CLUB HISTORY!

Charles Clegg, the president of Yorkshire County Cricket Club, decided to form Sheffield United in March 1889.

Within six years, The Blades had become one of the toughest opponents in English football as a great 30-year period saw them win the league title once, and finish runners-up twice. They also walked away with the FA Cup in 1899, 1902, 1915 and 1925, as well as being losing finalists in 1901 and 1936.

Things changed for United after World War Two, and between 1946 and 1976 the Bramall Lane side moved between the Championship and the top flight seven times.

By 1981, they hit their lowest point when they were relegated to League 2, but under influential bosses Dave Bassett and Neil Warnock the club returned to the top flight.

The Blades suffered relegation on goal difference back to the Championship on the final day of the 2006-07 season, a position from which they haven't recovered. Manager Kevin Blackwell will be hoping his side can return to the Premier League in 2010!

Bramall Lane

CLUB STATS!

Stadium: Bramall Lane
Capacity: 32,500
Formed: 1889
Nickname: The Blades
Manager: Kevin Blackwell
Captain: Chris Morgan
Record signing: James Beattie from Everton, £4 million
Biggest win: 10-0 v Burslem Port Vale, 1892
Biggest defeat: 13-0 v Bolton, 1890
Highest attendance: 68,287 v Leeds, 1936
Home kit: Red and white striped shirts, black shorts and socks
Away kit: White and burgundy shirts, shorts and socks
Honours: English League title (1), Championship (1), League 2 (1), FA Cup (4)

Sheffield United's 1915 FA Cup-winning team

⚽ Sheffield United were just 90 minutes away from a return to the Premier League in 2009, but it wasn't to be The Blades' day as they lost 1-0 to Burnley in the Championship play-off final!

⚽ The 2002-03 season under manager Neil Warnock will be remembered for Sheffield United's run to the semi-finals of both the FA and League Cups. The Blades lost them both!

⚽ Sheffield United have loads of famous fans who worship the Yorkshire club. The biggest of them all is Sean Bean, who played Boromir in Peter Jackson's The Fellowship Of The Ring!

Matt Kilgallon

SHEFFIELD WEDNESDAY

★ COCA-COLA CHAMPIONSHIP ★

FAB FACT!
Sheffield Wednesday are nicknamed The Owls, because Hillsborough is in a north-west part of the city that used to be called Owlerton!

Marcus Tudgay

Coca-Cola

A LEAGUE 1 PLAY OFF WINNERS
SHEFFIELD WEDNESDAY F.C

The Owls beat Hartlepool to clinch promotion from League 1 in 2005

CLUB HISTORY!

The Hillsborough side have worn blue and white shirts since they were formed by the Sheffield Wednesday Cricket Club in 1867, making them the fourth oldest existing league club after Notts County, Nottingham Forest and Chesterfield.

Wednesday played at various grounds in the city, including Highfield and Olive Grove, before moving to Owlerton in 1899. The club later renamed the stadium Hillsborough in 1912.

Wednesday were on fire in their early days, reaching the FA Cup final in 1890, winning the cup in 1896 and 1907, and bagging league titles in 1903 and 1904. A trophy wasn't lifted again until 1935.

The 1950s saw the club swap Championship football for the top flight on regular occasions. They then suffered heartache in the 1966 FA Cup Final after throwing away a 2-0 lead against Everton.

During the 1980s and 1990s, Wednesday were a top-flight club under Ron Atkinson and Trevor Francis, but they couldn't maintain their form and by 2003 were relegated to League 1. A play-off win under Paul Sturrock saw a Championship return in 2005!

Hillsborough

CLUB STATS!

Stadium: Hillsborough
Capacity: 39,812
Formed: 1867
Nickname: The Owls
Manager: Brian Laws
Captain: Darren Purse
Record signing: Paolo Di Canio from Celtic, £4.5 million
Biggest win: 12-0 v Halliwell, 1891
Biggest defeat: 10-0 v Aston Villa, 1912
Highest attendance: 72,841 v Man. City, 1934
Home kit: Blue and white striped shirts, black shorts, blue socks
Away kit: Yellow shirts, blue shorts and socks
Honours: English League title (4), Championship (5), FA Cup (3), League Cup (1), Community Shield (1)

Glory for Wednesday in the 1991 League Cup Final

⚽ Sheffield Wednesday's last victory in a major cup final was nearly 20 years ago, when Trevor Francis' side beat FA Cup holders Man. United 1-0 to win the League Cup!

⚽ The Owls are supported by some crazy fans. Paul Gregory, also known as Tango, never wears a shirt at away matches and the club's brass band can be always heard be at Hillsborough!

⚽ Sheffield Wednesday lost two cup finals to Arsenal in 1993. The Owls lost 2-1 in the FA Cup final replay, and also went down 2-1 to The Gunners in the League Cup final at Wembley!

Jermaine Johnson celebrates

CLUB LEGENDS!

MATCH checks out the club's greatest players!

ANDREW WILSON

Wednesday's fierce striker spent 16 seasons with the club, netting 216 goals in 545 appearances after joining from Glasgow Clyde back in 1900!

DAVID HIRST

Hirst scored one minute after coming on as a sub in his first match against Everton, and smashed home 149 goals for The Owls before leaving in 1997!

PAOLO DI CANIO

Nicknamed 'The Volcano', Di Canio was mega skilful and scored some class goals, but will be remembered for pushing over referee Paul Alcock in 1998!

SHREWSBURY TOWN

★ COCA-COLA LEAGUE 2 ★

CLUB STATS!

Stadium: The ProStar Stadium

Capacity: 9,875

Formed: 1886

Nickname: The Shrews

Manager: Paul Simpson

Captain: Graham Coughlan

Record signing: John Dungworth from Aldershot and Mark Blake from Southampton, £100,000

Biggest win: 11-2 v Marine, 1995

Biggest defeat: 8-1 v Norwich (1952) and Coventry (1963)

Highest attendance: 18,917 v Walsall, 1961

Home kit: Blue, amber and white shirts, shorts and socks

Away kit: Black, white and red shirts, shorts and socks

Honours:
League 1 (1979),
League 2 (1994),
Welsh Cup (1891, 1938, 1977, 1979, 1984 & 1985)

England Under-21 star Joe Hart (left)

CLUB HISTORY!

Shrewsbury were a non-league club until they joined the Football League in 1950, and just 11 years later they managed to reach the semi-finals of the League Cup. A ten-year spell in the Championship followed from 1979 to 1989, but by 2003 they had slipped into the Conference, even though they did bounce back at the first attempt via the play-offs. Shrewsbury have since played in League 2, just missing out on promotion in 2008-09 when Gillingham scored a 90th-minute winner in the play-off final at Wembley!

Play-off heartbreak in 2007

⚽ Shrewsbury used to pay a guy called Fred Davies to row out in his boat and rescue footballs that had been booted into the River Severn on matchdays!

⚽ The Shrews are the only club to reach two play-off finals at the new Wembley stadium. They played in the League 2 showdown in 2007 and 2009, but lost both games!

⚽ Man. City and England Under-21 keeper Joe Hart used to play for Shrewsbury. The local lad played 54 league games before joining Man. City in a £1.5 million deal in 2006!

SOUTHAMPTON
★ COCA-COLA LEAGUE 1 ★

FAB FACT!
The *mayflower* on the club's crest represents the ship that took the Pilgrims from Southampton to Plymouth in the USA in 1620!

CLUB STATS!

Stadium: St. Mary's Stadium

Capacity: 32,689

Formed: 1885

Nickname: The Saints

Manager: Alan Pardew

Captain: Kelvin Davis

Record signing: Rory Delap from Derby, £4 million

Biggest win: 9-3 v Wolves, 1965

Biggest defeat: 8-0 v Tottenham (1936) and Everton (1971)

Highest attendance: 32,104 v Liverpool, 2003

Home kit: Red and white striped shirts and socks, black shorts

Away kit: Yellow and blue shirts, yellow shorts and socks

Honours:
League 1 (1960),
Division Three South (1922),
FA Cup (1976)

The Saints celebrate their shock FA Cup win in 1976

CLUB HISTORY!

Southampton FC was formed by members of the St. Mary's Church of England Young Men's Association way back in 1885. A 31-year stay in the Championship began in 1922 and The Saints had to ground share with Pompey after a bomb landed on their old ground, The Dell, during World War Two. In 1966 they were promoted to the top flight, but were relegated in 1974, bouncing back four years later and finishing second in 1984. The Saints lost the FA Cup final in 2003 and their 27-year stay in the top flight ended in 2005, with another drop to League 1 in 2009!

Southampton v Brighton, 1898

⚽ Southampton have a mega rivalry with neighbours Portsmouth. Harry Redknapp was Saints boss in 2004-05 before returning to Pompey for a second spell!

⚽ Loads of current Premier League stars came through the club's youth academy, including Theo Walcott, Wayne Bridge, Gareth Bale and Chris Baird!

⚽ Southampton caused one of the biggest FA Cup final shocks of all-time when they beat mighty Man. United 1-0 in 1976. Bobby Stokes hit the winner in the 83rd minute!

SOUTHEND UNITED
★ COCA-COLA LEAGUE 1 ★

FAB FACT!
Shrimpers manager Steve Tilson is the fifth longest-serving boss in England. He took over as caretaker gaffer in November 1993!

CLUB STATS!

Stadium: Roots Hall
Capacity: 12,168
Formed: 1906
Nickname: The Shrimpers
Manager: Steve Tilson
Captain: Adam Barrett
Record signing: Stan Collymore from Crystal Palace, £750,000
Biggest win: 10-1 v Golders Green (1935), Brentwood (1968) and Aldershot (1990)
Biggest defeat: 9-1 v Brighton, 1966
Highest attendance: 31,090 v Liverpool, 1979
Home kit: Blue and white shirts, blue shorts and white socks
Away kit: Yellow and blue shirts and socks, yellow shorts
Honours:
League 1 (2006),
League 2 (1980),
Southern League Division Two (1907 & 1908)

Freddy Eastwood's rocket free-kick stuns Man. United in 2006

CLUB HISTORY!

The Blue Boar pub in Southend was the setting for the formation of the club in 1906, with The Shrimpers becoming a Football League side just 14 years later. Moving to Roots Hall in 1955, Southend bounced between the bottom two divisions before back-to-back promotions saw them finish 12th in the Championship in 1991-92 – the highest league finish in their history. After slipping down to the bottom flight, Steve Tilson's arrival in 1993 saw the start of the club's most successful period, and they just missed out on the play-offs in 2009!

⚽ Southend won back-to-back promotions in 2005 and 2006. After beating Lincoln 2-0 in the League 2 play-off final, they claimed the League 1 title a year later!

⚽ The Shrimpers reached two Johnstone's Paint Trophy finals on the bounce in 2004 and 2005, but lost them both 2-0 to Blackpool and Wrexham!

⚽ Back in 2006, Southend knocked holders Man. United out of the Carling Cup. Freddy Eastwood's stunning free-kick was the only goal of the fourth-round tie!

Ex-Southend boss Bobby Moore

STOCKPORT COUNTY
★ COCA-COLA LEAGUE 1 ★

FAB FACT!
County wore *blue and white* stripes after Argentina won the 1978 World Cup, but changed their kit after the UK fought them in the Falklands War!

CLUB STATS!

Stadium: Edgeley Park

Capacity: 10,812

Formed: 1883

Nickname: The Hatters

Manager: Gary Ablett

Captain: Michael Raynes

Record signing: Ian Moore from Nottingham Forest, £800,000

Biggest win: 13-0 v Halifax, 1934

Biggest defeat: 8-1 v Chesterfield, 1902

Highest attendance: 27,833 v Liverpool, 1950

Home kit: Blue and white shirts, blue shorts and white socks

Away kit: Orange and black shirts and shorts, orange socks

Honours:
Division Three North (1922 & 1937),
League 2 (1967)

Wayne Hennessey in action against Barnet in 2007

CLUB HISTORY!

Stockport County were formed in 1890, seven years after the club began playing as Heaton Norris Rovers, and became known as The Hatters because the town was famous for its hat-making. Since then Stockport fought to stay in the league on four occasions, but under Uruguayan boss Danny Bergara reached Wembley finals four times from 1992-94. After an impressive five-season stay in the Championship from 1998-2002, County slipped back to League Two, but won the play-off final against Rochdale in 2008!

⚽ Awesome Wolves and Wales keeper Wayne Hennessey set a Football League record with County in 2006-07 as Stockport went nine matches without conceding a goal!

⚽ Stockport had an amazing run in the 1996-97 League Cup. They beat Prem sides Blackburn, Southampton and West Ham on their way to the semi-finals!

⚽ The first ever Stockport County side played their home games at a park in Heaton Norris in the 19th Century, where they had to use a barn as a changing room!

Danny Bergara and Kevin Francis

FAB FACT!
Stoke Fans love singing 'Delilah' by ancient Welsh singer Tom Jones and were named the noisiest fans in the Premier League in 2008-09!

Liam Lawrence and Abdoulaye Faye

FAB FACT!
Rory Delap's monster long throws are legendary at the Britannia Stadium. He learnt to do them by throwing the javelin at school!

Stoke lift the League Cup in 1972

CLUB LEGENDS!

MATCH checks out the club's greatest players!

SIR STANLEY MATTHEWS

'The Wizard Of Dribble' burned past defenders as a right winger for Stoke. After two spells at the club, Matthews was 50 when he played his last match in 1965!

GORDON BANKS

Stoke's most-capped player with 36 England caps while at the Victoria Ground, Banks won the League Cup in 1972, one of his 246 appearances for Stoke!

PETER HOEKSTRA

Stoke's Player Of The Decade ripped up English defences from 2001 to 2004. The 6ft 3ins winger played 98 games for The Potters before retiring at 31 years old!

CLUB HISTORY!

Stoke may have been formed as early as 1863, but there is no evidence of any matches taking place. The Field Magazine's report that the club was created in 1868 is the club's starting date.

In 1878, Stoke moved to the Victoria Ground and became one of the Football League's original 12 teams in 1888-89.

A 17-year-old Stanley Matthews made his Stoke debut in 1932 as the club won promotion from the Championship, and for the rest of the decade The Potters took the top flight by storm.

Matthews left for Blackpool in 1947 and six years later Stoke were back in the Championship, but the England winger returned at the age of 46 and Stoke were promoted in 1963.

League Cup glory and FA Cup semi-final spots followed in the early 1970s, and Stoke spent a brief spell in the top flight in the 1980s. A period in League 1 was the club's low point from 1991-93.

Stoke then bagged two Johnstone's Paint Trophy wins, and after a forgettable spell in the Championship, they returned to the Prem after a draw against Leicester on the final day of 2007-08!

The Britannia Stadium

CLUB STATS!

Stadium: The Britannia
Capacity: 28,218
Formed: 1863
Nickname: The Potters
Manager: Tony Pulis
Captain: Abdoulaye Faye
Record signing: Dave Kitson from Reading, £5.5 million
Biggest win: 10-3 v West Brom, 1937
Biggest defeat: 10-0 v Preston, 1899
Highest attendance: 51,380 v Arsenal, 1937 (at the Victoria Ground)
Home kit: Red and white striped shirts, white shorts and socks
Away kit: Black and red shirts, black shorts and socks
Honours: Championship (2), League 1 (1), League Cup (1), Johnstone's Paint Trophy (2)

The Potters celebrate promotion to the Premier League in 2008

⚽ Stoke boss Tony Pulis is in his second spell in charge of The Potters. Johan Boskamp took over after Pulis was sacked in June 2005, but he was back in the hotseat a year later!

⚽ Stoke had a great first season in the Premier League in 2008-09. Their return to the top flight after 23 years saw the club finish 12th, and included wins against Tottenham and Arsenal!

⚽ The Potters' only victory in a major domestic cup final was nearly 40 years ago. They beat Chelsea in the 1972 League Cup Final thanks to goals from Terry Conroy and George Eastham!

Rory Delap winds up a long throw

SUNDERLAND

FAB FACT!
Sunderland became known as *The Black Cats* in 1997! Other suggestions for a new nickname were *The Miners*, *The Mackems* & *The Light Brigade!*

Kenwyne Jones

Captain Bobby Kerr lifts the FA Cup in 1973

CLUB HISTORY!

Schoolteacher James Allan, who was working in the city, set up Sunderland and District Teachers AFC in 1879, who became Sunderland a year later ahead of their first match against Ferryhill.

The club bagged the league title in just their second season in the Football League, and with Johnny Campbell scoring over 30 goals, Sunderland were champions again a season later.

More titles arrived in 1895, 1902, 1913 and 1936, while Sunderland even hit nine goals against arch rivals Newcastle in 1908. Their long stay in the top flight ended in 1958, and a last major trophy came in 1973 when they beat Leeds 1-0 in the FA Cup final.

After losing the 1985 League Cup Final and the 1992 FA Cup Final, Sunderland fought back to the Prem in the late 1990s, but were relegated with a record low of 19 points in 2003.

Roy Keane dragged Sunderland up from the bottom of the Championship to the title in 2007, but after a two-and-a-half year stay it was left to Ricky Sbragia to guide Sunderland to Prem safety. Steve Bruce took over ahead of the 2009-10 season!

The Stadium Of Light

The Black Cats parade the FA Cup at Wembley in 1937

⚽ Craig Gordon became the most expensive keeper in British football history when he joined from Hearts in August 2007. The Black Cats spent a massive £9 million on the Scotland star!

⚽ Before signing for Sunderland last summer, midfielder Lorik Cana used to play in France for Marseille. He's only the second Albanian player to score in the Champions League!

⚽ The cats on the club's crest are a tribute to the 1937 Cup Final, when Sunderland fan Billy Morris took a tiny black kitten to Wembley as a good luck charm and saw his side beat Preston 3-1!

CLUB STATS!

Stadium: Stadium Of Light
Capacity: 49,000
Formed: 1879
Nickname: The Black Cats
Manager: Steve Bruce
Captain: Lorik Cana
Record signing: Craig Gordon from Hearts, £9 million
Biggest win: 11-1 v Fairfield, 1895
Biggest defeat: 8-0 v Sheff. Wed (1911), West Ham (1968) and Watford (1982)
Highest attendance: 75,118 v Derby, 1933 (at Roker Park)
Home kit: Red and white striped shirts, black shorts and socks
Away kit: White and blue shirts, white shorts and socks
Honours: English League title (6), Championship (5), League 1 (1), FA Cup (2)

Grant Leadbitter

CLUB LEGENDS!

MATCH checks out the club's greatest players!

JIMMY MONTGOMERY

The Sunderland-born keeper made 627 appearances and is always remembered for his awesome double save against Leeds in the 1973 FA Cup Final!

NIALL QUINN

Sunderland's chairman arrived in the North East in 1996 as a striker from Man. City, and later became the first player to score at the Stadium Of Light!

KEVIN PHILLIPS

After forming a deadly strike partnership with Niall Quinn, Phillips netted 132 goals for Sunderland and played eight times for England!

FAB FACT!

Swansea's old *Vetch Field* stadium was built on a patch of ground where 'vetch' grew - a type of cabbage plant used to feed cows!

Garry Monk

Coca-Cola LEAGUE 1
CHAMPIONS 2008
SWANSEA CITY F.C.

Swansea storm to the League 1 title in 2008

CLUB HISTORY!

Football was exclusively played in North Wales before the game arrived in the south after a newspaper printed the rules in 1894. Swansea Town were formed in 1912, changing their name in 1970.

Before World War Two, Swansea won the Division Three South title in 1925, before finishing fifth in the Championship and reaching the FA Cup semi-finals the following season.

Another FA Cup semi-final appearance arrived in 1964, but The Swans were battling for survival in League 2 by the 1970s. The appointment of John Toshack in 1978 saw the club's fortunes change completely as they won promotion to the top flight in 1981.

Money problems saw Swansea back in League 2 by 1986, but yet another fightback was on the cards as the Welsh club won promotion to League 1 in 1988, then reached the play-offs in 1993.

Relegation to the Conference was avoided in 2003 and the club moved to the Liberty Stadium in 2005. A shoot-out defeat against Barnsley in 2006 saw The Swans miss out on promotion to the Championship, but the League 1 title soon followed in 2008!

The Liberty Stadium

CLUB STATS!

Stadium: Liberty Stadium
Capacity: 20,520
Formed: 1912
Nickname: The Swans
Manager: Paulo Sousa
Captain: Garry Monk
Record signing: Ashley Williams from Stockport, £400,000
Biggest win: 12-0 v Sliema Wanderers, 1982
Biggest defeat: 8-0 v Liverpool (1990) and Monaco (1991)
Highest attendance: 32,796 v Arsenal, 1968 (at Vetch Field)
Home kit: White shirts, black shorts and socks
Away kit: Red shirts, white shorts and socks
Honours: League 1 (1), Division Three South (2), League 2 (1), Johnstone's Paint Trophy (2), Welsh Cup (11)

Swansea v Peterborough, 1965

⚽ Swansea won promotion to the Championship in 2007-08 after topping League 1 with a massive 92 points. Striker Jason Scotland was the top scorer with 24 league goals!

⚽ The club's main rivals are Championship side Cardiff. In 50 league meetings, Swansea have won 18 games, the biggest a 5-1 victory in 1949, with 16 draws and 16 defeats!

⚽ Swans boss Paulo Sousa won 51 caps for Portugal. The classy midfielder was in the squad that reached the Euro 2000 semi-finals, before losing 2-1 to winners France!

Guillem Bauza

CLUB LEGENDS!

MATCH checks out the club's greatest players!

IVOR ALLCHURCH
The local lad had two spells at Swansea after World War Two. Allchurch's club record of 166 league goals still stands over 40 years after he retired!

LEE TRUNDLE
After signing from Wrexham in 2003, Trundle's showboating skills became famous on Soccer AM before he moved to Bristol City for a club record £1 million!

JASON SCOTLAND
The Trinidad & Tobago striker scored his 50th goal for the club in 2009 and was twice named in the PFA Team Of The Year before joining Wigan!

SWINDON TOWN
★ COCA-COLA LEAGUE 1 ★

CLUB STATS!

Stadium: *The County Ground*

Capacity: *14,800*

Formed: *1881*

Nickname: *Robins*

Manager: *Danny Wilson*

Captain: *Hasney Aljofree*

Record signing: *Joey Beauchamp from West Ham, £800,000*

Biggest win: *10-1 v Farnham United Breweries, 1925*

Biggest defeat: *10-1 v Man. City, 1930*

Highest attendance: *32,000 v Arsenal, 1972*

Home kit: *Red and white shirts, shorts and socks*

Away kit: *White and blue shirts, shorts and socks*

Honours:
*League 1 (1996),
League 2 (1986),
Southern League (1911 & 1914),
League Cup (1969),
Anglo-Italian Cup (1970)*

Swindon celebrate promotion in 1993

CLUB HISTORY!

After 41 years of playing non-league footy, Swindon joined the Football League in 1920 and chalked up their club-record 9-1 victory in the first game of the following season. The Robins' highlight over the next few decades was their League Cup win in 1969, before they set a League 2 record of 102 points on their way to the title in 1986. Glenn Hoddle led Swindon to the Prem in 1993, but after leaking 100 goals they suffered back-to-back relegations. Danny Wilson became Swindon's ninth boss in 11 years after taking over in December 2008!

⚽ Swindon won promotion to the Premier League in 1993. They'd been promoted three seasons earlier, but weren't allowed to go up after paying players illegally!

⚽ Swindon won the League Cup when they were playing in League 1. They shocked top-flight giants Arsenal 3-1 after extra-time at Wembley in 1969!

⚽ Over a 20-year spell, Swindon legend John Trollope set a Football League record at the County Ground. The defender played 770 matches – a record for one club!

League Cup winners, 1969

TORQUAY UNITED
★ COCA-COLA LEAGUE 2 ★

FAB FACT!
Leroy Rosenior was manager of Torquay for just ten minutes in 2007 before the club was taken over and he got sacked!

CLUB STATS!

Stadium: Plainmoor
Capacity: 6,104
Formed: 1899
Nickname: The Gulls
Manager: Paul Buckle
Captain: Chris Hargreaves
Record signing: Leon Constantine from Peterborough, £75,000
Biggest win: 9-0 v Swindon, 1952
Biggest defeat: 10-2 v Fulham (1931) and Luton (1933)
Highest attendance: 21,908 v Huddersfield, 1955
Home kit: Yellow and blue shirts, shorts and socks
Away kit: White shirts, shorts and socks
Honours: None

Torquay's black and white kit, 1953

CLUB HISTORY!

Sergeant-Major Edward Tomney set up Torquay in 1899. They merged with Ellacombe to form Torquay Town in 1910, sharing Plainmoor with Babbacombe until they merged in 1921. Then just six years later they were a Football League side. From 1972 the club struggled in League 2, and were nearly relegated twice to the Blue Square Premier in the 1980s. A shoot-out win against Blackpool in the 1991 League 2 Play-off Final saw promotion, but in 2007, after 80 years in the league, Torquay were relegated, returning in 2009!

The 1991 promotion party

⚽ After two seasons in the Blue Square Premier, Torquay bounced back to League 2 after beating Cambridge 2-0 in the play-off final at Wembley in 2009!

⚽ Sky Sports' Soccer AM presenter Helen Chamberlain is a massive Gulls fan. She goes to loads of games at Plainmoor and even has a Torquay United tattoo!

⚽ Torquay wore black and white striped shirts before changing to yellow and blue in 1954. Legend has it the new kit was based on the sand and sky of the seaside town!

TOTTENHAM HOTSPUR

★ BARCLAYS PREMIER LEAGUE ★

FAB FACT!
Tottenham manager Harry Redknapp is the uncle of Chelsea and England star Frank Lampard, who played under Harry at West Ham!

Robbie Keane

Jonathan Woodgate nets the winner in the 2008 Carling Cup Final

CLUB HISTORY!

Spurs were formed in 1882 when ex-students from Tottenham Grammar School and St. John's Presbyterian School teamed up. A year later the club was playing on Tottenham Marshes and wearing navy blue kits, later changing to red shirts in 1890.

Tottenham moved into White Hart Lane in 1899, before they became the only non-league club to win the FA Cup in 1901.

The 1961 Spurs side led by Danny Blanchflower were the first club in the 20th Century to win the double. Another FA Cup win followed a year later and in 1963 Spurs lifted the Cup Winners' Cup – Jimmy Greaves slammed home 37 league goals that season.

They won the League Cup twice and the UEFA Cup once in the 1970s, but were relegated in 1977. They bounced back just one season later and went on to pick up two more FA Cups in the 1980s, then won the the UEFA Cup again in 1984.

The highest Spurs have finished in the Premier League was fifth under Martin Jol in 2006. They beat Chelsea to win the Carling Cup in 2008, but lost to Man. United in the final the following season!

Spurs captain Alan Mullery lifts the UEFA Cup in 1972

⚽ After winning the Carling Cup against Chelsea in 2008, Spurs joined Man. United as the only Premier League club to win a trophy in each of the last six decades!

⚽ Spurs captain Robbie Keane had an awesome 2007-08 season. He won his first trophy after lifting the Carling Cup at Wembley and scored his 100th Premier League goal!

⚽ After scoring 27 goals in 70 Prem matches, Dimitar Berbatov left Tottenham for a club-record fee in 2008. Man. United snapped up the Bulgaria striker for £30.75 million!

White Hart Lane

CLUB STATS!

Stadium: White Hart Lane

Capacity: 36,310

Formed: 1882

Nickname: Spurs

Manager: Harry Redknapp

Captain: Robbie Keane

Record signing: Darren Bent from Charlton, £16.5 million

Biggest win: 13-2 v Crewe, 1960

Biggest defeat: 8-0 v Cologne, 1995

Highest attendance: 75,038 v Sunderland, 1938

Home kit: White and yellow shirts and socks, blue shorts

Away kit: Blue and yellow shirts, shorts and socks

Honours: English League title (2), Championship (2), UEFA Cup (2), European Cup Winners' Cup (1), FA Cup (8), League Cup (4)

Aaron Lennon

TRANMERE ROVERS

★ COCA-COLA LEAGUE 1 ★

FAB FACT!
ESPN Footy presenter Ray Stubbs is a massive Tranmere Fan. Stubbsy even played for the Wirral club in the 1970s!

CLUB STATS!

Stadium: Prenton Park

Capacity: 16,567

Formed: 1884

Nickname: The Rovers

Manager: John Barnes

Captain: Ian Goodison

Record signing: Shaun Teale from Aston Villa, £450,000

Biggest win: 13-0 v Oswestry United, 1914

Biggest defeat: 9-1 v Tottenham, 1953

Highest attendance: 24,424 v Stoke, 1972

Home kit: White shirts with blue trim, white shorts, white and blue socks

Away kit: Blue shirts, shorts and socks

Honours:
Division Three North (1938),
Johnstone's Paint Trophy (1990),
Welsh Cup (1935)

Liverpool legend John Barnes takes over at Prenton Park in 2009

CLUB HISTORY!

Tranmere lasted one season under their original name, Belmont, and wore blue shirts and white shorts in their early days. Rovers played in local leagues until they joined the Football League in 1921, then a young Dixie Dean made his debut in 1924. By 1975 the club were back in League 2 facing huge money problems, but under John King and John Aldridge they enjoyed a huge revival, finishing runners-up in the 2000 League Cup Final. Boss Ronnie Moore missed out on the 2009 play-offs and was replaced by John Barnes last summer!

⚽ The 2009-10 season marks Tranmere Rovers' 125th anniversary. The Merseyside club was formed when two cricket clubs merged way back in 1884!

⚽ Tranmere just missed out on the play-offs in 2008-09. Needing a win against Scunthorpe, Rovers conceded an 88th-minute equaliser and The Iron took their place!

⚽ Rovers boss John Barnes played 79 times for England. The wicked midfielder also won two league titles, two FA Cups and the League Cup as a Liverpool player!

Trophy time at Wembley in 1990

WALSALL
★ COCA-COLA LEAGUE 1 ★

FAB FACT!
Walsall beat Arsenal 2-0 in the FA Cup in 1933! The Gunners went on to win the top Flight the same season!

CLUB STATS!

Stadium: Banks's Stadium
Capacity: 11,230
Formed: 1888
Nickname: The Saddlers
Manager: Chris Hutchings
Captain: Mark Hughes
Record signing: Alan Buckley from Birmingham, £175,000
Biggest win: 10-0 v Darwen, 1899
Biggest defeat: 12-0 v Small Heath (1892) and Darwen (1896)
Highest attendance: 11,037 v Wolves, 2003
Home kit: Red shirts with white stripes, white shorts with red trim, red socks
Away kit: Green and grey striped shirts, grey shorts and socks
Honours:
League 2 (1960 & 2007)

Paul Merson

⚽ Giant keeper Clayton Ince is a Trinidad & Tobago legend. The 6ft 3ins stopper has won 73 caps for his country since making his debut against Barbados in 1997!

⚽ Sky Sports pundit Paul Merson was manager at Walsall between 2004 and 2006. He gave striker Matty Fryatt his first-team chance before selling him to Leicester!

⚽ Steven Gerrard's cousin, Anthony, used to play for Walsall. The tough-tackling defender played 158 games for The Saddlers before moving to Cardiff in 2009!

CLUB HISTORY!

Local rivals Walsall Town and Walsall Swifts merged to form The Saddlers in 1888. The club reached a Championship high of 14th place in 1962, before slipping back down to the bottom division in 1979. Plans to ground-share with Birmingham collapsed in the mid-1980s, before The Saddlers moved to Banks's Stadium in 1990. They won promotion from League 1 in 1999 and 2001, but relegation back to League 2 followed in 2006. Richard Money led them to the title by one point a season later, and now Chris Hutchings wants more success!

The Saddlers win promotion in 2001

WATFORD
★ COCA-COLA CHAMPIONSHIP ★

FAB FACT!
When *Sir Elton John* became club chairman in 1976, he appointed Graham Taylor as boss and took Watford all the way to the top Flight!

Jon Harley and John Eustace

Play-off success for The Hornets at Wembley in 1999

CLUB HISTORY!

The club had various name changes after being formed in 1881. They were known as Watford Rovers and West Herts, before Watford FC was finally chosen after merging with rivals St. Mary's.

Watford joined Division Three South in 1920 and moved into Vicarage Road two years later. They stayed in the bottom division until being promoted to League 1 in 1960, then went up again in 1969. An FA Cup semi-final appearance followed one season later.

The 1970s saw Watford drop to the bottom division, but a new era was about to begin under Graham Taylor in 1976, as the club returned to the top flight and reached the 1984 FA Cup Final.

After Taylor left to join Aston Villa, Watford slipped back into the Championship and it wasn't until he returned that they were back in the Premier League after winning the play-off final in 1999.

Taylor left for Villa again, and Ray Lewington guided Watford to the semi-finals of the FA Cup in 2003, and the League Cup in 2005. Aidy Boothroyd managed a Prem return in 2006, but left in 2008. His replacement, Brendan Rodgers, lasted just six months!

Watford's 1969 team celebrate winning promotion

⚽ The 2006-07 season saw Watford return to the Premier League for the first time since 2000. The Hornets also made the FA Cup semi-finals before losing 4-1 to Man. United!

⚽ Watford manager Malky Mackay also played for the club before hanging up his boots. The defender played 60 games for The Hornets from 2005-08 and scored five goals!

⚽ Two of England's top young stars have worn the yellow and black of Watford in recent seasons. Man. United's Ben Foster and Aston Villa's Ashley Young were both Vicarage Road heroes!

Vicarage Road

CLUB STATS!

Stadium: Vicarage Road
Capacity: 18,400
Formed: 1881
Nickname: The Hornets
Manager: Malky Mackay
Captain: Jay DeMerit
Record signing: Nathan Ellington from West Brom, £3.25 million
Biggest win: 10-1 v Lowestoft Town, 1926
Biggest defeat: 10-0 v Wolves, 1912
Highest attendance: 34,099 v Man. United, 1969
Home kit: Yellow shirts and socks, black shorts
Away kit: Black shirts, shorts and socks
Honours: League 1 (2), League 2 (1)

Tommy Smith

CLUB LEGENDS!

MATCH checks out the club's greatest players!

LUTHER BLISSETT

Watford's legendary striker still holds the club record for the most goals and appearances. He even scored a hat-trick on his full England debut!

JOHN BARNES

The skilful Jamaican-born winger was only 17 when he made his club debut in 1981 and smashed home 83 goals before joining Liverpool in 1987!

ASHLEY YOUNG

Before moving to Aston Villa in a record £9.65 million move in January 2007, the silky winger took Vicarage Road by storm from the youth to the first team!

Chris Brunt

FAB FACT! The Hawthorns is the highest ground in English League Football. Amazingly, it stands 168 metres above sea level!

The Baggies beat Birmingham to win the FA Cup in 1931

CLUB HISTORY!

Workers at Salter's Spring Works in West Bromwich formed the club in 1878. They had to walk to Wednesbury to buy their first football, which is why the name West Bromwich Strollers stuck.

By 1880, Strollers had become Albion and they won the FA Cup in 1888. Despite being one of 12 teams in the first Football League season, West Brom's success came in the FA Cup – winning the trophy again in 1892 and reaching two more finals by 1911.

Following World War Two, West Brom were promoted to the top flight in 1949 where they stayed for 24 years, finishing in the top five three years in a row in the late 1950s. The League Cup followed in 1966 and a Jeff Astle winner won the FA Cup in 1968.

Under charismatic boss Ron Atkinson, The Baggies reached the FA Cup semi-finals in 1978 and achieved third place in 1979. But by 1986, they were relegated and didn't return for 16 years.

They dragged themselves back to the top flight after dropping to League 1 in 1992-93, and despite a great escape in 2005, have been relegated under Gary Megson, Bryan Robson and Tony Mowbray!

The Hawthorns

CLUB STATS!

Stadium: The Hawthorns
Capacity: 27,877
Formed: 1878
Nickname: The Baggies
Manager: Roberto Di Matteo
Captain: Jonathan Greening
Record signing: Borja Valero from Real Mallorca, £4.7 million
Biggest win: 12-0 v Darwen, 1892
Biggest defeat: 10-3 v Stoke, 1937
Highest attendance: 64,815 v Arsenal, 1937
Home kit: Blue and white striped shirts, white shorts and socks
Away kit: Red shirts, blue shorts and socks
Honours: English League title (1), Championship (3), FA Cup (5), League Cup (1), Community Shield (2, 1 shared)

West Brom's 1888 FA Cup-winning team

⚽ West Brom's £1.5 million striker Simon Cox couldn't stop ripping the net in 2008-09. The former Swindon hitman scored 29 league goals, the highest in any division!

⚽ Under manager Bryan Robson, West Brom made Premier League history back in 2004-05 when they became the only team to survive in the top flight after being bottom at Christmas!

⚽ Baggies skipper Jonathan Greening owns a Champions League winners' medal. The midfielder was on the bench when Man. United won the 1999 final against Bayern Munich!

Jonathan Greening

MATCH checks out the club's greatest players!

JEFF ASTLE

The ex-England striker scored in every round of the 1968 FA Cup and netted in the 1970 League Cup Final – the first player to hit the net in two Wembley finals!

CYRILLE REGIS

The Baggies legend won the PFA Young Player Of The Year award in 1978, reached three cup semi-finals in five seasons and scored 112 goals for the club!

RUSSELL HOULT

Hoult was West Brom's keeper from 2001 to 2007 and played 213 games for the club. He kept an incredible 27 clean sheets in the 2002 title-winning side!

FAB FACT!
In the best-selling book *Harry Potter and The Philosopher's Stone*, Hogwarts student Dean Thomas admits he's a Hammers Fan!

Carlton Cole

Trevor Brooking and Frank Lampard Senior lift the FA Cup at Wembley in 1980

CLUB HISTORY!

hames Iron Works was the original name of the club, which was et up in 1895 by workers at the famous shipbuilding company. At the turn of the 20th Century, they changed their name o West Ham United and moved into Upton Park in 1904.

Promotion from Division Two followed in 1923, the same year that West Ham lost the first FA Cup final at Wembley to Bolton. The Hammers were relegated nine years later and didn't return o the top flight of English football until 1958.

The 1960s was a great time to be a West Ham fan, as the club won the FA Cup in 1964 and the Cup Winners' Cup a season later. Hammers stars Bobby Moore, Martin Peters and Sir Geoff Hurst also starred in England's World Cup-winning side of 1966.

Under manager John Lyall, they won the FA Cup in 1975 and 980, and almost won the league title in 1986, only to finish third. Since the creation of the Premier League in 1992, West Ham have played in all but three seasons. After Alan Curbishley resigned n 2008, Gianfranco Zola was appointed and finished ninth!

Hammers captain Bobby Moore collects the Cup Winners' Cup in 1965

⚽ West Ham fans love singing 'I'm Forever Blowing Bubbles'. Before a home match in 1999, a massive 23,680 fans blew bubbles for one minute, setting a Guinness World Record!

⚽ Loads of famous people from the world of movies, TV and politics support West Ham, including US President Barack Obama, Ray Winstone, Noel Edmonds and Russell Brand!

⚽ West Ham set an awesome record when they beat Arsenal to win the FA Cup in 1980. They were the last club from outside the top flight to lift the trophy, and had an all-English team!

Upton Park

CLUB STATS!

Stadium:	Upton Park
Capacity:	35,303
Formed:	1895
Nickname:	The Hammers
Manager:	Gianfranco Zola
Captain:	Matt Upson
Record signing:	Savio from Brescia, £9 million
Biggest win:	10-0 v Bury, 1983
Biggest defeat:	8-2 v Blackburn, 1963
Highest attendance:	42,322 v Tottenham, 1970
Home kit:	Claret and blue shirts and socks, white shorts
Away kit:	Blue shirts, shorts and socks
Honours:	Championship (2), European Cup Winners' Cup (1), FA Cup (3), Intertoto Cup (1)

Matt Upson

CLUB LEGENDS!

MATCH checks out the club's greatest players!

BOBBY MOORE

England's World Cup-winning skipper was captain of West Ham for over a decade and played 544 matches for the East London club!

SIR TREVOR BROOKING

The West Ham legend was used as a forward between 1967 and 1984, and scored the winning goal in the 1980 FA Cup Final with a header!

ROB GREEN

Greeno was the winner of the Hammer Of The Year award in 2008 and runner-up in 2009. He's now a regular in Fabio Capello's England squads!

WIGAN ATHLETIC
★ BARCLAYS PREMIER LEAGUE ★

FAB FACT!
Wigan star Jordi Gomez used to play for Barcelona's youth team, but left to join Espanyol and Swansea before joining The Latics in 2009!

Ben Watson celebrates

EMIERSHIP HERE WE COME!

WIGAN ATHLETIC AFC | PROMOTION 2005

Wigan storm into the Premier League in 2005

CLUB HISTORY!

The town's original football team, Wigan Borough, resigned from the Football League in 1931, and Wigan Athletic were formed at a public meeting a year later at the Queen's Hall.

The club bought Springfield Park for just £2,250 and wore red and white shirts in the early years. A clothing shortage after World War Two forced The Latics to change to blue shirts.

After years of non-league football, Wigan were finally elected to the Football League in 1978-79 and finished sixth in League 2. Promotion to League 1, where they stayed for ten years, followed in 1982 after they finished third with 91 points.

The only relegation in Wigan's history occurred in 1992-93, before JJB Sports owner Dave Whelan took over the club in 2005. Paul Jewell was appointed as the new manager in 2001.

With Nathan Ellington's goals, Wigan won promotion to the Championship in 2003 and the Prem in 2005, finishing tenth and losing to Man. United in the Carling Cup final. Steve Bruce arrived as boss in 2007, but was replaced by Roberto Martinez in 2009!

Skipper Charlie Bishop lifts the old Division Three trophy in 1997

⚽ Wigan are the youngest club in the Premier League. The Latics, who weren't formed until 1932, were only promoted to the top flight as Championship runners-up in 2005!

⚽ The Latics first became a league club when they won promotion from the Conference in June 1978. They replaced League 2 side Southport, who now play in the Blue Square North!

⚽ The most Wigan have ever received for a player was when Antonio Valencia moved to Prem champions Man. United in June 2009. The Ecuador international cost £16 million!

The DW Stadium

CLUB STATS!

Stadium: DW Stadium

Capacity: 25,138

Formed: 1932

Nickname: The Latics

Manager: Roberto Martinez

Captain: Mario Melchiot

Record signing: Charles N'Zogbia from Newcastle, £6 million

Biggest win: 7-1 v Scarborough, 1997

Biggest defeat: 6-1 v Bristol Rovers, 1990

Highest attendance: 27,526 v Hereford, 1953 (at Springfield Park)

Home kit: Blue and white striped shirts, blue shorts, white socks

Away kit: Amber shirts and socks, black and amber shorts

Honours: League 1 (1), League 2 (1), Johnstone's Paint Trophy (2)

Mario Melchiot

CLUB LEGENDS!

MATCH checks out the club's greatest players!

PAUL JEWELL

The Liverpool-born striker joined Wigan in 1984 and scored 35 goals in 137 games. Jewell then returned as manager in 2001 and led The Latics to the Prem!

NATHAN ELLINGTON

After joining from Bristol Rovers, 'The Duke' scored on his debut and was the top scorer in the Championship as Wigan won promotion to the Prem in 2005!

JIMMY BULLARD

The ex-painter and decorator was awesome in central midfield as Wigan won promotion to the Prem. Bullard also helped them reach the 2006 Carling Cup Final!

FAB FACT!
Wolves' stadium is named after *Benjamin Molineux*, who bought the land to build a house on in 1744, before it became the club's home in 1889!

Richard Stearman

Wolves celebrate winning the Championship title in 2009

Coca-Cola CHAMPIONSHIP CHAMPIONS 2009
WOLVERHAMPTON WANDERERS F.C.

CLUB HISTORY!

Wolves' turbulent history began in 1877 as a schoolboy team after the headmaster of St. Luke's School give a ball to some students. The club was originally named after the school, but then merged with Blakenhall Wanderers to become Wolverhampton Wanderers.

They beat Everton in the 1893 FA Cup Final, just four years after moving into their Molineux stadium. By the outbreak of World War Two, Wolves had reached three more FA Cup Finals, winning in 1908, and finished as runners-up in the top flight in 1938 and 1939.

After the war, Wolves became one of the biggest clubs in the country, winning three titles in the 1950s and lifting the 1960 FA Cup under Stan Cullis. The League Cup then followed in 1974.

Despite another League Cup win in 1980, the decade saw Wolves freefall to League 2, but in 2003 the club were back in the Prem after thrashing Sheffield United 3-0 in the play-off final.

Their stay was shortlived after they finished rock bottom the next season. Mick McCarthy took over in 2006 and within three seasons had taken the club back to the English top flight!

Billy Wright is chaired around Wembley after the 1949 FA Cup Final

⚽ Wolves bounced back to the Premier League in style in 2009 after being crowned Championship winners. Mick McCarthy's team won the title by seven points!

⚽ The last Wolves star to play for England was striker Steve Bull. The one-time factory worker won 13 caps under Sir Bobby Robson and played at the 1990 World Cup!

⚽ Wolves striker Sylvan Ebanks-Blake was the top scorer in the Championship in 2008-09. The former Plymouth hitman netted 25 goals, including a hat-trick against Norwich!

Molineux

CLUB STATS!

Stadium: Molineux
Capacity: 28,576
Formed: 1877
Nickname: Wolves
Manager: Mick McCarthy
Captain: Karl Henry
Record signing: Kevin Doyle from Reading, £6.5 million
Biggest win: 14-0 v Crosswell's Brewery, 1886
Biggest defeat: 10-1 v Newton Heath, 1892
Highest attendance: 61,315 v Liverpool, 1939
Home kit: Amber shirts and socks, black shorts
Away kit: White shirts, shorts and socks
Honours: English League title (3), Championship (3), League 1 (1), Division Three North (1), League 2 (1), FA Cup (4), League Cup (2), Johnstone's Paint Trophy (1)

Karl Henry

BILLY WRIGHT
After being told he would never play professional football, Wright spent 14 seasons with Wolves, made 541 appearances and won 105 England caps!

STEVE BULL
The club's record goalscorer netted 250 league goals in 13 years with Wolves. The 1987-88 season is remembered for Bull's 52 goals in all competitions!

JOLEON LESCOTT
The goalscoring England defender was just 17 when he made his Wolves debut, and was a key player in the side that won promotion to the Prem in 2003!

WYCOMBE WANDERERS

★ COCA-COLA LEAGUE 1 ★

FAB FACT!
Under Lawrie Sanchez, Wycombe reached the FA Cup semi-finals in 2001, only to get knocked out 2-1 by Liverpool at Villa Park!

CLUB STATS!

Stadium: Adams Park
Capacity: 10,000
Formed: 1887
Nickname: Chairboys
Manager: Peter Taylor
Captain: Michael Duberry
Record signing: Sean Devine from Barnet, £200,000
Biggest win: 5-0 v Hitchin Town (1994) and Burnley (1997)
Biggest defeat: 5-0 v Walsall, 1995
Highest attendance: 9,921 v Fulham, 2002
Home kit: Dark and light blue checked shirts, dark blue shorts, dark and light blue socks
Away kit: Black shirts, shorts and socks
Honours:
Blue Square Premier (1993),
Ryman League Premier Division (1956, 1957, 1971, 1972, 1974, 1975, 1983 & 1987),
FA Trophy (1991 & 1993)

Martin O'Neill's Wycombe side lift the FA Trophy at Wembley in 1993

CLUB HISTORY!

After being formed by a group of furniture makers back in 1887, it took 106 years for Wycombe to reach the Football League. Wanderers had amazing success under Martin O'Neill and Lawrie Sanchez, but were relegated back to League 2 during Tony Adams' first season in charge in 2004. The club remained in the basement division under former Celtic captain Paul Lambert, despite reaching the play-offs in 2008. Former England Under-21 boss Peter Taylor took over for the 2008-09 season and led the club to promotion at the first attempt!

⚽ Aston Villa manager Martin O'Neill had a top time as Wycombe boss. After guiding them into the Football League in 1993, he led them straight into League 1 in 1994!

⚽ Wycombe almost reached the 2007 Carling Cup Final. In the semi-finals, they held Chelsea to a 1-1 draw at home in the first leg before losing 4-0 in the second leg!

⚽ Peter Taylor won promotion to League 1 in his first season as Wycombe boss in 2008-09, beating Bury on goal difference to the last automatic spot!

Peter Taylor celebrates promotion

YEOVIL TOWN
★ COCA-COLA LEAGUE 1 ★

FAB FACT!
Glovers player-manager Terry Skiverton has been at Yeovil since 1999. The class centre-back has played over 300 games for the club!

CLUB STATS!

Stadium: Huish Park

Capacity: 9,665

Formed: 1895

Nickname: Glovers

Manager: Terry Skiverton

Captain: Stefan Stam

Record signing: Pablo Bastianini from Atletico Penarol de Rafaela, £250,000

Biggest win: 12-1 v Westbury United, 1923

Biggest defeat: 8-0 v Man. United, 1949

Highest attendance: 16,318 v Sunderland, 1949 (at Huish)

Home kit: Green and white hooped shirts, white shorts and socks

Away kit: Black and green shirts, black shorts and socks

Honours:
League 2 (2005),
Blue Square Premier (2003),
Ryman Premier League (1988 & 1997),
Southern League (1955, 1964 & 1971),
FA Trophy (2002)

Yeovil storm to the League 2 title in 2005   CHAMPIONS 2005

CLUB HISTORY!

Known as Yeovil Casuals in their early days, the Somerset club became Yeovil Town in 1907. In their non-league days they caused a massive FA Cup upset when they beat top-flight Sunderland 2-1 back in 1949. It wasn't until the arrival of Gary Johnson in June 2001 that Yeovil reached the Football League, bagging promotion in fine style in 2003, then again from League 2 in 2005. Two seasons later, Yeovil reached the League 1 play-off final, but lost 2-0 to Blackpool at Wembley. They narrowly avoided relegation by two points in 2009!

Yeovil shock Sunderland in 1949

⚽ Like Barnet's Underhill stadium, Yeovil's old Huish ground was famous for its sloping pitch. The club left it behind in 1990 when they moved to Huish Park!

⚽ Famous players to pull on the green and white kit of Yeovil include Southampton boss Alan Pardew and ex-Ipswich and Sunderland goal king Marcus Stewart!

⚽ Yeovil set a record when they won the Blue Square Premier in 2002-03. Gary Johnson's Glovers side beat runners-up Morecambe to the title by a whopping 17 points!

INDEX »

Arsene Wenger and Tony Adams celebrate winning the double

Barcelona win the 2009 Champions League

Blackburn Rovers

Cardiff City's Joe Ledley hits the net

2009 WINNERS

Chelsea lift the FA Cup in 2009

MK Dons storm to the League 2 title in 2008

Reading goalkeeper Steve Death in action

County Ground: 186, 222
Coventry City: 9, 19, 20, 30, 33, 37, 41, 48, 50, 55, 125, **140**, 160, 187, 212
Cox, Arthur: 149
Cox, Gershom: 17
Cox, Simon: 231
Coyle, Owen: 127
Craney, Ian: 104
Craven Cottage: 154, 155
Crawford, Jackie: 27
Crawford, Ray: 66
Crewe Alexandra: **143**, 145, 171, 187, 225
Crewe Alexandra 'A': 183
Croatia: 75, 77, 97, 102
Crosswell's Brewery: 237
Crouch, Peter: 27, 83, 197, 225
Crowe, Jason: 51
Crystal Palace: 9, 15, 17, 29, 30, 41, 122, 127, 129, 135, 138, **144**, 149, 170, 189, 214
Crystal Palace, The: 145
Cullis, Stan: 44, 237
Culverhouse, Ian: 41
Cummings, Tommy: 127
Curbishley, Alan: 135, 233
Curtis, George: 141
Curtis, Harry: 122
Czech Republic: 88, 89, 91, 92, 93, 95, 99
Czechoslovakia: 73, 77, 89, 90

D

Dagenham & Redbridge: **146**
Dalglish, Kenny: 29, 48, 173
Dambusters theme: 171
Darlington: 143, **147**, 151, 159, 193
Darlington Arena: 147
Dartford: 183
Darwen: 24, 127, 158, 227, 231
Davenham: 180
Davey, Simon: 111
Davidson, Callum: 199
Davies, Billy: 189, 199
Davies, Fred: 212

Davies, Kevin: 119, 139
Davies, Simon: 193
Davis, Kelvin: 213
Day, Mervyn: 29
Dean Court: 120
Dean, Bill 'Dixie': 16, 17, 20, 153, 226
Deane, Brian: 17
Death, Steve: 203
Deco: 82
Deepdale: 198, 199
Defoe, Jermain: 93, 225
Del Piero, Alessandro: 63, 81
Delap, Rory: 213, 217
Delaunay, Henri: 89, 90
Delaunay, Pierre: 89, 90
Delilah: 216
DeMerit, Jay: 229
Dempsey, Clint: 154
Denmark: 18, 77, 89, 90, 91, 93, 95, 96, 99, 102
Derby County: 9, 13, 19, 25, 27, 28, 33, 39, 51, 129, 132, 141, 147, **148**, 151, 153, 159, 171, 181, 185, 189, 197, 199, 213, 219
Derry, Shaun: 145
Devine, Sean: 238
Di Canio, Paolo: 211
Di Matteo, Roberto: 136, 182, 231
Di Stefano, Alfredo: 62, 65
Dial Square: 107
Dickinson, Jimmy: 197
Didi: 72
Diouf, El Hadji: 114
Distin, Sylvain: 197
Division Four: 193
Division One: 8, 27, 149, 169, 179, 191
Division Three: 156, 157, 181, 235
Division Three North: 121, 151
Division Three South: 131, 135, 145, 195, 197, 202, 221, 229
Division Two: 190, 204, 233
Dixon, Kerry: 203
Dixon, Lee: 51
Djorkaeff, Jean: 81
Djorkaeff, Youri: 81
Docherty, Tommy: 137

Doherty, Gary: 187
Don Valley Stadium: 206
Doncaster Rovers: 113, 122, 128, 138, 143, 146, 147, **150**, 165, 167, 170, 207
Dowie, Iain: 191
Doyle, Kevin: 203, 237
Dragons' Den: 181
Drake, Ted: 19, 137
Drogba, Didier: 50, 53, 61, 83, 137
Duberry, Michael: 238
Dublin, Dion: 19, 141
Dudek, Jerzy: 64
Duguid, Karl: 194
Dungworth, John: 212
Dunne, Richard: 28, 175
DW Stadium: 235
Dwight, Roy: 189
Dzajic, Dragan: 93

E

Eardley, Neil: 191
Earnshaw, Robert: 131, 149, 188
East End: 185
East Germany: 90
Eastham, George: 51, 217
Eastlands: 173, 174, 175
Eastville Stadium: 128
Eastwood, Freddy: 214
Ebanks-Blake, Sylvan: 195, 237
Eboue, Emmanuel: 18
Ecuador: 83, 235
Edgar Street: 160
Edgeley Park: 215
Edmonds, Noel: 233
Edwards, Keith: 209
Edwards, Rob: 117
Eintracht Frankfurt: 59, 62, 65
El Cant del Barça: 101
El Salvador: 77
Ellacombe: 223
Elland Road: 167
Ellington, Nathan: 229, 235
Elliott, Matt: 51

Elliott, Wade: 126
Elm Park: 203
Elmander, Johan: 119
England: 25, 27, 43, 54, 73, 74, 75, 76, 77, 78, 79, 81, 82, 83, 88, 89, 91, 93, 94, 97, 98, 99, 102, 108, 113, 117, 123, 131, 132, 134, 137, 139, 141, 142, 143, 145, 153, 158, 165, 169, 175, 177, 179, 183, 189, 190, 197, 199, 212, 219, 224, 225, 226, 229, 231, 233, 237, 238
Eriksson, Sven-Goran: 102, 175, 190
Escape To Victory: 165
Espanyol: 234
ESPN: 226
Estonia: 131
Eto'o, Samuel: 101
Euro '92: 95, 102
Euro '96: 43, 88, 89, 91, 92, 93, 94, 97, 99
Euro 1960: 99
Euro 1968: 99
Euro 1972: 88, 99
Euro 1980: 88
Euro 1984: 93, 96, 98, 99
Euro 1988: 91
Euro 2000: 88, 91, 92, 93, 97, 99, 143, 221
Euro 2004: 91, 93, 97, 98, 102
Euro 2008: 88, 89, 91, 97, 98, 102
Europa League: 155
European Champion Clubs' Cup: 59
European Championship: 87, 88, 90, 92, 93
European Championship Trophy: 89
European Cup: 12, 23, 43, 58, 59, 62, 66, 67, 70, 109, 148, 165, 173, 177, 189
European Cup Winners' Cup: 12, 131, 137, 153, 175, 225, 233
European Footballer Of The Year: 117
European Golden Shoe: 173, 177
European Nations' Cup: 90
European Player Of The Year: 177
Eusebio: 77, 79

The great Michel Platini

Ryan Giggs sinks Arsenal in the 1999 FA Cup semi-final

Evans, Roy: *173*
Everton: *8, 9, 10, 13, 15, 16, 17, 19, 20, 25, 26, 28, 32, 33, 34, 35, 38, 39, 41, 46, 49, 50, 109, 113, 119, 121, 149, 151,* **152,** *169, 173, 175, 179, 181, 190, 199, 209, 211, 212, 213, 237*
Ewood Park: *115*
Exeter City: *145,* **156,** *183*

F

FA Cup: *23, 29, 31, 32, 34, 35, 36, 38, 39, 40, 41, 44, 105, 107, 109, 113, 115, 117, 119, 120, 121, 125, 127, 131, 135, 136, 137, 141, 143, 144, 145, 146, 147, 149, 153, 155, 156, 157, 158, 160, 161, 163, 165, 167, 169, 170, 171, 173, 175, 177, 181, 182, 185, 186, 189, 190, 191, 195, 197, 199, 202, 209, 211, 213, 217, 219, 221, 225, 226, 227, 229, 231, 233, 237, 238, 239*
FA Trophy: *129, 180, 183*
Fabregas, Cesc: *18, 29, 107*
Fairfield: *219*
Farnham United Breweries: *222*
Faurlin, Alejandro: *202*
Faye, Abdoulaye: *216, 217*
Feethams: *147*
Fellaini, Marouane: *153*
Fenerbahçe: *176*
Ferdinand, Les: *17, 19, 29, 185, 202*
Ferdinand, Rio: *26, 167*
Ferguson, Darren: *192, 193*
Ferguson, Duncan: *28*
Ferguson, Hughie: *35, 131*
Ferguson, Sir Alex: *10, 21, 23, 25, 30, 34, 44, 48, 56, 67, 70, 177, 192*
Ferran, Jacques: *60*
Ferrari, Giovanni: *72*
Ferryhill: *219*
Feyenoord: *59, 60, 66, 70*
FIFA Club World Championship: *147*
FIFA Club World Cup: *85*
FIFA World Player Of The Year: *26, 177*

Figo, Luis: *63, 91*
Filbert Street: *169*
Finland: *155*
Finn Harps: *149*
Finney, Sir Tom: *199*
Finnigan, John: *138*
Fiorentina: *59*
Flamengo: *85*
Flamini, Mathieu: *15*
Fletcher, Steven: *127*
Flora: *67*
Floriana: *66, 165*
Fluminense: *85, 156*
Fontaine, Just: *76, 77*
Football League: *8, 109, 119, 127, 131, 137, 141, 142, 143, 146, 149, 151, 155, 159, 165, 171, 183, 193, 195, 207, 212, 214, 215, 217, 219, 222, 223, 226, 231, 235, 238, 239*
Forlan, Diego: *81*
Forrest, Jimmy: *34*
Forster, Bernd: *77*
Forster, Derek: *27*
Forster, Karlheinz: *77*
Forster, Nicky: *123*
Fortune, Quinton: *21*
Foster, Ben: *21, 46, 229*
Foster, Stephen: *111*
Foster, Steve: *147*
Foulke, William 'Fatty': *137, 209*
Fowler, Robbie: *14, 15, 17, 19, 20, 29, 48*
Foy, Chris: *155*
France: *73, 74, 75, 76, 77, 81, 83, 88, 89, 90, 91, 92, 93, 96, 98, 99, 107, 219, 221*
Francis, Gerry: *202*
Francis, Kevin: *27, 215*
Francis, Trevor: *27, 44, 113, 211*
Fratton Park: *16, 196, 197*
Freedman, Dougie: *145*
Freestone, Chris: *159*
Friday, Robin: *203*
Friedel, Brad: *19, 115*
Frost, Nick: *128*
Fry, Barry: *193*
Fryatt, Matty: *169, 227*
Fulham: *9, 17, 19, 20, 27, 33, 39, 54,* *123, 137,* **154,** *161, 163, 165, 186, 202, 223, 238*
Fuller, Barry: *157*

G

Galic, Milan: *93*
Gallowgate End: *185*
Galpharm Stadium: *161*
Garner, Joe: *133*
Garneys, Tom: *165*
Garrincha: *72, 77*
Gascoigne, Paul: *29, 43, 89, 97, 185*
Gattuso, Gennaro: *64*
Gazzaniga, Silvio: *73*
Gento, Francisco: *58, 61*
German Cup: *70*
Germany: *72, 73, 74, 75, 77, 81, 83, 88, 89, 90, 91, 92, 93, 95, 96, 102*
Gerrard, Anthony: *227*
Gerrard, Steven: *29, 36, 62, 63, 64, 77, 173, 227*
Gérson: *79*
Gigg Lane: *132*
Giggs, Ryan: *10, 19, 29, 37, 63, 177*
Gillespie, Keith: *28*
Gillespie, Steven: *142*
Gillett, Kenny: *110*
Gillingham: *120, 139,* **157,** *212*
Ginola, David: *15, 29*
Giresse, Alain: *93, 99*
Giuseppe Meazza Stadium: *68, 69*
Glanford Park: *207*
Glasgow Clyde: *211*
Glass, Jimmy: *133*
Gleeson, Stephen: *182*
Glossop NE: *139*
Glover, Lee: *206*
Goddard, Paul: *181*
Goethals, Raymond: *70*
Golden goal: *89*
Golders Green: *214*
Goldstone Ground: *123*
Gomes, Nuno: *91*
Gomez, Jordi: *234*
Goodison Park: *16, 20, 79, 153, 190, 199*

Goodison, Ian: *226*
Gordon, Craig: *219*
Gosling, Dan: *153*
Goss, Jeremy: *187*
Gradi, Dario: *143*
Graham, George: *56, 107*
Graham, Milton: *120*
Grant, Avram: *137*
Gray, Andy: *29, 54, 138*
Gray, Stuart: *186*
Grayson, Simon: *167*
Greaves, Jimmy: *17, 149, 225*
Greece: *81, 89, 90, 91, 93*
Green, Benny: *113*
Green, Paul: *151*
Green, Rob: *29, 233*
Green, Ryan: *160*
Greening, Jonathan: *231*
Gregory, Paul: *211*
Griffin Park: *122*
Grimsby: *138, 182, 207*
Grimsby Pelham: *158*
Grimsby Town: *158*
Grosso, Fabio: *81*
Guardiola, Pep: *63*
Gudjohnsen, Arnor: *97*
Gudjohnsen, Eidur: *97*
Guia, Ademir da: *81*
Guia, Domingos da: *81*
Guinness Premiership: *229*
Gunn, Bryan: *187*
Gylmar: *72*

H

Haan, Arie: *83*
Hagan, Jimmy: *209*
Hales, Derek: *135*
Halifax: *55, 215*
Hallam FC: *13*
Halliwell: *211*
Hamburg: *59, 60, 61, 70, 131*
Hammond, Dean: *142*
Hampden Park: *59, 65, 67, 99*
Hanks, Tom: *109*
Hanot, Gabriel: *60*
Hansen, Alan: *61*

Sir Geoff Hurst completes his World Cup final hat-trick in 1966

Sir Alf Ramsey talks tactics at Ipswich

Gianluca Vialli lifts the Champions League trophy for Juventus

Jermaine Beckford, Leeds United

Kellow, Tony: 156
Kelly, David: 51
Kempes, Mario: 77
Kendall, Howard: 153
Kennedy, Alan: 48, 61
Kennington Oval: 38
Kensington: 137
Kerr, Bobby: 219
Kerr, Scott: 171
Kewell, Harry: 29
Kezman, Mateja: 99
Khaki Cup Final: 137
Kidderminster: 129
Kilgallon, Matt: 209
King Edward VII: 143
King, John: 226
King, Ledley: 18, 225
King, Marlon: 110
Kinnaird, Arthur: 34, 35, 39
Kinnear, Joe: 189
Kinsella, Mark: 135
Kiraly, Gabor: 145
Kirichenko, Dmitri: 93
Kiss, Laszlo: 77
Kitson, Dave: 217
Klasnic, Ivan: 97
Klose, Miroslav: 72, 77, 96
Kluivert, Patrick: 92, 93, 94
Knight, Alan: 197
Knight, Zat: 118
Knill, Alan: 132
Kocsis, Sandor: 77
Koller, Jan: 95, 99
Komljenovic, Slobodan: 95
Konchesky, Paul: 36
Kone, Bakary: 83
Kostic, Bora: 62
KR Reykjavik: 66
Kucukandonyadis, Lefter: 75
Kuwait: 74

L

L'Equipe: 60
La Orejona: 59
Labone, Brian: 153

Lafleur, Abel: 73
Lambert, Paul: 142, 238
Lampard Senior, Frank: 233
Lampard, Frank: 13, 19, 53, 65, 137, 224
Langton, Bobby: 18
Lara, Cristian: 83
Laranjeiras Stadium: 156
Larsen, Henrik: 93
Larsson, Sebastian: 113
Latal, Radoslav: 99
Latchford, Bob: 50
Lato, Grzegorz: 75, 77
Laurent, Lucien: 77
Laursen, Martin: 109
Law, Denis: 177
Lawrence, Liam: 216
Lawrenson, Mark: 110
Laws, Brian: 207, 211
Layer Road: 142
Lazio: 26, 63
Le Roux, Yvon: 99
Leadbitter, Grant: 219
League 1: 109, 113, 115, 117, 120, 125, 127, 135, 137, 138, 142, 151, 155, 156, 157, 158, 159, 160, 161, 163, 167, 169, 170, 175, 179, 180, 181, 182, 185, 187, 191, 193, 195, 197, 202, 203, 207, 211, 213, 214, 215, 217, 221, 222, 226, 227, 229, 231, 235, 238, 239
League 2: 117, 119, 120, 121, 127, 131, 142, 143, 146, 147, 151, 157, 158, 159, 160, 163, 170, 171, 180, 182, 183, 186, 190, 193, 195, 197, 204, 205, 206, 209, 212, 215, 221, 223, 226, 227, 235, 237, 239
League Cup: 12, 35, 44, 45, 46, 49, 50, 54, 55, 56, 109, 113, 123, 125, 133, 137, 147, 158, 169, 173, 179, 183, 187, 189, 191, 193, 202, 205, 206, 209, 212, 214, 215, 217, 219, 222, 226, 229, 231, 237
Leamington: 142
Ledley, Joe: 131
Lee, Alan: 206
Lee, Francis: 19
Lee, Graeme: 151
Lee, Jason: 139

Lee, Robert: 14
Leeds United: 17, 19, 20, 26, 30, 33, 39, 47, 51, 59, 67, 121, 142, 151, 165, **166**, 167, 202, 209, 219
Leeds City: 167, 204
Leeds Road: 161
Leggat, Graham: 20
Lehmann, Jens: 61, 67, 91
Leicester City: 9, 17, 19, 24, 27, 39, 44, 47, 51, 117, 122, 129, 139, **168**, 182, 187, 197, 217, 227
Leicester Fosse: 24, 169, 188
Leitch, Archie: 23
Lennon, Aaron: 11, 27, 225
Lens: 107
Lescott, Joleon: 237
Le Tissier, Matt: 19
Lewington, Dean: 182
Lewington, Ray: 229
Lewis, Joe: 183
Lewis, John: 115
Leyton Orient: 27, 55, 127, 142, 146, **170**
Leytonstone: 146
Liberty Stadium: 221
Ligue 1: 70
Lincoln City: 51, 120, 147, **171**, 204, 207, 214
Lincoln United: 104
Linderoth, Anders: 81
Linderoth, Tobias: 81
Lineker, Gary: 29, 73, 77, 169
Lippi, Marcello: 61
Lita, Leroy: 179
Little, Brian: 56, 109
Littlewoods Challenge Cup: 49
Liverpool: 8, 9, 11, 12, 13, 14, 15, 16, 17, 19, 20, 25, 26, 32, 33, 35, 36, 39, 41, 46, 47, 48, 49, 50, 51, 52, 54, 56, 58, 59, 60, 61, 62, 63, 64, 65, 66, 107, 111, 119, 121, 125, 145, 149, 153, 155, 158, **172**, 173, 193, 195, 197, 199, 213, 214, 215, 221, 226, 229, 237, 238
Lofthouse, Nat: 119
Loftus Road: 202
Logan, Jimmy: 38
London: 137
London Road: 193
Long, Shane: 202

Loughborough: 107, 111
Low, Josh: 186
Lowestoft Town: 229
Lunt, Kenny: 160
Lupescu, Ionut: 81
Lupescu, Nicolae: 81
Luton Town: 39, 47, 49, 51, 53, 128, 207
Lyall, John: 233
Lyn Oslo: 167
Lyon: 155

M

Mabbutt, Gary: 37, 39
Macclesfield Town: **180**
MacDougall, Ted: 38
Mackail-Smith, Craig: 146, 192
Mackay, Malky: 229
Macken, Jon: 39
MacLean, Steve: 195
Madejski Stadium: 203
Magilton, Jim: 202
Maidstone United: 157
Maine Road: 11, 23, 175
Makaay, Roy: 62
Malbranque, Steed: 53
Maldini, Cesare: 81
Maldini, Paolo: 58, 61, 62, 65, 69, 75, 81
Malmo: 59, 70
Malta: 96
Manchester City: 9, 10, 13, 17, 18, 19, 23, 26, 27, 28, 33, 35, 39, 41, 47, 56, 109, 119, 123, 161, 171, 173, **174**, 175, 190, 197, 211, 212, 219, 222
Manchester United: 8, 9, 10, 11, 12, 13, 14, 15, 16, 17, 19, 21, 24, 25, 26, 29, 30, 32, 33, 34, 35, 37, 38, 39, 41, 43, 44, 46, 47, 48, 49, 50, 51, 55, 58, 59, 60, 61, 63, 65, 67, 85, 96, 97, 101, 115, 117, 120, 123, 125, 129, 142, 145, 147, 153, 155, 157, 159, 163, 164, 170, 174, **176**, 177, 181, 186, 187, 189, 191, 192, 195, 199, 202, 211, 213, 214, 225, 229, 231, 235, 239
Maniche: 82

Man. United win the 2009 Carling Cup

246 MATCH!

Maradona's handball breaks English hearts

Mansfield Town: *51, 55, 159, 202*
Maracana: *83, 84*
Maradona, Diego: *75, 79*
Margate: *38, 120*
Marine: *212*
Mariner, Paul: *165*
Marlet, Steve: *155*
Marseille: *60, 61, 70, 219*
Marsh, Rodney: *202*
Martin, Russell: *193*
Martinez, Roberto: *235*
Martins, Joao: *67*
Martyn, Nigel: *167*
Mascherano, Javier: *29*
Masek, Vaclav: *77*
Masser, Alf: *167*
Matthaus, Lothar: *74, 75, 91*
Matthews, Sir Stanley: *27, 38, 117, 217*
Mawene, Youl: *199*
Mayflower, The: *194*
Maynard, Nicky: *124*
McArdle, Rory: *205*
McAuley, Gareth: *165*
McCall, Stuart: *121*
McCann, Grant: *138*
McCarthy, Benni: *114*
McCarthy, Jon: *204*
McCarthy, Mick: *237*
McClaren, Steve: *125, 179*
McDermott, Terry: *29*
McFarland, Roy: *149*
McGrath, Lloyd: *141*
McGrath, Paul: *29, 109*
McIlroy, Sammy: *180, 183*
McIntyre, Johnny: *20*
McLeish, Alex: *113*
McManaman, Steve: *14*
McParland, Ian: *190*
McPhee, Stephen: *117*
Meadow Lane: *190*
Meazza, Giuseppe: *72*
Mee, Bertie: *107*
Megs and the Vootball Kids: *178*
Megson, Gary: *119, 212, 231*
Melchiot, Mario: *235*
Mellor, Neil: *198*
Mendieta, Gaizka: *95*

Mendonca, Clive: *135*
Mercer, Joe: *175*
Merson, Paul: *227*
Messi, Lionel: *59, 101*
Metreveli, Slava: *93*
Metz: *155*
Mexico: *73, 74, 77, 80, 81, 83*
Michels, Rinus: *102*
Middlesbrough: *9, 16, 19, 25, 27, 29, 33, 37, 41, 47, 49, 51, 56, 123, 125, 133, 135, 136, 139, 147, 160, 178*
Midland League: *193*
Mifsud, Michael: *55*
Milburn, Jackie: *185*
Mildenhall, Steve: *51*
Milla, Roger: *75*
Millennium Stadium: *41, 49, 122*
Miller, Brian: *127*
Millholme Bank: *133*
Mills, Pablo: *206*
Millwall: *41, 133, 155, 181, 195, 206, 207*
Millwall Rovers: *181*
Milner, James: *55*
Milosevic, Savo: *93*
Milutinovic, Bora: *74*
Mitchell, James Frederick: *33*
MK Dons: *182*
MLS: *165*
Molby, Jan: *48*
Molineux: *237*
Molineux, Benjamin: *236*
Monaco: *63, 221, 225*
Money, Richard: *227*
Monk, Garry: *220*
Montero, Julio: *81*
Montero, Paolo: *81*
Montgomery, Jimmy: *219*
Moore, Bobby: *43, 214, 233*
Moore, Ian: *215*
Moore, Ronnie: *226*
Moran, Kevin: *41*
Moran, Steve: *29*
Morecambe: *183, 239*
Morgan, Chris: *209*
Morgan, Marvin: *105*
Morocco: *73*
Morris, Billy: *219*

Morrison, Clinton: *140*
Mortensen, Stan: *38, 117*
Moss Rose: *180*
MOTD 2: *231*
Mother Noblett's Toffee Shop: *153*
Mourinho, Jose: *13, 137*
Mouyokolo, Steven: *163*
Mowbray, Tony: *231*
Moyes, David: *15, 125, 153, 199, 212*
Müller, Dieter: *92, 93*
Müller, Gerd: *66, 76, 77, 92, 93*
Mullery, Alan: *225*
Munich Air Disaster: *23, 175, 177*
Munich Tunnel: *22*
Murphy, Danny: *155*
Murphy, John: *117*
Murray, Scott: *125*
Myung-Bo, Hong: *80*

N'Zogbia, Charles: *235*
Nadal, Miguel Angel: *83*
Nadal, Rafael: *83*
National Football Museum: *35, 198*
National Hockey Stadium: *182*
Naylor, Richard: *167*
Neal, Phil: *48, 61*
Neeskens, Johan: *77*
Nejedly, Oldrich: *77*
Nelsen, Ryan: *115*
Neville, Gary: *63, 177*
Neville, Phil: *153*
New Brighton: *127*
New Brighton Tower: *151*
New Zealand: *115*
Newcastle United: *9, 13, 14, 16, 17, 19, 21, 25, 32, 33, 35, 39, 41, 47, 54, 111, 113, 115, 119, 121, 125, 133, 139, 147, 155, 160, 161, 171, 179, 184, 193, 195, 196, 202, 219, 235*
Newell, Mike: *17, 62, 158*
Newport: *185*
Newton Heath: *177, 237*
Nigeria: *74, 75, 77*
Ninian Park: *131*

Nistelrooy, Ruud van: *29*
Noble-Lazarus, Reuben: *111*
Nolan, Kevin: *119*
North End Cricket and Rugby Club: *199*
North Korea: *79*
North Lindsey United: *207*
North Queensland Fury: *19*
Northampton Town: *133, 156, 159, 186, 193*
Northern Ireland: *75, 113, 180, 225*
Northwich Victoria: *171*
Norway: *90, 99*
Norwich City: *9, 11, 25, 29, 41, 47, 49, 55, 56, 111, 119, 141, 143, 149, 157, 165, 187, 193, 206, 212, 237*
Nottingham Forest: *17, 19, 20, 23, 24, 27, 30, 33, 34, 39, 41, 47, 48, 49, 51, 54, 55, 59, 60, 70, 109, 113, 119, 129, 137, 139, 149, 157, 167, 169, 188, 189, 190, 191, 211, 215*
Notts County: *9, 13, 33, 38, 51, 111, 121, 139, 156, 159, 189, 190, 197, 204, 205, 211*
Notts Olympic: *169*
Nou Camp: *100, 137*
Novak, Dezso: *93*
Nugent, David: *132, 199*
Nuneaton Borough: *193*

O

O'Connor, Kevin: *122*
O'Connor, Martin: *51*
O'Driscoll, Sean: *151*
O'Hara, Jamie: *21*
O'Leary, David: *167*
O'Neill, Martin: *109, 169, 238*
Oakwell: *111*
Obama, Barack: *233*
Of London, Asprey's: *11, 89*
Ogrizovic, Steve: *19, 141*
Old Carthusians: *33*
Old Etonians: *32, 33, 34, 115*
Old Trafford: *9, 10, 22, 23, 24, 50, 55, 129, 174, 177, 185*
Oldham Athletic: *9, 29, 49, 50, 163,*

Jeremy Goss strikes against Bayern Munich

QPR's famous plastic pitch

Legendary Brazil striker Ronaldo

Brazil: 77
Ronaldo: 81
Ronaldo, Cristiano: 16, 26, 29, 91, 177
Rooney, John: 180
Rooney, Wayne: 26, 29, 82, 91, 93, 98, 176, 180
Roots Hall: 214
Roseberry Park: 183
Rosenborg: 62
Rosenior, Leroy: 223
Ross, Jimmy: 19, 38
Rossendale: 115
Rossendale United: 183
Rossi, Paolo: 77
Rotherham United: 47, 49, 121, 143, 190, **206**
Rotherham County: 206
Rotherham Town: 206
Rowlands, Martin: 202
Royal Engineers: 33
Royle, Joe: 191
Rugby World Cup: 141
Runcorn: 104
Rush, Ian: 20, 29, 39, 48, 49, 54, 173
Russia: 75, 76, 91, 93, 97
Ryder Cup: 35

S

Saha, Louis: 38, 153, 155
Salenko, Oleg: 76, 77
Salter's Spring Works: 231
Saltergate: 139
Sam, Lloyd: 134
Sampdoria: 61, 165
San Marino: 96
San Siro: **68**
Sanchez, Lawrie: 238
Sanchez, Leonel: 77
Sanchis, Manuel: 63, 81
Sand, Ebbe: 77
Sandygate Road: 13
Santos Laguna: 113
Santos, Djalma: 72
Santos, Nilton: 72

Saracens: 229
Saucedo, Ulises: 86
Saudi Arabia: 74, 83
Saunders, Ron: 56, 109
Savage, Robbie: 28
Savio: 233
Sbragia, Ricky: 219
Scales, John: 14
Scarborough: 50, 129, 171, 235
Schillaci, Salvatore: 77
Schmeichel, Peter: 19, 95, 96
Scholes, Paul: 10, 63
Schön, Helmut: 86
Schwarzer, Mark: 125, 178, 179
Schweinsteiger, Bastian: 96
Scifo, Enzo: 91
Scolari, Luiz Felipe: 81
Scotland: 38, 43, 48, 77, 82, 91, 97, 99, 125, 165, 219
Scotland, Jason: 221
Scott, Andy: 122
Scott, Paul: 132
Scunthorpe & Lindsey United: 207
Scunthorpe United: 117, 181, 182, 207, 226
Seaman, David: 35, 107
Seed, Jimmy: 135
Seedorf, Clarence: 59, 63, 94
Seeler, Uwe: 75
Selhurst Park: 29, 145
Senturk, Semih: 97
Sereni, Matteo: 165
Sevilla: 179
Sexton, Dave: 137
Shaddongate United: 133
Shankly, Bill: 158, 173, 199
Sharp, Billy: 207
Sharpe, Lee: 29
Shaw, Gary: 29
Shaw, Joe: 107
Shearer, Alan: 16, 17, 19, 20, 29, 88, 91, 93, 94, 115, 171, 185
Sheffield FC: 13
Sheffield United: 9, 13, 17, 28, 33, 35, 119, 127, 128, 131, 137, 190, 199, 204, 206, 207, **208**
Sheffield Wednesday: 9, 11, 13, 19, 25, 30, 33, 35, 38, 39, 41, 47, 49, 51,

113, 153, 160, 169, 170, 191, 207, **210**, 219
Sheffield Wednesday Cricket Club: 211
Sheridan, John: 139
Sheringham, Teddy: 19, 29, 94, 101, 142, 181
Sherwood, Steve: 19
Shevchenko, Andriy: 26, 64, 137
Shilton, Peter: 19, 27, 29, 49, 75, 81, 91, 170, 189, 195
Shorey, Nicky: 16, 203
Short, Craig: 28
Shrewsbury Town: 132, 141, 146, 157, **212**
Sidwell, Steve: 123, 203
Sillett, John: 141, 160
Silva, Gilberto: 107
Silva, Leonidas da: 77
Silver, Thomas Lyte: 35
Simonsen, Allan: 99
Simpson, Paul: 212
Simpson, Peter: 145
Sincil Bank Stadium: 171
Singers: 141
Sixfields Stadium: 186
SK Brann: 202
Skinner, Frank: 231
Skint Records: 123
Skiverton, Terry: 239
Slade, Russell: 123
Sliema Wanderers: 221
Slovakia: 99
Small Heath: 151, 227
Small Heath Alliance: 113, 117
Smicer, Vladimir: 64, 91, 95
Smith, Dean: 160
Smith, Gordon: 123
Smith, Jack: 119
Smith, Jim: 197
Smith, Joe: 117
Smith, Mark: 143
Smolarek, Ebi: 81
Smolarek, Wlodzimierz: 81
Snodin, Ian: 151
Soccer AM: 221
Soccer Walk Of Fame: 85
Solskjaer, Ole Gunnar: 101
Song, Rigobert: 82

Sonko, Ibrahima: 202
Souness, Graeme: 115, 173
Sousa, Paulo: 221
South Africa: 75, 81
South Korea: 77, 80, 81, 83
South Shore: 117
Southall, Neville: 121, 153
Southampton: 9, 17, 19, 27, 33, 39, 41, 47, 49, 50, 104, 132, 139, 186, 212, **213**, 215, 239
Southend United: 39, 105, 117, 122, 138, 142, 151, 163, **214**
Southern, Keith: 116
Southgate, Gareth: 94, 179
Southport: 183, 191, 235
Spain: 58, 59, 81, 88, 89, 90, 91, 92, 93, 95, 96, 97, 99, 102
Speroni, Julian: 145
Sporting Lisbon: 60, 67, 119
Spotland Stadium: 55, 205
Springfield Park: 235
St. Andrew's: 112, 113
St. Etienne: 59
St. James Park: 113, 156, 185
St. Jude's: 202
St. Ledger, Sean: 198
St. Martins: 160
St. Mary's: 229
St. Mary's Stadium: 213
Stabile, Guillermo: 77
Stade de Reims: 59
Stade Dudelange: 62, 66
Stadelmann, Jurg: 59
Stadium Of Light: 219
Stadiummk: 182
Stallone, Sly: 165
Stam, Stefan: 239
Stamford Bridge: 65, 137, 170, 173
Standard Liege: 153
Stanley Park: 153
Stanley Villa: 104
Stanley, Willie: 141
Stead, Jon: 164
Stearman, Richard: 236
Steaua Bucharest: 60, 61, 66, 179
Stein, Brian: 53
Stevens, Gary: 153
Stewart, Damion: 200
Stewart, Fred: 131

Glory for Spain at Euro 2008

Tottenham show off the UEFA Cup in 1972

Uruguay strike in the 1950 World Cup Final

West Ham captain Bobby Moore collects the European Cup Winners' Cup

Wolves win the FA Cup in 1949

MATCH would like to thank these people for their help in producing the Book Of Football Records

Cris Freddi, author of The Complete Book Of The World Cup and The England Fact Book, for all his football facts and stats. **Billy Robertson** at Action Images and **Martin Ellis** at PA Photos for allowing us to use football pictures from their archives. **Andrew Barringer** at Luton Town FC, **Anthony Herlihy** at MK Dons FC, **Julian Jenkins** at Cardiff City FC, **Iain Johnstone** at Rochdale FC, **Tom Loakes** at Notts County FC, **Deano Standing** at Millwall FC, **Richard Stanton** at Macclesfield Town FC, **Martin Walker** at Darlington FC, **Gareth Willsher** at Northampton Town FC, **Dave Milner** for his Hallam FC picture, **Rex Page** at the Burton Mail and **David Triggs** at The Chester Chronicle.

Ole Gunnar Solskjaer scores the winner in the 1999 Champions League Final